Documenting China

DOCUMENTING CHINA

A Reader in Seminal Twentieth-Century Texts

Compiled and Introduced by
Margaret Hillenbrand and Chloë Starr

University of Washington Press

Seattle & London

This publication was supported
in part by the Donald R. Ellegood
International Publications Endowment.

University of Washington Press
PO Box 50096, Seattle, WA 98145, USA
www.washington.edu/uwpress

Library of Congress Cataloging-in-Publication Data

Documenting China : a reader in seminal twentieth-century texts /
compiled and introduced by Margaret Hillenbrand and Chloë Starr.
p. cm.
Includes bibliographical references.
ISBN 978-0-295-99127-6 (pbk. : acid-free paper)
1. Chinese language—Textbooks for foreign speakers—English. 2. Chinese
language—Readers. I. Hillenbrand, Margaret, 1972– II. Starr, Chloë, 1971–
PL1129.E5.D63 2011
495.1'82421—dc23 2011012399

The paper used in this publication is acid-free and meets the minimum
requirements of American National Standard for Information Sciences—
Permanence of Paper for Printed Library Materials, ANSI Z39.48–1984.∞

CONTENTS

PREFACE

Is it possible to present a selection of texts that documents a modern nation's psyche and collective history? This collection of essays, writings, and speeches sets out to answer this question by marking a series of pivotal moments in twentieth-century Chinese textual history. From Mao Zedong to Dai Jinhua, and from Taiwan to Tiananmen, the texts introduce some of the most contentious themes and personalities of China's recent past. These writings spurred their original readers to reform the Chinese language, to take up the challenge of modernization, to rally to the nation's cause, and to react against the diktats of central government. They offer insights into the formation of national agendas that are by turns engrossing and disturbing. The texts presented here both reflect and create history: they document moments of intellectual, social, or political change, and they exhort their readers to act decisively upon it. In most cases, the texts have also made their authors' reputations, setting them apart as outstanding thinkers, rhetoricians, or politicians. They thus read as both a history and a biography of twentieth-century Chinese thought and illustrate how seminal texts interact with one another to generate history. This collection differs from other advanced readers and compilations of writings by specific individuals in the clear witness it provides to the way in which both action and reaction have emerged from the written word in China's recent past.

The aims of *Documenting China* are two-fold: to present a series of texts which will challenge and extend the reading abilities of advanced language learners, and to encourage greater understanding of China's turbulent modern history. In compiling this volume, we have sought to address a problem that we observe regularly with students: namely, that a critical gap exists between the proficiency that can be attained after three or four years' intensive study of Chinese and the rather more elusive ability to handle real, raw, primary sources with confidence. This reader provides the training necessary to bridge this gap. Designed for advanced undergraduate students, master's level graduates, and students in master's and doctoral programs in Chinese Studies, it can be studied by individuals seeking an advanced level of reading comprehension or by seminar groups and classes as a basis for discussion. The texts selected are deliberately longer than those found in standard Chinese-language readers, and glossaries are selective rather than exhaustive. The readings are arranged more or less chronologically, but the vocabulary lists are not cumulative, and the individual sections can be read in any order.

The texts selected here are not intended as passages for intensive bursts of meticulous and stylistically polished translation. Rather than word-for-word translation or sentence-by-sentence accuracy, this volume encourages students to read for sense, to grasp challenging pieces whose overall argument is what counts. These are documents to be perused and précised, their main points extracted and their intellectual and literary contours described. This kind of extensive reading also allows students to assimilate many different language styles, registers, and discursive modes. These are *written* texts: how the message is encoded and narrated is key to their impact, and due attention to this encoding and narration can begin to turn language students into literary and cultural critics. For this reason, the texts are presented in both long (complex) form and simplified characters, and their eighty-year timespan exposes students to the complexities of language in different periods. Some are much simpler than others; the key is their breadth of style and rhetoric.

Historical understanding is equally germane to our objectives. In terms of selection, the political, social, and cultural impact of the text has been the prime criterion; and as these articles move from the early days of modern vernacular Chinese (白花 *baihua*) writings in the 1910s through to the beginnings of the hypertext age, they provide a series of illuminating snapshots of changing contexts and ideologies. These are almost exclusively elite texts, written in the main by politicians and intellectuals. Other texts may have had a penetrating effect at the grassroots level, and there are several literary writings that might have earned their place in a political history of twentieth-century China; but the texts chosen here are distinctive in the documentary record they provide of self-conscious attempts to bring change. Some do so by direct appeal to readers, others by their record of political speeches, and others still by highlighting—through discussion or transcript—facets of life intended to provoke outrage or incite reform. The volume is deliberately wide-ranging, including texts in the fields of philosophy, literary history, political science, gender studies, media and popular culture, neonationalist discourse, democratization movements, and international relations. At the same time, each essay, article, or speech plunges the reader right into the throes of a passionately fought debate. As a result, the student who knows little of, say, tensions in Sino-Japanese relations, will gain real insight into the sources of current problems as he or she comes to terms with the given text, while a student with greater knowledge will be able to focus on the nuances of the particular piece and its role in ongoing debate. The chapter prefaces give a concise but in-depth introduction to each article and to the debate that it has engendered, as well as providing suggestions for further reading. Each topic can be used as the basis of a research assignment, either to develop bibliographic and archival skills, or to form the raw material for more sustained inquiry.

Outline of the Reader

Documenting China begins as China comes to terms with the enormity of the end of imperial rule. The Peking University intellectual Hu Shi drew on decades of dissent and debate among scholars as he wrote his famous series of articles calling for literary and language reform. For Hu, language reform, the emergence of a vernacular literature, and hopes for national rejuvenation were tightly bound together. Hu Shi's writings gave momentum to a new wave of radicalism that championed mass education and continuing political reform, and led toward the famed debates of the May Fourth era. Just as Hu Shi's articles were carried in new media, so too did magazines and journals for a range of interest groups begin to proliferate in the early twentieth century. *The Ladies' Journal* was one of the earliest, running from 1915 onward and initiating debate between traditional notions of womanhood and Western feminism. How should the "new woman" be educated, and what was her role in a modern society? Editorials, articles, and advertisements present answers. Sun Yat-sen's "Three People's Principles" rounds off this section of pieces from the first two decades of the century. Sun's famous three-part program for democracy was a blueprint not just for revolution, but for the reform and governance that could transform radicalism into workable political praxis.

Mao Zedong's "Talks at the Yan'an Forum" laid down his vision of cultural practice in a communist state. Aimed at winning over intellectuals, the talks set out the role that intellectuals should play vis-à-vis the masses in promoting the revolution. That Mao, still a guerrilla leader, should produce an arts policy for his future state is indicative of the standing of culture in Chinese society; these talks have been much cited and debated ever since. Ding Ling and Wang Shiwei's articles, also written in the early 1940s, depict another side of the Yan'an era: critical engagement with the darker side of the Communist Party leadership, its hidden hierarchies, and sexual power plays. The rectification campaign that followed publication of these articles was thorough, and became a brutal model for later reeducation movements in the People's Republic of China.

The excerpts from state-run journal *Red Flag*, with their flamboyant yet totalizing rhetoric, shine a light on the ways and means through which continuous revolution was pursued in Mao's China. Just as the champions of revolution are described in metaphors that tap the elemental forces of the universe, so are its supposed enemies vilified in the language of demonology. Every bit as illuminating is the unadorned prose through which the young dissident Yu Luoke expressed his deep disenchantment at the injustices of the new class war. His essay "On Family Background," which protested the absurdities of a world in which only those "born red" could be true Communists, was part of a powerful countercurrent that flowed against the great wave of Cultural Revolution discourse during the late 1960s. It won him many admirers among disenfranchised Chinese youth, but ultimately cost him his life.

The next three readings chart the extraordinary decade of the 1980s, from the exhilarating days of democratic flourishes and economic opening up to the West, to the violent crackdown of 1989 and the inevitable reorientation inwards. The preface to Zhang Liang's volume *June Fourth—the True Story*, which purportedly documents meetings between China's leaders within Zhongnanhai from April to June 1989, explores the debates that waged within the Party over the nature of reform. *River Elegy* and *China Can Say No* document the changing tenor of the times in equally contrasting, but more culturalist, ways. The former, an emotionally charged appeal to a future symbolized by the seafaring spirit, the West, and the great blue yonder beyond China's shores was succeeded only a few short years later by *China Can Say No*, a neonationalist polemic that is as much an exercise in xenophobia as it is a paean to Chineseness.

China in the 1990s is the subject of the next cluster of writings. Deng Zhenglai and Jing Yuejin's groundbreaking essay on civil society in China tries to broker a different kind of relationship between the state and the people, one that rewrites power relations from the ground up, and creates the possibility of a more participatory social world. Dai Jinhua's essay, by contrast, hints at something close to nostalgia for the old days of autocracy, when Tiananmen Square was a place steeped in political meaning and intellectuals were people whose opinion mattered. Now, according to Dai, the squares of old are consumer plazas, while the rhetoric of middle-class belonging hides a swelling underclass, and many intellectuals prefer selling out to standing up and being counted. All the while, the resurgence of religious belief during the 1990s has led to questioning of the role that faith can play in modern communist China. The philosopher Liu Xiaofeng was one of the first to comment on the recent growth of Christianity among Chinese intellectuals, and his 1991 article looks at what the term "cultural Christian" might mean from theological and societal perspectives.

Documenting China ends with China and its place in the world: the Taiwan question, Sino-Japanese relations, and the possible promise of China's peaceful rise. In the case of Taiwan, the last three decades have witnessed an intense interrogation of the links between ethnicity and identity, as people across the spectrum ask themselves whether they are Chinese, Taiwanese, or both. China's relationship with Japan is no less tortuous: economic expediency, political rivalry, and the unburied past jostle for position in a diplomatic forcefield that governments have often manipulated at will. Yet all the while, the notion of China's peaceful rise— first articulated by Zheng Bijian in 2003—seemed to give the lie to China's flashes of belligerence. Promising a smooth path to superpower status, Zheng and his ilk argued for a China that was cosmopolitan, accommodating, and alert to the needs of the East Asian region. The Chinese government's response to this promise, and its progression to other slogans and campaigns is, of course, another story.

This volume began life as a selection of readings for a master's course in modern documentary texts at the School of Oriental and African Studies, University of London, on which both of the volume editors have taught. We would like to thank Professor Michel Hockx, the course's original architect, for generously allowing us to use some of his texts and ideas. We would like to offer our sincere thanks to Lorri Hagman and her team at Washington University Press for their vision, help and encouragement in producing this volume. Lorri Hagman's painstaking editorial work has been much appreciated. We are also very grateful to Fang Jing in Oxford, Xiao Min in Beijing, and Liu Boyun and Ding Yuting in New Haven for their various suggestions and for helping to check the text for accuracy.

Margaret Hillenbrand
Chloë Starr
2011

Documenting China

1. CULTURAL REFORM

On Constructive Literary Revolution
Hu Shi

The centrality of literature and literary reform to China's revolution in the early twentieth century might surprise outsiders. No matter how much the reformers sought to model themselves on the West, this aspect of cultural remaking made theirs a peculiarly Chinese revolution. To understand why the creation of a new literature was key to the program of reforming the nation, we need to glance back at what was being replaced. By 1905, when the state examinations were abolished, the empire was already on the brink of chaos, and the calls of many scholars to "save the nation" were born out of a real and urgent sense of this imminent doom. Immediate and practical solutions were needed to avoid not only political but societal breakdown. Overthrowing the current Manchu imperial ruling house was not enough: the reformers wanted a thorough rejuvenation of society, a makeover that would safeguard China from the kind of humiliations that the Western powers and Japan had been inflicting on the country in a series of defeats and unequal treaties since the 1840s. The Sino-Japanese War of 1895 and the Boxer Rebellion of 1900 had further weakened imperial authority, partly because the Qing dynasty (1644-1911) rulers had failed to act promptly and shore up China's damaged sense of national pride. Many thinkers of the time believed that the way forward was to adopt those aspects of Western society that had contributed to the West's ascendance. Science and democracy became key rallying terms.

Imperial China had been governed for centuries by a small number of elite scholars, recruited through a national examination system. The purpose of scholarship was eminently practical: to create individuals morally fit to carry out state rule. Education and governance were tightly bound together. This system, which required that candidates for office demonstrate a close textual knowledge of the classical canons (unchanged since around the twelfth century), was seen by many in the late Qing as one of the greatest obstacles to reform. A new curriculum was needed for a new era: one that taught useful subjects, such as engineering and armament design, foreign languages, math, chemistry, and agriculture, and not just philosophy, poetry, and moral righteousness. China had been left behind in the struggle for world supremacy, and in order to catch up, she needed to model herself on the West. For the intellectuals who fretted over China's predicament, the solutions were plain: modern education and democratic politics. Schools and universities set up by foreign missionaries had begun to introduce alternative schooling systems, but new technologies and new curricula could not easily be taught in the old written language of China. This language was thought too inflexible to accommodate imported terms and scientific language, and it was so distant from spoken Chinese that years of education were required to attain any useful proficiency. Language reform was therefore vital.

There were at least two stages to China's literary revolution. The first, championed by late nineteenth-century reformers, argued for raising the status of fiction and revamping it as a tool of moral and social education. The new fiction was to be a socially inspiring literature expressed in the vernacular language. Its works were to be instruments for change, means of influencing and galvanizing the population, tools for progress in the absence of political solutions. Fiction was also, needless to say, a strategy for making one's name, especially for intellectuals with no obvious role in government. Politico-literary discussions filled the new journals that sprang up in the wake of innovative printing technologies and a growing newsprint industry.[1] Scholars such as Liu Shipei and Zhang Binglin developed arguments for writing fiction into the literary canon, and they devised a new theoretical mode to allow for its study. *Wenxue* 文学, one of the four traditional classes of learning, came to include fiction and referred more closely to literature in the Western sense in the years after 1895.[2] Reformers such as Liang Qichao and Yan Fu promoted their understanding of the political and social purpose of fiction, and ensured the spread of this view among authors.

The second stage of literary reform followed on from fiction's new-found status and from this exponential growth in literary production and its distribution. This phase, spearheaded by Hu Shi (1891-1962), called for an abandonment of literary language (文言 *wenyan*) for all forms and genres of writing, and for a wholesale adoption of modern vernacular Chinese (白话 *baihua*) instead. Widespread use of the vernacular in fiction had begun in the late Qing, but Hu Shi advocated extending this to all literature, even that which had by generic definition been the preserve of classical Chinese. Hu continued to press for a socially inspiring literature; like Liang Qichao, he wanted the "new literature" to adhere to certain moral frames, and he castigated some late Qing works for their "depravity."

Hu, like most of his intellectual contemporaries, had received a classical education, in his case supplemented by modern-style teaching in a high school in Shanghai. His experiences as a student of philosophy in the United States, first at Cornell and then at Columbia for graduate work under a Boxer Indemnity scholarship, were formative for his later

---

1. On the debates in the new fiction magazines, see Shu-ying Tsau, "The Rise of 'New Fiction,'" in Doleželová-Velingerová, ed., *The Chinese Novel at the Turn of the Century*, 18-37.

2. See Huters, "A New Way of Writing"; and Hsia, "Yen Fu and Liang Ch'i-ch'ao," in *C. T. Hsia on Literature*, 223-46.

thinking.[3] One of Hu Shi's great interests was poetry, and his poems published in *New Youth* (新青年 Xin Qingnian) in 1918 were pioneering in their use of *baihua*. It was, however, as a critic that Hu Shi had most impact on society. Throughout the 1910s, Peking University was the epicenter of iconoclastic activity, and in 1917 Hu Shi joined its Faculty of Letters. His seminal article "Preliminary Comments on Literary Reform" was published in *New Youth* in 1917, and was followed a year later by his article "On Constructive Literary Revolution." These were later heralded as the spur for the literary revolution, and Hu's "Eight Don'ts"—or how not to write literature—were taken as programmatic for new writing. Over the next few years, *baihua* was adopted in schools, newspapers, and magazines, and by writers of new fiction.

In his article "On Constructive Literary Revolution" Hu Shi scathingly claims that contemporary literature survives only because nothing better has appeared. *Wenyan* is a dead language and cannot breathe life into the present. The finer ancient poets used *baihua*, as did the great vernacular novels of late imperial China—and this, according to Hu, offers a starting point for the development of a new language for literature. As a counterpoint to the "Eight Don'ts," he proposes four positives, and his criteria center around what is topically relevant and emotionally appealing to contemporary readers. The article discusses at length the relationship between a new literature and a literary national language (国语 *guoyu*). For Hu, a new literature preceded a new language, and those writing the new literature were also the creators of the new language. The precedents for this, he argues, come from medieval European literatures.

Hu's essays are much more than radical theorizing: he also suggests practical means whereby authors could develop this new literature. Much of the vernacular literature of the late Qing fails to meet his standards because of its formulaic nature, poor characterization, or limited scope. Chinese literature needed broader range, more disparate source material, greater imaginative power, and stronger structures. The models for language reform were Ming and Qing novels, but the inspiration for literary structures was foreign: English and French essayists, American short story writers, European dramatists. China needed a national translation program to ensure that the best of foreign literature was continuously available. It would take, he anticipated, thirty to fifty years to complete the reforms.

It is difficult to assess the direct contribution of the new literature to social or political revolution. As the reformers soon discovered, highly politicized or didactic literature does not always make for enjoyable reading, and more populist fiction soon grabbed back its market share. But

---

3. See McDougall and Louie, *The Literature of China*, 34-37.

language reform and educational change certainly had a great impact on China's development, and the close connection between literary and political reform meant that radical ideas in one field fed into a wider cultural transformation. It was, in part, the successes that the reformers scored in remolding the literary sphere—for so long the marker of social power in China—that gave them the courage to progress to broader political rethinking. In terms of literature, the chief legacy of Hu Shi, Chen Duxiu, and their fellow critics lies in the fact that the works written in the wake of their theorizing won the title "modern Chinese literature," a taxonomic convention that lasted for most of the twentieth century. According to this model, the literary revolution was triggered by the desire for social change, and modern literature began with the socially concerned short stories that Lu Xun published from 1918 onwards. Perhaps as a direct consequence of this linkage between literature and reform, the backdrop to literary works has tended paradoxically to garner more attention than the texts themselves. Indeed, for many critics literary modernity specifically denoted novels of social satire rooted in an antitraditional stance.[4] Recent challenges to this paradigm have emerged,[5] but its longevity testifies to the enduring persuasiveness of the May Fourth reformers.

Excerpted from *Xin qingnian* 4/8 (1917), 289-97.

Further Reading

Chow Tse-tsung. *The May Fourth Movement: Intellectual Revolution in Modern China.* Cambridge, Mass.: Harvard University Press, 1960.

Doleželová-Velingerová, Milena, ed. *The Chinese Novel at the Turn of the Century.* Toronto: University of Toronto Press, 1980.

Feng, Liping. "Democracy and Elitism: The May Fourth Ideal of Literature." *Modern China* 22/2 (1996), 170-96.

Hsia, C. T. *C. T. Hsia on Chinese Literature.* New York: Columbia University Press, 2004.

Huters, Theodore. "A New Way of Writing: The Possibilities for Literature in Late Qing China, 1895-1908." *Modern China* 14/3 (1988), 243-376.

Lee, Leo Ou-fan. "Literary Trends I: The Quest for Modernity 1895-1927." In John K. Fairbank, ed. *Cambridge History of China,* vol. 12: 451-504. Cambridge: Cambridge University Press, 1983.

---

4. See Lee, "Literary Trends I," 451-52.

5. David Der-wei Wang, for example, has discerned signs of reform and innovation long before the May Fourth era. These so-called "incipient modernities" were subsequently denied and repressed as the discourse of Western modernity took over. As Wang observes, by the time Yan Fu and Liang Qichao were proposing their reforms, "Chinese fictional convention had shown every sign of disintegrating and reinventing itself." See Wang, *Fin-de-siècle Splendor,* 4.

McDougall, Bonnie S., and Kam Louie. *The Literature of China in the Twentieth Century*. London: Hurst, 1997.

Mitter, Rana. *A Bitter Revolution: China's Struggle with the Modern World*. Oxford: Oxford University Press, 2004.

Schwartz, Benjamin I. *Reflections on the May Fourth Movement: A Symposium*. Cambridge, Mass: Harvard University Press, 1972.

Wang, David Der-wei. *Fin-de-siècle Splendor: Repressed Modernities of Late Qing Fiction, 1849-1911*. Stanford: Stanford University Press, 1997.

Yingjin, Zhang. "The Institutionalization of Modern Literary History in China, 1922-1980." *Modern China* 20/3 (1994), 347-77.

Hu Shi

建設的文明革命論

胡适

一

我的《文學改良芻議》發表以來，已有一年多了。這十幾個月之中，這個問題引起了許多很有價值的討論，居然受了許多很可使人樂觀的回應。我想我們提倡文學革命的人，固然不能不從破壞一方面下手。但是我們仔細看來，現在的舊派文學實在不值得一駁。甚麼桐城派的古文哪，文選派的文學哪，江西派的詩哪，夢窗派的詞哪，聊齋志異派的小說哪，——都沒有破壞的價值。他們所以還能存在國中，正因為現在還沒有一種真有價值，真有生氣，真可算作文學的新文學起來代他們的位置。有了這種「真文學」和「活文學」，那些「假文學」和「死文學」，自然會消滅了。所以我望我們提倡文學革命的人，對於那些腐敗文學，個個都該存一個「彼可

文學改良芻議	Wénxué gǎiliáng chúyì	Hu's "Tentative Suggestions for Literary Reform," which appeared in *New Youth* on January 1, 1917
駁	bó	*v* refute; dispute
桐城派	Tóngchéng pài	Tongcheng School, named after a county in Anhui that produced several famous prose writers whose style was imitated by later Qing writers
文選派	Wénxuǎn pài	Wenxuan School, named after sixth-century anthology of exemplary poetry and prose
江西派	Jiāngxī pài	Jiangxi School, successors of Song dynasty poetry school associated with Huang Tingjian 黃庭堅
夢窗派	Mèngchuāng pài	Mengchuang School, named after a collection of *ci* 詞 poems by Southern Song poet Wu Wenying 吳文英
聊齋志異派	Liáozhāi zhìyì pài	followers of the style of Pu Songling's 蒲松齡 famed c collection of short stories of the supernatural from the early Qing

6

取而代也」的心理，個個都該從建設一方面用力，要在三五十年內替中國創造出一派新中國的活文學。

我現在做這篇文章的宗旨，在於貢獻我對於建設新文學的意見。我且先把我從前所主張破壞的八事引來做參考的資料：

一，不做「言之無物」的文字。

二，不做「無病呻吟」的文字。

三，不用典。

四，不用套語爛調。

五，不重對偶：——文須廢駢，詩須廢律。

六，不做不合文法的文字。

七，不摹仿古人。

八，不避俗話俗字。

這是我的「八不主義」，是單從消極的，破壞的一方面著想的。

自從去年歸國以後，我在各處演說文學革命，便把這「八不主義」都改作了肯定的口氣，又總括作四條，如下：

一，要有話說，方才說話。這是「不做言之無物的文字」一條的變相。

二，有甚麼話，說甚麼話；話怎麼說，就怎麼說。這是二、三、四、五、六諸條的變相。

三，要說我自己的話，別說別人的話。這是「不摹仿古人」一條的變相。

四，是甚麼時代的人，說甚麼時代的話。這是「不避俗話俗字」的變相。這是一半消極，一半積極的主張。一筆表過，且說正文。

言之無物	yánzhī wúwù	lacking in substance; devoid of
無病呻吟	wúbìng shēnyín	moan without being ill; affectation
典	diǎn	allusions; literary quotations
套語	tàoyǔ	conventional expressions
爛(瀾)調	làn(lán) diào	slander; poor phrases
駢	pián	parallel(isms); antithetical couplets
摹仿	mófǎng	imitate; model on
八不主義	"Bābùzhǔyì"	"Eight Don'ts"

7

二

我的「建設新文學論」的唯一宗旨只有十個大字：「國語的文學，文學的
國語」。我們所提倡的文學革命，只是要替中國創造一種國語的文學。有
了國語的文學，方才可有文學的國語。有了文學的國語，我們的國語才可
算得真正國語。國語沒有文學，便沒有生命，便沒有價值，便不能成立，
便不能發達。這是我這一篇文字的大旨。

　　我曾仔細研究：中國這二千年何以沒有真有價值真有生命的「文言的
文學」？我自己回答道：「這都因為這二千年的文人所做的文學都是死
的，都是用已經死了的語言文字做的。死文字決不能產出活文學。所以中
國這二千年只有些死文學，只有些沒有價值的死文學。」

　　我們為什麼愛讀《木蘭辭》和《孔雀東南飛》呢？因為這兩首詩是用
白話做的。為甚麼愛讀陶淵明的詩和李後主的詞呢？因為他們的詩詞是用
白話做的。為甚麼愛杜甫的《石壕吏》、《兵車行》諸詩呢？因為他們都
是用白話做的。為甚麼不愛韓愈的《南山》呢？因為他用的是死字死
話。……簡單說來，自從《三百篇》到於今，中國的文學凡是有一些價值有
一些兒生命的，都是白話的，或是近於白話的。其餘的都是沒有生氣的古
董，都是博物院的陳列品！

木蘭辭	"Mùláncí"	folk song from the Northern and Southern dynasties
孔雀東南飛	"Kǒngquè dōng nán fēi"	"The Peacock Flies Southeast," Han dynasty *yuefu* poem, also known as "Jiao Zhongqing's wife" (Jiāo Zhòngqīng qī 焦仲卿妻)
陶淵明	Táo Yuānmíng	famous Eastern Jin poet and literatus (365-427)
李後主	Lǐ Hòuzhǔ	posthumous title of Li Yu (937-78), Southern Tang ruler and poet
杜甫	Dù Fǔ	renowned Tang poet (712-70)
韓愈	Hán Yù	Tang prose writer and poet (768-824)
三百篇	Sānbǎi piān	another name for the *Book of Odes* (Shijing 詩經)

再看近世的文學：何以《水滸傳》、《西遊記》、《儒林外史》、《紅樓夢》，可以稱為「活文學」呢？因為他們都是用一種活文字做的。若是施耐庵、邱長春、吳敬梓、曹雪芹，都用了文言做書，他們的小說一定不會有這樣生命，一定不會有這樣價值。

讀者不要誤會，我並不曾說凡是用白話做的書都是有價值有生命的。我說的是，用死了的文言決不能做出有生命有價值的文學來。這一千多年的文學，凡是有真正文學價值的，沒有一種不帶有白話的性質，沒有一種不靠這個「白話性質」的幫助。換言之，白話能產出有價值的文學，也能產出沒有價值的文學；可以產出《儒林外史》，也可以產出《肉蒲團》。但是那已死的文言只能產出沒有價值沒有生命的文學，決不能產出有價值有生命的文學；只能做幾篇《擬韓退之〈原道〉》或《擬陸士衡〈擬古〉》，決不能做出一部《儒林外史》。若有人不信這話，可先讀明朝古文大家宋濂的《王冕傳》，再讀《儒林外史》第一回的《王冕傳》，便可知道死文學和活文學的分別了。

為甚麼死文字不能產生活文學呢？這都由於文學的性質。一切語言文字

水滸傳	*Shuǐhǔzhuàn*	*Outlaws of the Marsh*, Ming novel attr. to Shi Nai'an 施耐庵
西遊記	*Xīyóujì*	*Journey to the West*, Ming novel attr. to Wu Cheng'en 吳承恩
儒林外史	*Rúlín Wàishǐ*	*The Scholars*, Qing novel by Wu Jingzi 吳敬梓
紅樓夢	*Hónglóumèng*	*The Dream of Red Chambers*, also known as *The Story of the Stone* (石頭記 *Shítou jì*), Qing dynasty novel by Cao Xueqin 曹雪芹 and Gao E 高鶚
肉蒲團	*Ròupútuán*	*The Carnal Prayer Mat*, salacious Ming dynasty novel attr. to Li Yu 李漁
韓退之	Hán Tuìzhī	style name (*zi* 字) of Han Yu
陸士衡	Lù Shìhéng	Jin poet and minor official (261-303)
宋濂	Sòng Lián	late Yuan—early Ming prose writer (1310-81) noted for his characterization

的作用在於達意表情；達意達得妙，表情表得好，便是文學。那些用死文
言的人，有了意思，卻須把這意思翻成幾千年前的典故；有了感情，卻須
把這感情譯為幾千年前的文言。明明是客子思家，他們須說「王粲登
樓」、「仲宣作賦」；明明是送別，他們卻須說「陽關三迭」、「一曲渭
城」；明明是賀陳寶琛七十歲生日，他們卻須說是賀伊尹、周公、傅說。
更可笑的，明明是鄉下老太婆說話，他們卻要他打起唐宋八家的古文腔
兒；明明是極下流的妓女說話，他們卻要他打起胡天游、洪亮吉的駢文調
子……請問這樣做文章如何能達意表情呢？既不能達意，既不能表情，那
裏還有文學呢？即如那《儒林外史》裏的王冕，是一個有感情、有血氣、

王粲登樓	"Wáng Càn dēnglóu"	"Wang Can Ascends the Tower," short title of a Yuan *zaju* drama, based on Han dynasty characters
仲宣	Zhòngyí	style name of Wang Can (177-217)
陽關三迭	"Yángguān" sāndié	"repeat the 'Yang Pass Tune' three times," referring to a song based on a poem by the famous Tang poet Wang Wei 王维 (701-761) that was traditionally used as a metaphor for parting
一曲渭城	"Yī qǔ Wèi Chéng"	Wang Wei's poem "Parting at Wei Cheng," also used as a metaphor for parting. Wei Cheng was a town on the Wei River just north of the Tang capital Chang'an, from which one began the journey west
陳寶琛	Chén Bǎochēn	scholar-official and tutor (1848-1935) to the last emperor, Xuantong 宣统 (Puyi 溥仪, 1906-67)
伊尹	Yī Yǐn	Duke of Yi
周公	Zhōu Gōng	Duke of Zhou
胡天游	Hú Tiānyóu	poet and specialist in parallelisms (1696-1758)
洪亮吉	Hóng Liàngjí	Hanlin Academy scholar (1746-1809) ranked second in state exams in 1790

能生動、能談笑的活人。這都因為做書的人能用活言語活文字來描寫他的生活神情。那宋濂集子裏的王冕，便成了一個沒有生氣，不能動人的死人。為甚麼呢？因為宋濂用了二千年前的死文字來寫二千年後的活人；所以不能不把這個活人變作二千年前的木偶，才可合那古文家法。古文家法是合了，那王冕也真「作古」了！

因此我說，「死文言決不能產出活文學」。中國若想有活文學，必須用白話，必須用國語，必須做國語的文學。

三

上節所說，是從文學一方面著想，若要活文學，必須用國語。如今且說從國語一方面著想，國語的文學有何等重要。

有些人說：「若要用國語做文學，總須先有國語。如今沒有標準的國語，如何能有國語的文學呢？」我說這話似乎有理，其實不然。國語不是單靠幾位言語學的專門家就能造得成的；也不是單靠幾本國語教科書和幾部國語字典就能造成的。若要造國語，先須造國語的文學。有了國語的文學，自然有國語。這話初聽了似乎不通。但是<u>列位</u>仔細想想便可明白了。天下的人誰肯從國語教科書和國語字典裏面學習國語？所以國語教科書和國語字典，雖是很要緊，決不是造國語的利器。真正有功效有勢力的國語教科書，便是國語的文學，便是國語的小說、詩文、戲本。國語的小說、詩文、戲本通行之日，便是中國國語成立之時。試問我們今日居然能拿起筆來做幾篇白話文章，居然能寫得出好幾百個白話的字，可是從甚麼白話教科書上學來的嗎？可不是從《水滸傳》、《西遊記》、《紅樓夢》、《儒林外史》，……等書學來的嗎？這些白話文學的勢力，比甚麼字典教科書都還大幾百倍。字典說「這」字該讀「<u>魚彥反</u>」，我們偏讀他做「者

| 列位 | lièwèi | "all of you"; everyone |
| 魚彥反 | yú yàn fǎn | method for indicating the pronunciation of a character in classical Chinese. (Hu's point is that modern Chinese has drawn on vernacular literary usage to alter the meanings and pronunciations of written classical Chinese.) |

個」的者字。字典說「麼」字是「細小」，我們偏把他用作「甚麼」、「那麼」的麼字。字典說「沒」字是「沉也」，「盡也」，我們偏用他做「無有」的無字解。字典說「的」字有許多意義，我們偏把他用來代文言的「之」字，「者」字，「所」字和「徐徐爾，縱縱爾」的「爾」字......總而言之，我們今日所用的「標準白話」，都是這幾部白話的文學定下來的。我們今日要想重新規定一種「標準國語」，還須先造無數國語的《水滸傳》、《西遊記》、《儒林外史》、《紅樓夢》。

所以我以為我們提倡新文學的人，盡可不必問今日中國有無標準國語。我們盡可努力去做白話的文學。我們可儘量採用《水滸傳》、《西遊記》、《儒林外史》、《紅樓夢》的白話。有不合今日的用的，便不用他；有不夠用的，便用今日的白話來補助；有不得不用文言的，便用文言來補助。這樣做去，決不愁語言文字不夠用，也決不用愁沒有標準白話。中國將來的新文學用的白話，就是將來中國的標準國語。造中國將來白話文學的人，就是制定標準國語的人。

我這種議論並不是「向壁虛造」的。我這幾年來研究歐洲各國國語的歷史，沒有一種國語不是這樣造成的。沒有一種國語是教育部的老爺們造成的。沒有一種是言語學專門家造成的。沒有一種不是文學家造成的。我且舉幾條例為證：

一，義大利。五百年前，歐洲各國但有方言，沒有「國語」。歐洲最早的國語是義大利文。那時歐洲各國的人多用拉丁文著書通信。到了十四世紀的初年，義大利的大文學家但丁 (Dante) 極力主張用義大利話來代拉丁文。他說拉丁文是已死了的文字，不如他本國俗話的優美。所以他自己的

麼	me	*suff, interrog. part.* now used in compounds; classical (mā) fine; small
之, 者, 所	zhī, zhě, suǒ	*de* 的 has taken over the functions of various classical Chinese particles, such as 之 (to denote the genitive), and 者 and 所 (to nominalize)
向壁虛造	xiàngbì xūzào	make up; fabricate
拉丁文	Lādīngwén	Latin

12

傑作《喜劇》，全用脫斯堪尼 (Tuscany)（義大利北部的一邦）的俗話。這部《喜劇》，風行一世，人都稱他做「神聖喜劇」。那「神聖喜劇」的白話後來便成了義大利的標準國語。後來的文學家巴卡嘉 (Boccacio, 1313-1375) 和洛倫 (Lorenzo de Medici) 諸人也都用白話作文學。所以不到一百年，義大利的國語便完全成立了。

　　二，英國。英倫雖只是一個小島國，卻有無數方言。現在通行全世界的「英文」，在五百年前還只是倫敦附近一帶的方言，叫做「中部土語」。當十四世紀時，各處的方言都有些人用來做書。後來到了十四世紀的末年，出了兩位大文學家，一個是是趙叟 (Chaucer, 1340-1400)一個是威克列夫 (Wyclif, 1320-1384)。趙叟做了許多詩歌，散文都用這「中部土語」。威克列夫把耶教的《舊約》、《新約》也都譯成「中部土語」。有了這兩個人的文學，使把這「中部土語」變成英國的標準國語。後來到了十五世紀，印刷術輸進英國，所印的書多用這「中部土語」，國語的標準更確定了。到十六、十七世紀，Shakespeare 和「伊裏沙白時代」的無數文學大家，都用國語創造文學。從此以後，這一部分的「中部土語」，不但成了英國的標準國語，幾乎竟成了全地球的世界語了！

　　此外，法國、德國及其它各國的國語，大都是這樣發生的，大都是靠著文學的力量才能變成標準的國語的。我也不去一一的細說了。

　　義大利國語成立的歷史，最可供我們中國人的研究。為甚麼呢？因為歐洲西部北部的新國，如英吉利、法蘭西、德意志，他們的方言和拉丁文相差太遠了，所以他們漸漸的用國語著作文學，還不算希奇。只有義大利是當年羅馬帝國的京畿近地，在拉丁文的故鄉，各處的方言又和拉丁文最

神聖喜劇	*Shénshèng xǐjù*	Dante's *La Divina Commedia*
中部土語	Zhòngbùtǔyǔ	Middle English (dialect); Chaucer was instrumental in securing the London dialect as standard Middle English
舊約	Jiùyuē	Old Testament
新約	Xīnyuē	New Testament
印刷術	yìnshuāshù	*n* printing
伊裏沙白時代	Yīlǐshābái shídài	Elizabethan era (now 伊莉莎白)
京畿	jīngjī	the capital and its environs

近。在義大利提倡用白話代拉丁文，真正和在中國提倡用白話代漢文，有同樣的艱難。所以英、法、德各國語，一經文學發達以後，便不知不覺的成為國語了。在義大利卻不然。當時反對的人很多，所以那時新文學家，一方面努力創造國語的文學，一方面還要做文章鼓吹何以當廢古文，何以不可不用白話。有了這種有意的主張（最有力的是 Dante 和 Alberti 兩個人），又有了那些有價值的文學，才可造出義大利的「文學的國語」。

我常問我自己道：「自從施耐庵以來，很有了些極風行的白話文學，何以中國至今衰不曾有一種標準的國語呢？」我想來想去，只有一個答案。這一千年來，中國固然有了一些有價值的白話文學，但是沒有一個人出來<u>明目張膽</u>的主張用白話為中國的「文學的國語」。有時<u>陸放翁</u>高興了，便做一首白話詩；有時<u>柳耆卿</u>高興了，便做一兩白話的小說。這都是不知不覺的自然出產品，並非是有意的主張。因為沒有「有意的主張」，所以做白話的只管做白話，做古文的只管做古文，做八股的只管做八股。因為沒有「有意的主張」，所以白話文學從不曾和那些「死文學」爭那「文學正宗」的位置。白話文學不成為文學正宗，故白話不曾成為標準國語。

我們今日提倡國語的文學，是有意的主張。要使國語成為「文學的國語」。有了文學的國語，方有標準的國語。

明目張膽	míng mù zhāng dàn	blazenly; flagrantly
陸放翁	Lù Fàngwēng	Southern Song poet and nationalist (1125-1210)
柳耆卿	Liǔ Qíqīng	Northern Song poet and official (987-1052)

2. SOCIAL REFORM

Excerpts from *The Ladies' Journal*

The impact of the women's periodical press in Shanghai in the early twentieth century stems from three interlocking revolutions in Chinese society: technological, gender and political. Debates on women's role in society did not spring into the magazine pages from nowhere: women and their male advisors had been contemplating for decades how "new" or "modern" women should behave. The growth of women's education—with greater numbers taught in missionary or local schools in China—together with increasing numbers of Chinese who traveled abroad and were influenced by ideas on women's emancipation and by the very different family ideologies that they encountered, provoked a deep questioning of how women could most appropriately play their part in a changing society. For many, this question was essentially about what women could contribute to the renovation of China. Liang Qichao held that the twin goals of strengthening the nation and preserving the race depended on educated mothers and wives. For others, the demise of the Qing dynasty, and the shifting of social hierarchies that followed, invoked a more philosophical and personal response to public perceptions of what constituted a good, genteel woman. In the novels and travelogues of the late Qing, women who wanted to be both modern and modest were negotiating the challenges of new horizons and a more international world. Could education be reconciled with marriage? Could a woman travel alone? Could female literati (閨秀 *guixiu*) make a free love match without being dubbed unchaste?[1] Parallel debates reappeared in the 1920s as newspaper columns showcased arguments about "pseudo-modernity"—women who displayed the external accoutrements of modernity, but whose interior transformations had not rendered them politically or morally modern.[2] Much of the debate, unsurprisingly, was conducted by men.

The role of the press, and of the magazine sector in particular, was pivotal both in developing the content of women's education, and in creating a community of like-minded men and women committed to change.[3] The traditional Chinese belief in the power of the written word was enhanced by the advent of rapid, mass printing, and by distribution networks which transcended local interests. It was with good reason that the early reformers sought to harness the power of the press; and magazines like

---

1. See Ellen Widmer, "Gentility in Transition: Travels, Novels, and the New *Guixiu*," in Daria Berg and Chloë Starr, eds. *China and the Quest for Gentility*.

2. See, for example, Louise Edwards, "Policing the Modern Woman in Republican China."

3. On the role of the press in forming an imagined community, see Leo Ou-fan Lee, *Shanghai Modern*, 45-46.

New Youth (新青年 Xin qingnian) were crucial for the nurturing of young idealists—and later, Communists—of both genders. The new media had begun as early as the 1870s to create an implied readership that was no longer exclusively male nor highly literate, and the inclusion of women as audience can be seen as a part of the universalizing drive of these early reformers. *Shen Bao* (申報 Shenbao, est. 1872), the first modern Chinese newspaper, aimed to include peasants, workers and merchants among its readers, and numerous other newspapers and journals appeared with a more readable style, designed to allow the semi-literate, including women, to benefit from new thinking. Adding further scope were pictorial magazines, whose images introduced readers to the world of urban life.[4] By 1907, the female revolutionary Qiu Jin was editing a journal, *Chinese Women's Newspaper* (中國女報 Zhongguo nübao), in simplified *wenyan*, which aimed at encouraging national sentiment in semi-literate female readers.

Shanghai formed the epicenter of the new print industry. By the 1890s more than a hundred publishers were operating from the city—a tenfold increase since the 1860s—and several thousand titles were in circulation.[5] The new presses also led to new types of texts being bought and sold, as reference works and dictionaries supplemented "leisure reading" materials. *The Ladies' Journal* (婦女雜誌 Funü zazhi) was one of approximately nine magazines printed by the Commercial Press in Shanghai, which also published textbooks, "repositories" of information, and flagship journals such as *Eastern Miscellany* (東方雜誌 Dongfang zazhi). *The Ladies' Journal*'s monthly circulation of around 10,000 copies post-1919 made it one of the most successful female journals of the era; and it was also one of the most long-lived, with a print run that extended from 1915 to 1932.[6] The Commercial Press had bookstores in twenty-eight cities across China, as well as in Hong Kong and Singapore, thus ensuring good circulation. Most of the magazines had a mixture of writing styles and content, from short stories to factual pieces, adverts, and editorials. Unlike many of its peer journals which targeted a female audience, *The Ladies' Journal* was at various points edited by women, such as the Wellesley- and Cornell-educated Zhu Hu Binxia, whose degree successes were printed in block type alongside her name, in case readers were not aware of her progressive credentials.[7] Journalists on the magazine were mostly in their twenties and thirties, and there was a high turnover of editors. Writers also rotated their positions frequently, and an interest in women's affairs was not necessarily a requirement, as shown by the appointment of Zhang Xichen to the editorship in 1921, when the writer Mao Dun (Shen Yanbing)—who had at

4. Barbara Mittler, *A Newspaper for China?*, 248-52.
5. For an extended analysis, see Alexander Des Forges, *Mediasphere Shanghai*.
6. Jacqueline Nivard, "Women and the Women's Press: The Case of *The Ladies' Journal* (Funü zazhi) 1915-1931," 37.
7. Lee, *Shanghai Modern*, 51.

least written on women's emancipation—could not be persuaded to take on the role.[8]

The Ladies' Journal presented a mix of articles on marriage, family life, science, health and medicine. Feminism and patriotism were key themes in the early issues. Foreign and Chinese examples of family life vied for attention with romantic fiction and historical biographies of virtuous or heroic women; articles on fashion were juxtaposed with calls for women's suffrage. Several commentators have noted the ambiguities and tensions in the women's movement in China, as debates about modernity, women's representation, and feminism were interwoven with notions of nationalism and strategies for reform which prescribed a limited sphere for women.[9] Was gender equality an end in itself, or was it subordinate to the national interest? To what degree should China strive to emulate the West in its fashioning of the new woman? The vacillation in views and themes reflected wider movements in society, and traced the sharp turns in political power as the Nationalist era took hold. Women now had to strive to ensure that their intellectual worth was regarded as valid in the new construction of women, and many struggled with the dismissal of female talent and its replacement by physical beauty as a marker of genteel femininity. Double standards persisted, with women expected to embody new ideologies as well as to support them vocally. Semantically, while *xin qingnian* denoted progressive ideas, "new woman" (新女性 *xin nüxing*) usually characterized a modern lifestyle, if not little more than a fashion sense.[10] Moreover, while reformist intellectuals had provided the main current of thought on women throughout the first two decades of the century, the militarized social order of the Guomindang soon suppressed much of the earlier debate. As those in commercial and military sectors rose to power under the Nationalists, former literati were sidelined, along with the causes they espoused.[11]

Commentators have analyzed four main phases in the history of *The Ladies Journal*, which roughly correspond to changing political phases. A sudden shift in thinking on traditional morality following May Fourth, for example, was succeeded in the late 1920s by a return to a more conservative approach. Free love and free divorce had taken over from discussions of monogamy and nuclear families, only to be later subsumed under the emphasis on women as "good mothers and good wives" (良妻賢母 *liangqi xianmu*, also as 賢妻良母 *xianqi liangmu*). Articles on eugenics

---

8. Nivard, "Women and the Women's Press," 46-7.

9. A good starting point is Carol C. Chin's article "Translating the New Woman: Chinese Feminists View the West, 1905-15," 490-518.

10. Jeesoon Hong, "The Chinese Gentlewoman in the Public Gaze: Ling Shuhua in Twentieth-Century China and Britain," in Berg and Starr, eds. *China and the Quest for Gentility*, 235-252.

11. For a discussion of the modern female as synecdoche for governance, see Edwards, "Policing the Modern Woman in Republican China," 115.

and birth control which appeared in the more liberal phase of the magazine's life provoked lively responses from readers as the new "democratic" press began to flex its muscles. The magazine remained a commercial venture, however, and when opinions were too transgressive, personnel shifts could be expected. From 1925 onward, the journal carried fewer foreign translations, and began to sway back to traditional values, although there was a brief final flowering of left-wing views in 1930-31.[12]

Scholars have noted that transitions in the figure of the new woman across Republican era magazines mirror these basic ideological shifts. As Barbara Mittler observes, the new woman who initially emerged in Shanghai women's magazines of the late Qing was somewhat masculine in appearance. Depicted as an equal to men, she was full of confidence, a heroine ready to save China. Yet over time many journals began to replace this independent pioneer, clad in male attire, with a different type of new woman, a perfect "femme," who was less a citizen and more of an accomplished, modern mother for China's new citizens. The discourse of equality and liberation ceded to one which stressed instead the woman's role in the household, and her traditional skills of "cooking, cleaning, and caring." By the 1930s, the pendulum had swung again, and certain magazines began to show a different type of new woman: a *new* new woman, who railed against conservative definitions of her role and who indulged her distaste for men. This *new* new woman could cope perfectly well without a man, and reshaped the perfect woman into a fusion of the best features of both genders. The perfect new woman was superior to men, and no longer needed masculine approval for her actions.[13] Yet perhaps the key point was the constant fluidity of female representation; and the figure of the new woman would continue to shift in tune with political currents right up to the Communist era and beyond.

1. Excerpted from Hu Huaichen, "Lihun wenti," *Funü zazhi* 6/7 (1920), 12.

2. Excerpted from Li Sanwu (pseud.), "Ziyou lihun lun," *Funü zazhi* 6/7 (1920), 1-8.

---

12. Jacqueline Nivard provides an outline of phases in the magazine's history in her "Women and the Women's Press," 38.

13. Barbara Mittler, "In Spite of Gentility—Women and Men in *Linglong* (Elegance), a 1930s Women's Magazine," in Berg and Starr, eds. *China and the Quest for Gentility*, 208-34.

Further Reading

Barlow, Tani E. "Theorizing Woman: *Funü, Guojia, Jiating*" (Chinese Woman, Chinese State, Chinese Family). In Inderpal Grewal and Caren Kaplan eds., *Scattered Hegemonies: Postmodernity and Transnational Feminist Practices.* Minneapolis and London: University of Minnesota Press, 1994.

Berg, Daria, and Chloë Starr, eds. *China and the Quest for Gentility: Negotiations Beyond Gender and Class.* London: Routledge, 2007.

Bray, Francesca. *Technology and Gender: Fabrics of Power in Late Imperial China.* Berkeley and Los Angeles: University of California Press, 1997.

Chiang, Yung-chen. "Womanhood, Motherhood and Biology: The Early Phases of *The Ladies' Journal*, 1915-25." *Gender and History* 18/3 (2006), 519-45.

Chin, Carol C. "Translating the New Woman: Chinese Feminists View the West, 1905-15." *Gender and History* 18/3 (2006), 490-518.

Des Forges, Alexander. *Mediasphere Shanghai*: *The Aesthetics of Cultural Production.* Honolulu: University of Hawaii Press, 2007.

Edwards, Louise. "Policing the Modern Woman in Republican China." *Modern China* 26/2 (April 2000), 115-47.

Hockx, Michel. *Questions of Style: Literary Societies and Literary Journals in Modern China, 1911-1937.* Leiden: Brill, 2003.

Judge, Joan. *The Precious Raft of History: The Past, the West, and the Woman Question in China.* Stanford: Stanford University Press, 2008.

Lee, Leo Ou-fan. *Shanghai Modern: The Flowering of a New Urban Culture in China, 1930-1945.* Cambridge, Mass.: Harvard University Press, 1999.

Mittler, Barbara. *A Newspaper for China? Power, Identity, and Change in Shanghai's News Media, 1872-1923.* Cambridge, Mass.: Harvard University Asia Center, 2004.

Nivard, Jacqueline. "Women and the Women's Press: The Case of *The Ladies' Journal* (Funü zazhi) 1915-1931." *Republican China* 10/16 (1984), 37-56.

Orliski, Constance. "The Bourgeois Housewife as Laborer in Late Qing and Early Republican Shanghai." *Nannü* 5/1 (2003), 43-68.

Yeh, Catherine Vance. *Shanghai Love.* Seattle: University of Washington Press, 2006.

胡懷琛：離婚問題

離婚問題原是婚姻問題裏的一個小問題。因為婚姻問題包括結婚，離婚，改嫁，廢妾等等許多的事。所以離婚一件事。算是婚姻問題裏的一部份。我因為婚姻問題太大。一時不能說完。現在對於離婚，有了感觸，便先寫出來。這一部份研究研究。

　　中國人普通的習慣，說到離婚問題，便不成問題。因為他們說離婚是當然不可能的事。便是迫於不得已離了婚。男女二人，都算抱恨終身，決不能恢復本來的名譽。

　　但是在中國的法律上說，離婚問題，也算不成問題，因為法律並不禁止離婚。既然不絕對禁止，到了必要的時候便可以離。不到必要的時候，原不必離。倘然在法律上有絕端禁止之條，那麼對於這法律贊成反對，自然生出問題來。現在法律既不禁止，所以不成問題。

　　照以上兩方面看起來，雖同是不成問題，然二方面極端反對。現在作者是立於贊成離婚問題的一方面，和作者反對的，便是普通的習慣。所以我所研究的也便是普通習慣，我的話很長。在下面分開來細細的講。

　　（一）習慣不必是真理。凡是一種習慣。便是多數的人認他為真理。然而他終不是真理。譬如數十年前，以女子不必讀書為真理。現在人人都知道是錯誤了。離婚問題也是這樣，不過他的關係，更複雜一點罷了。

　　（二）習慣也不是無所憑藉的，無論甚麼事。既然成了一種習慣。他必有個原因。斷不是憑空成立的。也不是一天養成的。無論何事，都是如此。便說到離婚，普通的習慣，為甚麼把他當一件壞事？他也有個原因。這個原因是甚麼？我現在也不能確切指出。大約是防止淫蕩的意思。這個意思，不是不好。

改嫁	gǎijià	remarry (of a woman)
廢妾	fèiqiè	*v ob* dismiss a concubine
抱恨終身	bàohèn zhōngshēn	be filled with lifelong remorse
贊成	zànchéng	approve of; assent to
憑藉	píngjiè	grounds; evidence
憑空	píngkōng	groundless; out of thin air
淫蕩	yíndàng	loose morals; licentious behavior

但是後來的人走向極端去了。無論怎樣，總不可以離婚。離婚便算一件極不名譽的事。因一個防止淫蕩的原因便造成現在婚姻上無限的痛苦。實在可歎得很！

照上面看來，我可得著一個判斷如下：（一）不能離婚之說，並非真理，（二）不能離婚之說，也有根據。現在我們討論這事，便有下手處了。第一辯明不能離婚之說並非真理。第二既知他的根據不錯，我們只可利用他，矯正他走入極端，却不可攻擊他。詳細說明如下：

『一』辯明不能離婚之說並非真理。男女性情不合，品行不齊。兩方面均願意離婚，當然可以離婚，如不離婚，便生出下面各種的害處。（甲）女子與他人<u>私通</u>。（乙）男子<u>娶妾宿娼</u>或與他女子不正式結婚。（丙）男女各<u>灰心短氣</u>。對於職務，成績不佳。（丁）彼此<u>鬱鬱不樂</u>，多病早死。女子尤多。（戊）或女子被男子所累，或男子被女子所累，在交際場中減少其榮譽，有此種種害處，救濟的唯一方法，便是離婚。又有人說：『男女性情不同，品行不齊，固然難於<u>偕老</u>。但這是結婚時不謹慎的結果。倘然結婚時謹慎選擇。自不至有離婚的事情發生。』我說不然。（甲）現在多數的男女所受的婚姻痛苦多半是他父母替他造就的。不能怪他自己選擇不慎。何以却要他永受痛苦，（乙）便說是自由選擇的。一個人的品行。前好後壞，也是常有的事，在當初又何能知道他後來要變壞。到後來變壞了，如不贊成他壞便不能一天同居。如要贊成他壞，便是被逼迫喪失了自己的品格，世上最可痛心的事，再沒有比此更甚的了。處在這個時候，非離婚不可，而且誤認不離婚是真理，更生出或男或女不能自立的惡習慣來，這種以女子為多數，男子為少數，普通的女子，不能自立，或不願自立，只是<u>倚賴</u>男子，終日坐食或且任意遊玩。他的心理，既然嫁了這個男子，可以供給我的衣食，我又何必要自立，落得倚賴他。

甲, 乙, 丙, 丁	jiǎ, yǐ, bǐng, dīng	A, B, C, D (counting via the ten Heavenly Stems)
私通	sītōng	illicit relationships
娶妾宿娼	qǔqiè sùchāng	take concubines and visit prostitutes
灰心短氣	huīxīn duǎnqì	downhearted; depressed
鬱鬱不樂	yùyùbúlè	depressed; melancholy
偕老	xiélǎo	grow old together (husband, wife)
倚賴	yǐlài	be dependent on; rely on

　　男子雖不願意，却也無法，不得不供給他，男子既然被他所累，在精神上經濟上都受了莫大的影響。對於學問，對於事業，多不能發展。或且有意做壞事騙錢，供給妻子的<u>揮霍</u>，弄到後來，自己的品格喪完了。固不消說，還要間接害了他人。求他的根源，都是由於不能離婚來的，倘然早離了婚。男子固然不受累，女子也知道非自立不能處世。只須有一分的能力，便要做一分的事情了。斷不再坐食遊玩了。並不必有離婚的實事發現，女子纔得覺悟。只須將（不能離婚）的<u>謬見</u>打破了。女子早知自警。決不敢存了倚賴之心了。這是就男子一方面說。如就女子一方說，也是有的，我親自聽見人家說：有某某女教習，他的丈夫貪懶怕做事。只靠妻子度日。連一家的人，都靠妻子度日。這個現象豈不奇怪。我想一個男子，總有一分能力。做一分的事。何至坐在家裏靠妻子度日。倘然將（不能離婚）的謬見打破了，他豫防著妻子要求離婚，他決不敢如此了，現在造成這個現象，豈非是（不能離婚）四個字害了他們麼？照以上各方面看起來，不能離婚的謬見，是應該打破的了。

　　（二）利用不能離婚的根據。不能離婚說的根據，便是防止淫蕩。這句話我在前面早說過了。防止淫蕩我們總不能說他是錯。不過防止淫蕩和離婚完全是兩件事。舊式人的謬見，把離婚當做淫蕩，把不離婚當做不淫蕩，這句話我們不可不先行辯明。但是現在多數主張離婚的人，不曾把這句話辯明，你只管提倡離婚。他們只當你是提倡淫蕩，這樣豈不是愈弄愈壞。這件事雖然只怪舊式的人頭腦太不清楚，却也怪新式的人不會<u>措辭</u>，使他們生出誤會來。所以我說凡是提倡離婚的人。一面須要極力攻擊淫蕩。使舊式的人知道淫蕩和離婚不同。一面也須<u>自礪</u>，切不可偶然陷於淫蕩的嫌疑，方減少反對離婚的阻力。而且防止淫蕩，也是新人格裏必不可少的事。我們須要和提倡離婚同時並進，再說一句，便是世上的事。最怕走入極端，以前因防止淫蕩，變成絕對禁止離婚的大害。現在切不可因為提倡離婚，便又走向極端去了，在提倡的人，我知道他決沒有這事發生，

揮霍	huīhuò	squander
謬見	miùjiàn	erroneous views or opinions
措辭	cuòcí	choice of wording; diction
自礪	zìlì	temper; steel oneself

但恐一般沒有澈底覺悟的人，借著這個潮流胡鬧，也是不能免的事。所以提倡的時候，不可不豫防。

提倡離婚，果然如此做去，自然可以收獲效果。只是在現在的時代，有三個難解決的問題，不得不再要研究。

（一）現在已嫁的女子，多數沒有自立的技能。離婚以後，他怎麼度日。難道便置之不問麼？

（二）現在舊習慣沒有完全革除。譬男子對於女子。要求離婚，在男子認為不算甚麼事，却是女子於離婚以後，為習慣的束縛，不能再嫁。這也是一件極不平的事。

（三）在童兒沒有<u>公育機關</u>以前，倘然有了兒女，被他牽制，却又如何解決？

以上三個問題，實在難解決，我們要解決時，第一要養成女子有自立的技能。第二要改移社會的習尚，承認娶再嫁之婦，第三要組織兒女公育機關。然這三件事是不是一天能辦得到？這句話我實在不敢說。這三件事一天辦不到。便是離婚問題一天難解決。

然而難解決只管難解決，我們却不可不向前做去。在這過渡時候，中間也有許多危險，但這許多危險，我們是認為不能免的。總而言之：我們切不可<u>因噎廢食</u>，却不能<u>貪食致病</u>。

公育機關	gōngyù jīguā	(institutions of) public education
因噎廢食	yīnyē fèishí	"give up eating for fear of choking"
貪食致病	tānshí zhìbìng	"be so greedy as to make oneself ill"

李三㐫： 自由離婚論

NB. English terms below appear as in the original

本誌第三號，四珍君介紹瑞典<u>愛倫凱</u>女士所作『愛情與結婚』一書。他的書裏面詳說愛情的性質，愛情和結婚的關係，把愛情這件東西，看做結婚的中心要素。(Centre element) 很為<u>精密週到</u>，<u>不偏不倚</u>，合乎<u>中庸</u>。我是在近代婦女問題學者裏面，最佩服最景慕愛女士的。所以現在也學<u>東施效</u><u>顰</u>作一篇文章，拿他的自由離婚論作根據，另外稍微附加我自己的意見，參合而成，覺得可以和四珍君的那篇『愛情與結婚』互相發明的地方不少。

但是我們要想明白愛女士的自由離婚，必須先明白愛女士的愛情與結婚。因為自由離婚這件事，是性的理論上新道德 (New morality) 的問題，是對於舊道德 (Old morality) 的一種革命。必定愛情和結婚，先有不可離的關係，然後自由離婚，才能夠成為一種問題。為甚麼呢？<u>愛氏</u>主義，結婚必有愛情做他的基礎。反過來說，就是無愛情的男女，不能結婚。再從此意推開，就是從前雖有愛情，可以結婚，而且既經結婚，但是現在男女兩方面的愛情，卻已到了完全消滅的程度。這時<u>天倫</u>的樂趣，一點也沒有，還說甚麼<u>夫唱婦隨</u>，不如分離各便為妙。這就是愛女士主張自由離婚的根本理由。現在我為研究的順序起見，先把愛女士關於新道德方面愛情和結婚的<u>綱要</u>，略微附帶的說明一下，然後再入本題，便不致招語出無根的譏誚了。

愛倫凱	Àilún Kǎi	Ellen Key (1849-1926), Swedish writer and social reformer
精密	jīngmì	precise; accurate
週到	zhōudào	thorough
不偏不倚	bùpiān bùyǐ	impartial
中庸	zhōngyōng	the golden mean
東施效顰	Dōngshī xiàopín	the ugly Dong Shi knitting her brows in imitation of the beauty Xi Shi, only to make herself uglier; blind imitation
愛氏	Àishì	Ms. Key
天倫	tiānlún	natural bonds between family members
夫唱婦隨	fūchàng fùsuí	the husband sings and the wife follows: domestic harmony
綱要	gāngyào	outline; essentials

關於性的倫理愛女士代表的著述『愛情與結婚』裏面，依愛氏自己的說明：『一方對於<u>種族改良</u>的要求，和他方從格外增加愛情求其幸福的個人要求中間，看出適當平衡調和的計畫。』這就是新道德的<u>要旨</u>。因而我們從這樣計畫，引出兩個問題：一個是種族的改良：(Species of improvement) 一個是愛情的幸福。(Love of happiness) 若是和舊道德對比起來，恐怕愛情的幸福，是他的議論的焦點 (Focus) 呢？

愛倫凱女士，是近代有名的個人主義 (Individualism) 學者。對於個人 (Individual) 的幸福，非常重視。把個人的幸福之一，求之於各個人的愛情要求的裏面。極力主張愛情的價值。同時又把性的道德的全部根源，擺在愛情的底下，照這樣看來，雖把愛女士的思想，叫做一種『愛情教』，(Love Religion) 也沒有甚麼不行的。

把愛情作為根源的愛倫凱女士，對於性的道德裏面最重大的結婚道德，定下一種倫理法典 (Ethic Statute) 他說：『無論甚麼結婚，有愛情的，便是道德的；雖經過法律上的手續形式，如果毫無愛情，便是不道德的。』就是依愛女士所說結婚生活上道德的或不道德的標準，全然因愛情的有無而決定。至於是否經過法律上的手續形式，並不成為問題，可以撇開不論。簡括的說，愛女士所主張的<u>精髓</u>，結婚必根於實質上的愛情，法律上的手續形式，一概可以不要。男女若是兩下有愛情的時候，無論怎樣，總可能夠結婚。假若不是這樣，便始終不能夠結婚。大約愛女士關於結婚道德是一個形式廢除論者呢！

因為愛女士把愛情的有無，做為結婚道德的不道德的標準，那麼當然引出第二個性的道德的特色，就是他有名的自由離婚論。愛女士以為愛情雖是結婚的唯一要義，但是若說男女的愛情是一件終身不變的東西，恐怕無論甚麼人，總不敢相信，譬如現在有男女兩個人，他二十歲的時候，愛情非常熱烈濃厚，<u>似漆如膠</u>，到了三十歲乃至四十歲的時候，勢易時移，

種族改良	zhǒngzú gǎiliáng	"improving the race"; eugenics
要旨	yàozhǐ	main idea; gist
精髓	jīngsuǐ	essence
似漆如膠	sìqīrújiāo	like glue and lacquer; deep love
一絲毫	yīsīháo	at all; one little bit

說是他們兩人的愛情，仍然和二十歲的時候一絲毫不差，始終如一，
對於這個論斷，可以說沒有那一個人，敢於大膽的點頭稱是。所以愛女士
一面說明愛情和結婚的關係；一面又主張自由離婚。他說：『不能够保持
永久的愛情，和不能够保持長生不老一樣。能够保持的，不過對於生命和
愛情，加以最好的注意罷了。』因而對於離婚，他以為是心靈的世界上：
和感覺的世界上；一種不能够預知的變動，無論甚麼人，都能作無條件的
要求。愛女士的意見如此。這就是他的自由離婚論心理的根據。從此類推
起來，那向無愛情的<u>強制結婚</u>，或由父母做主；或因勢利關係；一切男女
無意識的結合，照理都應當許他自由分離，這是不用說的。愛氏既拿愛情
做為結婚的基礎，臨了歸結到自由離婚，自是當然的徑路。從這一點看起
來，所謂一夫一婦外面的形式，不待說已是破壞無餘的了。

　　愛女士的自由離婚論發表以後，很有許多主張『舊道德』的學者，極
端反對他的結婚道德：竟至罵他為道德上虛無主義。(Moral Anarchism) 把
嚴格的終身一夫一婦的結合，做為<u>性的倫理</u>的根本，就是把嚴格一夫一婦
的形式，做為性的道德第一條件。他所根據的理由，以為：『確定形式的
結婚，纔能够說是堅固永久自我的表現。個人在無責任的狀態時候，對於
別人的生活，<u>動輒</u>容易斷行給他一種重大影響的決心。但是確定形式的結
婚，在這時候，已經奪去他的行為的自由，最能強制的<u>駕馭</u>他。因為順住
性的方面<u>一時的衝動</u>和情念而行動時，我們便完全失却洞察和先見，而且
要從我們自己的人格的自然，和人生一般的秩序上，脫離孤立，無所憑
依。所以婚姻要民法上的形式來表示性的關係外面的結果，警戒外面的責
任。一旦依民法上的形式成立以後，便當為永續的，不能隨意變更。』又
說：『離婚太易的結果，決不得安安穩穩的過幸福的社會生活。一般人承
認自由離婚，不過出於一時的氣忿和利己心，並沒有甚麼道理。』以上所
講的是反對派的主張。

強制結婚	qiángzhì jiéhūn	forced marriage
性的倫理	xìng de lúnlǐ	sexual ethic
動輒	dòngzhé	easily; frequently
駕馭	jiàyù	control; master
(一時的)衝動	chōngdòng	act on impulse; the spur of the moment
洞察	dòngchá	insight; ability to see clearly

反對派從舊道德立論，本乎<u>基督教</u>的主旨，來說明結婚道德。那麼當然和愛女士的新道德不相容。他一面提倡一夫一婦形成的<u>嚴守</u>，一面又講<u>良心</u>力克己力和<u>禁慾生活</u>的必要。他所主張的愛情，是精神的和靈的。他以為基督的人格，是最高尚的。所以想論兩性問題，除非基督，纔能有此資格。否則也必要古代教裏面的<u>大聖徒</u>。因為基督教的感情，是忘我的無我的愛和強烈精神的向上慾的作用。既是基督教忘我的愛的作用，他的愛情，自然從<u>空疎</u>感覺的領域脫離，而為高尚精神的愛情。就是想拿良心力克己力和禁慾主義來澈底的嚴守一夫一婦的關係。對於兩性間衝動和情念的世界，用一夫一婦的確定形式，意志的征服了他。這就是他舊道德根本的義意所在啊。

依反對派所說：『愛氏主張我們的人格，無論是善是惡，都應當<u>放任</u>於強烈色情的刺戟。人類是本能<u>卑劣</u>的奴隸，單為性慾而生存的。就是僅僅性慾的誘惑，纔是唯一的實在。其餘一切人生的目的或任務，不過是<u>幽靈</u>是形像罷了。』這樣一種批難，不免流於偏見和誤解。上面已經說過，愛氏拿愛情做性的道德的中心，把結婚外面的形式，置之度外，極力撇開，而鼓吹離婚的自由。但是愛氏所提倡的，果如反對派所說，是那麼卑俗的嗎？這必定要先看愛氏的愛情觀，然後纔能夠破他的誤謬。愛氏愛情觀，決不是像那反對派批難的放縱無度，又不像是反對派偏於精神的和靈的愛情。他所說的愛情，是一方面極肉慾的；同時他方面又極靈的。恰如<u>法蘭西</u>多數學者所說：『既非以感覺反對靈魂；同時又非以靈魂反對感覺。』實在是『靈肉一致的愛情。大凡無靈魂感覺本位的愛情，是本能的

基督教	Jīdūjiào	Christianity
嚴守	yánshǒu	strictly observe
良心	liángxīn	conscience
禁慾生活	jìnyù shēnghuó	ascetic life
大聖徒	dàshèngtú	great saints; sages
空疎	kōngshū	empty; lacking in substance
放任	fàngrèn	indulge; give free rein to
卑劣	bēiliè	base; despicable
幽靈	yōulíng	specter; ghost
法蘭西	Fǎlánxī	France; French

衝動的愛情，就是所謂『自由戀愛』；無感覺靈魂本位的愛情，是<u>空靈</u>的愛情。這兩種都不是愛女士所取。不僅為他所不取，而且極端的批難他。對於後面空靈的愛情，尤為格外極端的批難。世人把這種空靈的愛情，認為非常純潔，看得怎麼高尚，極力去尊敬他，這實在是基督教禁慾主義<u>釀成</u>的一個<u>弊害</u>。所以<u>蔑視</u>感覺、絕滅肉慾的，決不能算完全的愛情。因為愛情無所<u>附麗</u>的緣故，愛情既無所附麗，愛情兩個字，尚從何處說起。這是我希望大家注意的。

愛女士固然是破壞一夫一婦永續的形式學者，但是他在理想的境地，也未嘗不講究一夫一婦永續的形式，相信永續的一夫一婦的可能。他說：『愛情進化的過程，就是使人類達到一夫一婦的境地。』他的『愛情與結婚』的書裏面，有『愛情的進化』(Love of Evolve)一章，研究愛情進化的過程。以為他的最後境地，拿男女相互感覺和心靈的結合；慾望和義務的結合：自我主義和自我<u>獻奉</u>的結合：做人格的結合之愛情基礎。照此看來，愛氏愛情觀的理想方面，既有這樣高尚的意味，那麼像反對派所說，愛氏主張的愛情，是放縱無度的<u>官能</u>的追求，和肉慾的滿足許多話，全然是誤解偏見，在社會學上，毫無甚麼價值，不待煩言而解的了。

愛女士的自由離婚論是從倫理的方面社會的方面立論。除去他心理學的根柢以外，更能彀做現代結婚制度所釀成的弊害救濟策。雖然不是計出萬全，竟得比那嚴守一夫一婦形式所生的弊害較少。所以他說：『自由離婚，縱含有許多弊害，但是對於從野鄙的習慣；最無恥的買賣性交；最可痛的心靈虐殺；最無人道的殘害；和近代生活諸方面；所生出來的各種對於自由極野蠻的侵害等，因結婚而已經釀出，或正在醞釀的，和自由離婚比較起來，他的弊害程度，尤為重大。』這話實在不錯。如上面所講，愛氏於愛情進化理想的境地，相信一夫一婦制的可能，但是一轉眼看來，現

空靈	kōnglíng	empty; hollow
釀成	niàngchéng	breed; lead to
弊害	bìhài	harm; drawback
蔑視	mièshì	despise; scorn
附麗	fùlì	attach self to; rely on
獻奉	xiànfèng	offering; sacrifice
官能	guānnéng	sense; sensory

代實際社會上一般人，每每戴住一夫一婦的<u>假面具</u>，<u>肆行</u>他的多夫多婦主義。男子於正妻以外，<u>宿娼納妾</u>；女子於本夫以外，私結情人。這樣醜怪的事情，到處都有，廉恥毫無。所謂<u>野鄙</u>的習慣，最無恥的買賣性交，在一夫一婦的美名底下，公然實行。社會對於他，並不覺得希奇詫異。因為甚麼緣故，有這樣怪現象呢？又怎樣能夠補救這樣怪現象呢？從社會的立腳地看起來，愛倫凱女士的自由離婚論，要不外把這個問題做為出發點而考察的。

那麼上面所說的怪現象，現代戴住假面具的一夫一婦制，就是他的原因。換句話說，就是各個人不明白愛情意義的緣故，也就是不明白戀愛的自由和戀愛的選擇的緣故，再換句話說，就是他的唯一主要原因，在於不明白個人愛情完成的幸福，而拘於社會犧牲的要求。可是自由離婚，却很能夠救濟這樣怪現象的。為甚麼呢？惟有過那無意義<u>脫壳</u>的形骸結婚生活的男女，纔能夠做法律和習慣的犧牲，接續著過他的無意義醜怪的共同生活，秘密做不正當的性交，而能夠做他代替的。就是公然離婚。這不獨當事人的男女兩方面的利益，也是種族全體的幸福呢！

不過因為自由離婚，發生一種問題，就是離婚當事人生有子女的時候。在這個時候，愛女士仍然無<u>躊躇</u>的主張自由離婚。他說：『有子女也不是希奇的事，事實上夫婦關係，因為不能繼續，至於離婚，這是自己的過失。那麼對於所生的子女，不能免除共同養育的義務。但是他們養育子女也不必同居一室，不妨各自分居。』就是愛氏的意思，雖有子女，應當教育，也可以離婚。夫婦關係，既然到了義絕，便一點情趣都無。那麼又何必因為子女的緣故，勉強繼續那毫無情趣的夫婦關係，再事同居，徒然格外墮落離婚當事人的人格，而且格外給兒童一種無價值的感化。所以在這個時候，應當毅然決然的離婚，

假面具	jiǎmiànjù	mask; hypocrisy
肆行	sìxíng	wantonly
宿娼納妾	sùchāng nàqiè	visit prostitutes, take concubines
野鄙	yěbǐ	unruly and vulgar
脫壳	tuōké/qiào	remove the shell of something
躊躇	chóuchú	hesitate

不必顧慮。至於子女的撫養義務，隨便由男女那方面負擔，都沒有甚麼障礙的。自由離婚有兩種利益：一種是當事人的利益；一種是他們子女的利益。第一種利益，已經在上面各處說過。至於第二種利益，愛女士說：『離婚若是因兩親間性格或起見的不投而起的，那麼兒童自他的父母離婚以後他的狀態，格外要好。因為這個時候，兒童由他的父親和母親意志相反互相傾軋的痛苦境地逃了出來的緣故。』這又是一定的道理，不用我再饒舌了。

　　照上面所說看來，自由離婚，並不是結婚的破壞，寧可說是結婚保存的第一條件。不過外形上雖是同一自由離婚論，又各因提倡的人人生觀不同，他的內容，因而各別。就是愛倫凱女士等理想家所主張的自由離婚，看前面所講的，決不是拿自由戀愛做根柢。他所尊重的，不是『自由戀愛』(Free Love) 乃是『戀愛的自由』(Love of Freedom) 不是自由的戀愛乃是自由和責任相伴的戀愛。戀愛的自由，就是愛情不受脅迫，不加勉強的意思。自由戀愛不是這樣就是無論對於甚麼人，聽我高興，要戀愛便戀愛，毫無拘束限制的意思。兩下對比起來，兩個當然是不同的。然而很有許多人，把這兩個不同的名辭，混為一談。殊不可解自由戀愛是著眼在唯物觀的人生觀偏於性慾的肉體的方面。戀愛的自由便和他相反是在唯心的人生觀偏於精神的靈魂的方面，有這兩種差別，所以雖是同一自由離婚，因為出發點不同，他的歸宿，便自不得不有區別。現在正是新理想主義勃興時代，愛女士唯心的人生觀，當然可以合於時代要求暢行無阻的。那麼一般學者罵他為 (Moral Anarchism) 的，恐怕要自悔失言了。

顧慮	gùlǜ	have misgivings; worry
脅迫	xiépò	intimidate; coerce
唯物觀	wéiwùguān	materialist viewpoint
唯心的	wéixīnde	idealist
暢行無阻	chàngxíngwúzǔ	unimpeded; without obstruction

3. REFORM AND REVOLUTION

The Three People's Principles
Sun Yat-sen

Sun Yat-sen (Sun Yixian, Sun Zhongshan, 1866-1925) was one of the most prolific writers and thinkers of the first decades of the twentieth century. He was the founder and leading voice of a succession of revolutionary groups, whose aims evolved from reform and self-strengthening to a platform of "driving out the barbarian Manchus, restoring China to the Chinese, and creating a republic." By 1905, when Sun was back in Europe establishing new student revolutionary groups, land reform had been added to the pledge; and when the Revolutionary Alliance (同盟會 Tongmenghui) was formed in Japan later that year, succeeding Sun's Society for the Revival of China (興中會 Xingzhonghui), the equalization of land rights remained alongside the overthrow of the state in Sun's famous four-point declaration. The Tongmenghui manifesto set out a timetable for a three-stage path to democracy, envisaging China first governed by military law, then a six-year period under a provisional constitution, followed by full-blown democratic government by the people, locally and nationally. It was around this time that Sun first began to believe that the fall of the last imperial dynasty might take place during his own lifetime.[1] Sun, who "started life as an iconographer and died an icon,"[2] not only lived to see it happen, but became, briefly, the first president of the Republic of China.

Sun Yat-sen's thought and his political activity were inextricably intertwined. Although there were numerous cells of revolutionary activists extant during the late Qing, and reformists such as Liang Qichao and Kang Youwei gained a public voice by venting opposition in the new press, it would be difficult to separate the course of revolutionary activity from the life of Sun prior to the Wuchang revolt which sparked the revolution in October 1911. The international nature of the revolution, fomented in Japan and financed through the United States, is well known, but Sun spent more than a decade switching back and forth between centers of activity in Yokohama, Tokyo, London, Brussels, Berlin, Hong Kong, California, and Honolulu, as he sought support and brokered new revolutionary groups among overseas Chinese. Both Sun and the groups he founded suffered numerous setbacks and failures, underwent re-thinking and re-organization, and were forced to form a makeshift set of alliances with secret societies and other anti-Qing groups. Sun was expelled from China in 1895 following the unsuccessful Canton revolt, imprisoned in London in 1896, and took flight from Japan in 1907 following Qing government pressure.

---

1. George T. Yu, *Party Politics in Republican China*, 45.
2. John Fitzgerald, *Awakening China*, 26.

Internal dissent, division, leadership splits, and abortive insurrections characterized the erratic progress toward revolution.

Sun's *Three People's Principles* (三民主義 Sanmin zhuyi)—his politico-philosophical prescription for a new and triumphant China—was a long time in the making. As it germinated from early versions in 1905 to the final written edition in 1924, the Chinese empire fell; Sun founded the Nationalist Party (Guomindang), only to see it banned in 1913; the Chinese language was radically changed; a student protest movement altered the course of the nation. When Sun re-formed the Nationalist Party in Shanghai in 1920, the unfavorable international situation forced a change of outlook, and the party began to look to the Comintern and the Soviet Union for inspiration. Sun's tripartite program of democracy differed from other revolutionary writings in that it was not just a plan for an initial coup, but a comprehensive program for reform and governance. Sun's thought developed from its initial focus on the nation-state, with concomitant ideas on race, national destiny, and social Darwinism, to a deep concern with citizenship and civic republicanism after the fall of the Qing.[3] Sun read widely and thought much about the welter of issues facing China as the country sought the economic and social stability necessary to ensure the well-being of its new citizens. He produced an array of writings on defense issues, foreign policy, law, post-war industrial readjustment, and land utilization. In the manner of a Confucian philosopher, his works were not bound by time and space but took in the whole span of human society. The Three People's Principles were both ideological doctrine and concrete measures for the reconstruction of China, "a spiritual creed to inspire and galvanize the Chinese people to fulfill his revolutionary vision."[4] Sun's mentors and influences included political thinkers from Rousseau to Montesquieu, Mill to Marx, as well as Henry George (whose ideas on taxation and land nationalization were set out in his *Progress and Poverty*), and possibly also the Swiss thinker J. K. Bluntschli (who wrote on the need for a strong central state).[5] He was also deeply influenced by the humane socialism of his own Christian beliefs.

The *Three People's Principles* took initial shape during hours spent in the reading room of the British Museum in 1896-97, according to Sun's later memoirs. During this early period in exile, Sun developed his theory of governance under the three principles of nationalism, democracy, and socialism. His preliminary ideas were published in newspapers such as *People's Newspaper* (民報 Minbao), where the term *Sanmin zhuyi* was first used in 1905. By 1912, when the revolution propelled him to the presidency, Sun was able to declare the realization of the first two principles complete, while the third constituted the task ahead. By the time

---

3. Rana Mitter, *A Bitter Revolution*, 139-41.
4. Sidney H. Chang and Leonard H. D. Gordon, *All Under Heaven*, 24.
5. On the latter, see Audrey Wells, *The Political Thought of Sun Yat-sen*, 31-35.

Sun was drawing his thinking together in the great compendium *Reconstruction of the State* (建國大綱 Jianguo dagang, 1924), his ideas were widely known among radicals and politicians. To the deep distress of Sun, whose "blood and heart" went into their writing, his papers and foreign library were destroyed by fire when his ally Chen Jiongming rebelled in Canton in 1922. Sun had used his time residing in Shanghai's French concession in 1919 to systematize his thought, and the waste of all this effort was galling. The version of the *Three People's Principles* now in circulation is the edited transcript of a series of extempore lectures that Sun gave in 1924. As Sun wrote in the preface to this edition, he had had no time to prepare these lectures and no reference material at hand; in organization and substance, therefore, these lectures were much inferior to the cindered version. They were produced to meet the "urgent need" of the Nationalist Party for his guiding thought in their attempts to win hearts and minds in China, and Sun hoped that others would improve and complete the text.[6] Sun was not just being modest: critics have written of the "repetitive, convoluted and even misleading arguments of the lectures," which were drafted as Sun fought terminal cancer.[7] Yet although the text is hasty, it benefits from the simple and direct language of oral delivery; and his plea for it to be seen as a work in progress signals both the collaborative nature of his politics and his adherence to traditional Chinese textual practices.

Nationalism, or *minzu zhuyi* 民族主義, was the focus of the first six lectures, and the immediate object of the revolution. Sun believed that a deep-rooted consciousness of the nation was needed in order to unite the Chinese people, and thus to achieve the dual aims of removing the oppressive Manchus and resisting Western aggression and economic imperialism. The term *minzu*, a Japanese neologism, was not without its problems, since it conflated ethnicity with nationhood (whereas Sun at this stage identified five groups in the state: the Chinese, Mongol, Manchu, Tibetan and Muslim peoples). Sun appealed to the common language, religion, and blood ties that united the Han people as a way of melding local clan or family affiliations and promoting an overarching loyalty to the state. Sun praised China's traditional strengths and values, advocating the retention of that which was good in classical learning. Yet at the same time, China, just like Japan before it, would be well advised to adopt selectively from the West.

The second series of Sun's lectures was devoted to democracy, or *minquan* 民權. The term suggests "people's rights" or "people's powers," but Sun used it to mean the people's sovereignty, or their exercise of state power,

---

6. Sun Yat-sen, *Guofu quanji* (國父全集 The Complete Works of Sun Yat-sen; Taibei: Zhonghua jinian guofu bainian danchen shou bei weiyuanhui, 1974), Vol. 1, Preface, 1.
7. Fitzgerald, *Awakening China*, 9.

choosing not to use the alternative *minzhu* 民主. Sun, who possessed "an almost mystical faith in the inevitability of democracy's succeeding in China," [8] linked democratic governance to the ideal systems of the philosophers Confucius and Mencius. Aware of the problems of a new political system for a people long used to autocracy, Sun believed the Chinese needed educating into democracy. He linked democracy to the second of the French triad, *egalité* (and, incidentally, *liberté* to his *minzu*), but argued that—contrary to Western democracy, with its insistence on liberty—China had too much individual freedom and needed rather more discipline. Sun divided national power into two conceptual parts: democratic power, held by the people, and executive power, held by the government. China needed a centralized democracy, but one in which the whole people participated. If they could go beyond the representative government of the West, they would outdo it in democracy. Sun approved of the U.S. model of powers divided between executive, legislative, and judicial spheres, but added two more in the Chinese case: an examination system (to determine the best candidates for government) and a censorial sphere (to check government power). These together formed his Five Power Constitution. The centrality of the rule of law, and the secondary place of military power, were the core of his philosophy.

The final and incomplete set of four lectures discussed the "people's livelihood," *minsheng* 民生, often equated with "socialism." In the late 1910s, Sun's political power was at a low ebb, while at the same time warlord politics had left the economy fragile. Sun aimed to raise national economic well-being and overcome rural poverty, focusing in his lectures on food and textile production. He wanted a more equitable distribution of wealth, and to this end sought capital regulation and equalization of land ownership, following Henry George's model. Large industries such as banking and the railways were to be nationalized, but Sun challenged the core economic claims of Marxism. For Sun, China could still avoid both oppressive Western capitalist excesses, and the solutions to them that Communists proposed through class war and proletarian dictatorship. His later Communist critics would claim that Sun Yatsenism engendered a bourgeois-democratic revolution, lacking class awareness and settling for capitalism rather than the end goal of communism. Sun, for his part, never regained the power or health to test his ideas in practice, but it is far from clear that the Guomindang implemented them as he would have wished.

Excerpted from Sun Yat-sen, *Guofu quanji*, vol. 1 (Taibei: Zhonghua jinian guofu bainian danchen shou bei weiyuanhui, 1974), 122-26, adapted.

---

8. Chang and Gordon, *All under Heaven,* 108.

Further Reading

Bedeski, Robert E. "The Concept of the State: Sun Yat-sen and Mao Tse-tung." *China Quarterly* 70 (1977), 338-54.

Chang, Sidney H., and Leonard H. D. Gordon. *All Under Heaven: Sun Yat-sen and His Revolutionary Thought*. Stanford: Hoover Institution Press, 1991.

Fitzgerald, John. *Awakening China: Politics, Culture and Class in the Nationalist Revolution*. Stanford: Stanford University Press, 1996.

Godley, Michael R. "Socialism with Chinese Characteristics: Sun Yatsen and the International Development of China." *Australian Journal of Chinese Affairs* 18 (1987), 109-25.

Gregor, A. James and Maria Hsia Chang. "Nazionalfascismo and the Revolutionary Nationalism of Sun Yat-sen." *Journal of Asian Studies* 39/1 (1979), 21-37.

Greiff, Thomas E. "The Principle of Human Rights in Nationalist China: John C. H. Wu and the Ideological Origins of the 1946 Constitution." *China Quarterly* 103 (1985), 441-61.

Mitter, Rana. *A Bitter Revolution: China's Struggle with the Modern World*. Oxford: Oxford University Press, 2004.

Wells, Audrey. *The Political Thought of Sun Yat-sen: Development and Impact*. Basingstoke: Palgrave, 2001.

Whiting, Allen S. "A New Version of San Min Chu I." *Far Eastern Quarterly* 14/3 (1955), 389-91.

Yu, George T. *Party Politics in Republican China: The Kuomintang, 1912-1924*. Berkeley: University of California Press, 1966.

———. "The 1911 Revolution: Past, Present, and Future." *Asian Survey* 31/10 (1991), 895-904.

三民主義：民生主義 Lecture 1

諸君：

　　今天來講<u>民生主義</u>，什麼叫做民生主義呢？"民生"兩個字是中國向來用慣的一個名詞。我們常說什麼"<u>國計民生</u>"，不過我們所用這句話恐怕多是<u>信口</u>而出，不求甚解，未見得涵有幾多意義的，但是今日科學大明，在科學范圍內拿這個名詞來用於社會經濟上，就覺得意義無窮了。我今天就拿這個名詞來下一定定義，可說民生就是人民的生活，社會的生存、國民<u>生計</u>、群眾的生命便是。我現在就是用民生二字，來講處國近百十年來所發生的一個最大問題，這個問題就是社會問題，故民生主義就是社會主義，又名共產主義，即是<u>大同主義</u>。欲明白這個主義，斷非幾句定義的話可以講得清楚的；必須把民生主義的演講從頭到尾，才可以徹底明白了解的。

　　民生問題，今日成了世界各國的潮流。推到這個問題的來歷，發生不過一百幾十年。為什麼近代發生這個問題呢？簡單言之，就是因為這幾十年來，各國的<u>物質文明</u>極進步，工商業很發達，人類的的生產力忽然增加。著實言之，就是由於發明了機器，世界文明先進的人類便逐漸不用人力來做工，而用天然力來做工，就是用天然的汽力、火力、水力及電力來代替人的氣力，用金屬的銅鐵來替代的筋骨，機器發明之后，用一個人管理一副機器，便可以做一百人或一千人的工夫，所以機器的生產力和人工的生產便有大大的分別。在沒有機器以前，一個最勤勞的人，最多不過是做兩三個人的工夫，斷不能做得十個人以上工夫。照此推論起來，一個人

民生主義	mínshēngzhǔyì	The Principle of the People's Livelihood
國計民生	guójì mínshēng	national welfare
信口	xìnkǒu	blurted out
生計	shēngjì	livelihood
大同主義	dàtóng zhǔyì	Utopianism; belief in Great Harmony
物質文明	wùzhìwénmíng	material civilization

的生產力，就本領最大、<u>體魄</u>最強和最勤勞的人說，也不過是大過普通人十倍。平常人的生產力都是相等的，沒有什麼大差別，至於用機器來做工的生產力，和用人做工的生產力兩相比較，便很不相同，用人來做工，就是極有能干而兼勤勞的人，隻可以駕乎平常人的十倍；但是用機器來做工，就是用一個很懶惰和很尋常的人去管理，他的生產力也可以駕乎一個人力的幾百倍，或者是千倍，所以這幾十年來機器發明了之后，生產力比較從前就有很大的差別。我們拿眼前的可以証明的事實來說一說，比方在廣州市街上所見最多的人，莫如運送的苦力，這種苦力就叫做<u>挑夫</u>，這種挑夫的人數，佔廣州市工人中一大部分，挑夫之中體魄最強壯的人，最重的隻可以挑二百斤東西，每日不過是走幾十裡路遠，這種挑夫是很不容易得的。尋常的挑夫，挑了幾十斤重，走了幾十裡路遠，便覺得很辛苦。如果拿挑夫和運送的機器來比較，是怎麼樣的情形呢？象廣州市黃沙的火車，運送貨物，一駕火車頭可以拖二十多架貨車，一架貨車可以載幾百擔重的貨物，一架火車能夠載幾百擔，二十多架火車便能夠載一萬擔。這一萬擔貨物，用一架火車頭去拉，隻要一兩個人管理火車頭的機器，或者要幾個人管理貨車，一日便可以走幾百裡。譬如廣東的<u>粵漢鐵路</u>，由黃沙到韶關約有五百裡的路程，象從前專用人力去運貨物，一個人挑一擔，一百個人一百擔，如果有一萬擔貨物，就要有一萬個工人。用工人所走的路程計算，一個人一天大概隻能夠走五十裡，五百裡的路程就要走十天的時間。所以一萬擔貨物，從前專用人工去運送，就要一萬個工人，走十天之久，現在用火車去運送，隻要八點鐘的時間，一直便由黃沙到韶關，所用工人最多不過是十個人。由此便知道用十個人所做工便可以替代一萬人，用八點鐘便可以替代十天。機器和人工比較的相差，該是有多少呢！用火車來運送的工，不但是用一個人可以替代一千人。用一點種可以替代一日，是很便利迅速的。就是以運貨的工錢來說，一個工人挑一擔貨物，走五十裡路遠，每天大約要一元。要用一萬工人，跳一萬擔貨物，走

體魄	tǐpò	physique
挑夫	tiāofū	porter (carrying a shoulder pole)
粵漢鐵路	Yuè-Hàn tiělù	Guangdong-Wuhan (Hankou) railway

十天的路，統共就要十萬元。如果用火車來運送，頂多不過是幾千元，機器和人工的比較，單拿挑夫來講便有這樣的大差別，其他耕田、織布、做房屋以及種種工作，也是有幾百倍或幾千倍的差別。所以機器發明了之后，世界的生產力便生出一個大變動。這個大變動，就是機器佔了人工，有機器的人便把沒有機器的人的錢都賺去了。再象廣州沒有經過<u>鴉片戰爭</u>以前，是中國獨一的<u>通商口岸</u>，中國各省的貨物都是先運來廣州，然后再由廣州運去外洋；外國的貨物也是先運到廣州，然后由廣州運進各省，所以中國各省的進出口貨物，都是經過湖南、江西，走南雄、樂昌，才到廣州。因為這個原因，所以南雄、樂昌到韶關的這兩條路、在當時沿途的挑夫是很多的，兩旁的茶館飯店也是很熱鬧的。后來<u>海禁</u>大開，各省的貨物或者是有海船運到廣西，或者是由上海，天津直接運送到海洋，都不經過南雄，樂昌到韶關的這兩條路，所以由南雄、樂昌到韶關兩條路的工人，現在都減少了。從前那兩條路的繁盛，現在都變成很荒涼了。到了粵漢鐵路通了火車之后，可以替代人工，由廣州到韶關的挑夫更是<u>絕跡</u>。其他各地各國的情形都是一樣。所以從機器發明了之后，便有許多人一時失業，沒有工做，沒有飯吃。這種大變動，外國叫做實業革命。因為有了這種<u>實業革命</u>，工人便受很大的痛苦。因為要解決這種痛苦，所以近幾十年來便發生社會問題。

這個社會問題，就是今天所講的民生主義。我今天為什麼不學外國直接來講社會主義，要拿民生這個中國古名詞來替代社會主義呢？這是很有道理，我們應該要研究的。因為機器發明以后，經過了實業革命，成為社會問題，便發生社會主義。所以社會主義之發生已經有了幾十年，但是這幾十年中，歐美各國對於社會主義，還沒有找出一個解決方法，現在還

鴉片戰爭	Yāpiàn Zhànzhēng	Opium Wars (1840-42; 1856-60)
通商口岸	tōngshāng kǒuàn	trading port (incl. treaty ports after 1840s)
海禁	hǎijìn	ban on maritime trade with foreign countries
絕跡	juéjì	vanish; be stamped out
實業革命	shíyè gémìng	industrial revolution

是在劇烈戰爭之中。這種學說和思想現在流入中國來了。中國一班新學者也是拿他來研究。因為社會主義，現在中國很流行，所以共產主義現在中國也是很流行。中國學者拿社會主義和共產主義來研究，想尋一個解決方法，也是很艱難的。因為外國發明這種學理已經有了幾十年，到現在還不能夠解決，此時傳入中國。我們就想要解決，當然是不容易的。我們要研究這個問題，便要先把他的<u>源委</u>、性質和定義來研究清楚。共產主義和社會主義兩個名詞，現在外國是一樣並稱的，其中辦法雖然各有不同，但是通稱的名詞都是用社會主義。現在中國有人把社會主義同社會學兩個名詞作一樣的看待，這實在是混亂。這種混亂，不但專是中國人有的，因為社會這個名詞在英文是"<u>梳西乙地</u>"，社會學是"<u>梳西柯羅之</u>"，社會主義是"<u>梳西利甚</u>"。這三個字頭一半的英文串字都是相同的，所以許多人便生出混亂。其實英文中的社會主義"梳西利基"那個字，是從希臘文變出來的，希臘文社會主義的願意是"同志"，就象中國俗話說是"<u>伙計</u>"兩個字一樣，至於說到社會學的范圍，是研究社會的情狀、社會的進化和人類生活的問題，就是研究人民生計的問題。所以我作民生主義替代社會主義，始意就是在<u>正本清源</u>，要把這個問題的真性質表明清楚。要一般人一聽到這個名詞之后，便可以了解。因為社會主義已經發生了幾十年，研究這種學理的學者不知道有千百家，所出的書籍也不知道有千百種。其中關於解決社會問題的學說之多，真是<u>聚訟紛紜</u>。所以外國的俗語說，社會主義有五十七種，究竟不知那一種才是對的。由此便可見普通人對於社會主義無所適從的心理了。歐戰發生了之后，社會的進步很快，世界潮流已經到了解決問題的時期。凡是從前不理會社會主義的人，在此時也跟上社會主義的路來走。就時勢的機會講，社會黨應該可以做很多事，應該可以完

源委 (often 原委)	yuánwěi	the whole story; details
"梳西乙地"	"shūxīyǐdì"	society
"梳西柯羅之"	"shūxīkēluōzhǐ"	sociology
"梳西利甚"	"shūxīlìshèn"	socialism
伙計	huǒji	mate, partner
正本清源	zhèngběn qīngyuán	clarify thoroughly; get to source
聚訟紛紜	jùsòngfēnyún	at variance; widely divided opinions

全解決社會問題。但是社會黨的內部，便生出許多紛爭。在各國的社會黨，一時風起雲涌，發生種種派別，其中最著名的有所謂共產黨、國家社會黨和社會民主黨。各黨派之復雜，幾乎不止五十七種。所以從前旁觀者對於社會黨派別之復雜的批評，至此時正所謂<u>不幸而言中</u>。至於歐戰沒有發生以前，世界各國隻有贊成社會主義和反對社會主義的兩種人。反對的那種人，大多數都是資本家，所以從前隻有反對社會主義的資本家同社會黨來戰爭。到歐戰發生了以后，反對的人都似降服了，社會黨似乎可以<u>乘機</u>來解決社會問題。不過當時贊成社會主義的人，在事前沒有想到好辦法，所以社會黨內部便臨時生出許多紛爭。這種紛爭，比較從前反對派和贊成派的紛爭，更要厲害。所以社會問題至今不能解決，我們到了今日還是要來研究。在從前資本家、工人和學者反對社會主義的時候，所有世界各國贊成社會主義的人，不論是本國外國，都是認為同志。到了近來，不但是德國的社會黨反對俄國的社會黨，或者是俄國的社會黨反對英國、美國的社會黨，有國際的紛爭；就是一國的社會黨內部，也演出種種紛爭。所以社會問題愈演愈紛亂，到現在還找不出一個好方法來解決。

今天我所講的民生主義，究竟和社會主義有沒有分別呢？社會主義中的最大問題，就是社會經濟問題。這種問題，就是一班人的生活問題。因為機器發明以后，大部分人的工作都是被機器奪去了，一班工人不能夠生存，便發生社會問題。所以社會問題之發生，原來是要解決人民的生活問題，故專就這一部分的道理講，社會問題便是民生問題，所以民生主義便可說是社會主義的本題。現在各國的社會主義，各有各的主張，所以各國解決社會問題的方法也是各有不同。社會主義到底是民生主義中的一部分呀，或者民生主義是社會主義中的一部分呢？實業革命以后，研究社會問題的人不下千百家，其中研究最透徹和最有<u>心得</u>的，就是大家所知道的馬克思。馬克思對於社會問題，好象<u>盧梭</u>對於民權問題一樣，在一百多年以

不幸而言中	bùxìngéryánzhòng	predictions have unfortunately come true
乘機	chéngjī	to seize an opportunity
心得	xīndé	what one learns from working or studying
盧梭	Lúsuō	Jean Jacques Rousseau

前歐美研究民權問題的人，沒有那一個不是崇拜盧梭為民權中的聖人，好象中國崇拜孔子一樣；現在研究社會問題的人，也沒有那一個不是崇拜馬克思做社會主義中的聖人。在馬克思的<u>學說</u>沒有發表以前，世界上講社會主義的，都是一種陳義甚高的理論，離事實太過。而馬克思專從事實與歷史方面用功，原原本本把社會問題的經濟變遷，<u>闡發</u>無遺。所以后來學者把社會主義的人分作兩派：一是叫做"<u>烏托邦派</u>"，這個烏托邦和中國<u>黃老</u>所說的<u>華胥氏</u>之國意思相同；一是叫做"科學派"，專從科學方法去研究社會問題之解決。至於烏托邦派是專從理想上來把社會改良成一個安樂的國家，便有這種<u>子虛烏有</u>的寄托。這種寄托是由於人類受了很多痛苦，那些極有道德和悲天憫人的人，見了很不忍心但是沒有力量去改良，所以隻好說理想上空話，作一種<u>寄托</u>。中國俗話說："天生一條虫，地生一片葉；天生一隻鳥，地生一條虫。"這幾句話的意思，就是說有了虫就有葉來養，有了鳥就有虫來養。但是人類的天然形體不完全，生來沒有羽毛，必需衣以<u>御寒</u>，必需食以養生。在<u>太古</u>吃果實的時候，地廣人稀，人人都是很容易覓食，不必做很多的工就可以生活。到了漁獵時代，人民就要打魚獵獸，才可以有魚肉吃，才可以生活，就是要做工才有飯吃。到了<u>游牧</u>時代，人類要從事畜牧才可以生活，當時人人都是逐水草而居，時常遷徒，所有的工作便是很辛苦勤勞。至於農業時代，人類要樹藝五穀才可以生活，彼時人類的生活更是復雜，所有的工作更是辛苦勤勞。到了工商時代，遇事都是用機器，不用人力，人類雖然有力也沒有用處，想去賣工，找不到雇主。在這個時候，便有很多人沒有飯吃，甚至於餓死，所受的痛

學說	xuéshuō	doctrine; theory
闡發	chǎnfā	elucidate; explicate
烏托邦派	Wūtuōbāng pài	Utopianists
黃老	Huáng-Lǎo	Huangdi 黃帝 and Laozi 老子; Huang-Lao Daoism
華胥氏	Huàxūshì	mythical state reached in dream (from the Liezi 列子)
子虛烏有	zǐxū wūyǒu	fictitious; non-existent
寄托	jìtuō	to place (one's hope on)
御寒	yùhán	to keep out the cold
太古	tàigǔ	time immemorial
游牧	yóumù	nomadic

苦不是一言可盡。一般道德家，見得天然界的禽獸不用受痛苦尚且可以得衣食，人類受了痛苦反不容易得衣食，這是很可憫的；想要減少這些痛苦，令人人都可以得衣食，便發明了社會主義的學說，來解決這個問題。所以從前一般講社會主義的人多半是道德家，就是一般贊成的人，也是很有良心、很有道德的。隻有在經濟上已經成功、自私自利、不顧群眾生活的資本家才去反對，才不理社會問題。這個問題既然是為世界大多數人謀生活的問題，先知先覺的人，發明了這個道理之后，自然可以的多數人的同情心來表示贊成。所以這個學說一經出世之后，便組織得有社會黨。社會黨一經成立之后，團體便一天發達一天，一天加大一天，擴充到各國。但是從前講社會主義的人都是烏托邦派，隻希望造一個理想上的安樂世界，來消滅人類的痛苦；至於怎麼樣去消滅的具體方法，他們毫沒有想到。到了馬克思出世之后，便用他的聰明才智和學問經驗，對於這些問題作一種透徹的研究，把古人所不知道和所不能解決的都通通發明出來。他的發明中全憑著經濟原理。他照經濟原理作透徹的研究之后，便批評從前主張社會主義的人，不過是有個人的道德心和群眾的感情作用；其實經濟問題，不是道德心和感情作用可以解決得了的。必須把社會的情狀和社會的進化研究清楚了之后，才可以解決。這種解決社會問題的原理，可以說是全憑事實，不尚理想。至於馬克思所著的書和所發明的學說，可說是集幾千年來人類思想的大成。所以他的學說一出來之后，便<u>舉世風從</u>，各國學者都是信仰他，都是跟住他走；好象盧梭發明了民權主義之后，凡是研究民權的人都信仰盧梭一樣。從馬克思以后，社會主義裡頭便分兩派，一個是烏托邦派，一個是科學派。烏托邦的情形，剛才已經講過了。至科學派，是主張用科學的方法來解決社會問題。因為近幾十年來，物質文明極發達，科學很<u>昌明</u>，凡事都是要憑科學的道理才可以解決，才可以達到圓滿的目的。就是講到社會問題的解決方法，也是要從科學一方面研究清楚了之后，才可以得出結果。

| 舉世風從 | jǔshìfēngcóng | the whole world follows (the example) |
| 昌明 | chāngmíng | well-developed; glorious, bright |

4. RECTIFICATION

Thoughts on March Eighth
Ding Ling

Wild Lilies
Wang Shiwei

The early 1940s was a period of intense and sustained challenge for the Chinese Communist Party and its fledgling government in Yan'an. To the south, it was blockaded by the Nationalists, while eastward the Japanese threatened, squeezing resources and cutting off access routes. At the same time, the "Yan'an way" was at the peak of its persuasive powers, and making new converts all the time as its reputation grew as a place of sanctuary and idealism. In the succinct words of Timothy Cheek, "Drought, Nationalist spies, illiterate peasants and haughty intellectuals bedevilled the Shaan-Gan-Ning government;"[1] and Party cadres found themselves stretched, both logistically and ideologically. Under pressure, the behavior of some began to slip from the standards which they themselves had set. Mao's response was swift, and came in the form of a Rectification Campaign (整风运动 *Zhengfeng yundong*) launched against errant party members. The public form of this contest was a long period of cadre education and investigation, beginning in 1938 but entering a new stage of *Blitzkrieg* in the spring of 1942. The CCP itself and virtually all scholars agree that the Party developed successful ways to prosecute the Revolution—militarily, socially, ideologically—during this movement. Its professed targets were bureaucratism, dogmatism, sectarianism, and a failure to cherish the masses—all problems which were indeed growing steadily out of hand. But in a truer sense, rectification was a vehicle custom-built to create ideological unity within the CCP on the basis of Mao Zedong Thought. And in the inaugural move of a power play which would soon become established pattern, Mao used the campaign both to consolidate his personal authority and to weed out his political opponents.

Mao's rivals fell into two loose alliances: the "Russian Returned Students" who grouped themselves around former party leader Wang Ming; and the loose cannons in the theoretical think-tanks and literary institutions of Yan'an. Wang Ming was a Marxist-Leninist cast in the classical mould, whose close ties to the Soviet Union and the Comintern on the one hand, and determined advocation of a united front with the Nationalists against Japan on the other, increasingly drew Mao's ire. The other group—the focus of this chapter—were more motley in composition, and included

---

1. Timothy Cheek, "The Fading of Wild Lilies: Wang Shiwei and Mao Zedong's Yan'an Talks in the First CPC Rectification Movement," 28.

Ding Ling, Wang Shiwei, Ai Qing, Xiao Jun, He Qifang, and Liu Xuewei. Disparate as they were, these latter antagonists shared a vision of the role which art and literature—and, by natural extension, the intellectuals who were the standard-bearers of this culture—should play within a revolutionary world. Members of the literary intelligentsia such as Ding Ling and Wang Shiwei believed, almost as a mantra, in the ethos of remonstrance. They were loyal to the Party; and, just like devoted servants of the state from Qu Yuan onwards, their loyalty compelled them to speak out whenever they witnessed travesty. But their roots were also of more recent origin. In particular, the desire of the Party's critics for an independent voice showed their lingering allegiance to the spirit of the May Fourth Movement, with its individualism, cosmopolitanism, and faith in the transformative powers of debate.

These intellectuals saw rectification as their chance to drag Yan'an's dark side into the open, and they pressed their case in the mistaken belief that it would meet with favor from the leadership. The two essays excerpted here, Ding Ling's "Thoughts on March Eighth" and Wang Shiwei's "Wild Lilies," appeared in 1942 during a flurry of bold writing which had been launched late the year before by the publication in *Liberation Daily* (解放日报 Jiefang ribao) of Ding Ling polemical piece "We Need Critical Essays" (我们需要杂文 Women xuyao zawen). At the time, Ding was editor of the newspaper's literary page—on which her own essay had appeared—and a well-known stalwart on the intellectual scene. Wang Shiwei, by contrast, was a junior cultural apparatchik, but one in a hurry to make his idealistic mark. "Wild Lilies" was published a few days after Ding Ling's "Thoughts on March Eighth," and it bravely picked up Ding's gauntlet. Both writings have a startling candor, and both openly invoke the spirit of Republican China's premier essayist, Lu Xun. They depict Yan'an as a shady paradise, rife with sexual inequality, intellectual stiflement, and croneyism: a place which might have lauded itself loudly on its egalitarian spirit, but was busy practising the politics of hierarchy on the ground. Perhaps it was naïve of Ding and Wang to expect otherwise: after all, Yan'an was a guerrilla government and, as Gregor Benton and Alan Hunter explain, the regime "insisted like any other military establishment on discipline, regimentation, secrecy, top-down command, and the concentration of power at the center."[2] Ding and Wang's essays reveal the effects of this dirigisme on the real lives of Yan'an residents, and their writing homes in on themes of justice and morality. Long used to seeing itself as the arbiter of precisely these virtues, the Party was constitutionally disinclined to tolerate so blunt a critique.

If anything, Ding Ling's essay is the more circumspect of the two,

---

2. Gregor Benton and Alan Hunter, "Introduction," in Benton and Hunter, eds., *Wild Lily, Prairie Fire*, 6.

although it still packs a punch. Ding's subject is the status of women cadres in Yan'an, and her argument chimes closely with Julia Kristeva's later insights into the dangerous irreconcilability of the revolutionary and feminist causes. Women cadres imbibed as truth the Party word that their own liberation would follow in the wake of a liberated nation; but the realities of life in Yan'an were beginning to suggest a different story, in which peasant education, military victory, and land reform pushed women's rights to the bottom of the pile. To make matters worse, sexual politics in the Communist utopia worked to make even this lowly position untenable. Whatever its rhetoric touted, daily praxis in Yan'an legislated against both traditional domesticity and radical activism as proper paths for women: in the words of Yi-tsi Mei Feuerwerker, "They were forever the objects of attention or criticism, damned if they married or didn't, had children or didn't, stayed home or didn't."[3] And while revolutionary aesthetics might have preached against feminine frivolity, male cadres were as keen as ever on nubile, pretty women. Indeed, Ding Ling is discreetly scathing about those Yan'an men who divorced their plain or ageing wives on the grounds of their "political backwardness," only to "trade up" to a younger model soon after. Hung-Yok Ip makes the same point more poignantly when she observes that female long marchers—the heroines of yesteryear—were excluded from the weekly dance party once they had lost their looks.[4] At the core of Ding Ling's critique is bitter dismay at this rift between theory and practice, between dreams of equality and the reality of whispered or direct discrimination.

This same apprehension of rift runs through Wang Shiwei's "Wild Lilies." The essay appeared in two parts on the literature page of *Liberation Daily*, the first published on March 13, and the second ten days later. Comprising a preface and four short critical essays (杂文 *zawen*), Wang's doomed piece begins by pleading the cause of Yan'an youth and ends by damning the remote autocracy of its elders. Youth is precious to Wang, and he opens his essay with the story of Li Fen, a young female revolutionary who was martyred in 1928, and with whom Wang himself had been deeply in love. This opening salvo, as Apter and Cheek have noted, is a "cry from the heart" *à la* Lu Xun, a way of writing politics which "personalizes the world of stylized public experience"[5] at a time when the leadership was turning decisively toward coercive consensus. After laying out these credentials of sincerity, Wang goes on to acknowledge that tough conditions in Yan'an weigh heavily on the morale of its young people. But

---

3. Yi-Tsi Mei Feuerwerker, "In Quest of the Writer Ding Ling," 73.

4. Hung-Yok Ip, "Fashioning Appearances: Feminine Beauty in Chinese Communist Revolutionary Culture," 345.

5. David E. Apter and Timothy Cheek, "Introduction: The Trial," in Dai Qing, *Wang Shiwei and "Wild Lilies*," xvii. Cheek also argues elsewhere that, in a nod to Lu Xun's more satirical bent, Wang intends a contrast between the piety of Li Fen and the more brazen appeal of Jiang Qing, Mao's new wife. See Cheek, "The Fading of Wild Lilies," 34.

he insists that their real malaise can be traced back to the policy of privilege (特殊主义 *teshuzhuyi*), which had created three classes of clothing and five grades of food—and then assigned them according to rank not need. Yan'an was making little effort to hide its pecking order, and Wang warns that this system will both sap the Party faith and blight future recruitment. Most stingingly of all, he argues that high rank, far from functioning as the open door to perks and benefits, should be married to the spirit of austerity. Only then might Yan'an's cadres really work together.

Both Ding Ling and Wang Shiwei felt the wrath of the Party for daring to claim their right to remonstrance. In the initial days and weeks which followed the publication of their essays, loud murmurs of support for their views were audible; but as the machinery of rectification shifted into gear, these voices grew silent or changed their tone. Public condemnations of Wang Shiwei began to appear in April; Mao's Talks at the Yan'an Forum on Art and Literature (the subject of chapter 4) took place in May; and by June the campaign was operating at full throttle, structured around fierce anti-Wang meetings in which the writer was harangued by his opponents. On June 11, Ding Ling herself denounced Wang and recanted her own beliefs in a penitent self-criticism which would go some way toward salvaging her career. Yet Wang held out. This stubbornness, coupled with his increasing isolation in Yan'an, allowed the Party to transform him into a negative model, an incarnation of the sins which rectification had set out to purge. His name struck from the Party register, Wang was imprisoned until the spring of 1947, when he was brutally executed as the Red Army evacuated Yan'an. All the while, his name and the shame which he had suffered were written into CCP lore, both as a warning to others and—more insidiously—as part of the evolving manual on the management of dissidence which Communist leaders would find themselves consulting again and again in the future.

1. Ding Ling. "Sanbajie yougan." In Fan Qiao and Lu Jin, eds. *Ding Ling zawen*. Beijing: Zhongguo guangbo dianshi chubanshe, 1997, 614-18.

2. Wang Shiwei. "Ye Baihehua." *Mingbao yuekan* 5 (1988), 4-5.

Further Reading

Apter, David E., and Timothy Cheek. "Introduction: The Trial." In Dai Qing, *Wang Shiwei and "Wild Lilies": Rectification and Purges in the Chinese Communist Party, 1942-1944*, xvii-xxxi. Armonk: M. E. Sharpe, 1994.

Barlow, Tani E. "Introduction." In Tani E. Barlow and Gary J. Bjorge, eds. *I Myself Am a Woman: Selected Writings of Ding Ling*, 1-45. Boston: Beacon Press, 1989.

Benton, Gregor. "The Yenan Literary Opposition." *New Left Review* 92 (1975), 93-106.

————, and Alan Hunter. "Introduction." In Benton and Hunter, eds. *Wild Lily, Prairie Fire: China's Road to Democracy, Yan'an to Tiananmen, 1942-1989*, 3-68. Princeton: Princeton University Press, 1995.

Cheek, Timothy. "The Fading of Wild Lilies: Wang Shiwei and Mao Zedong's Yan'an Talks in the First CPC Rectification Movement." *Australian Journal of Chinese Affairs* 11 (1984), 25-58.

Feuerwerker, Yi-Tsi Mei. "In Quest of the Writer Ding Ling." *Feminist Studies* 10/1 (1984), 65-83.

Goldman, Merle. *Literary Dissent in Communist China*. Cambridge, Mass: Harvard University Press, 1967.

Ip, Hung-Yok. "Fashioning Appearances: Feminine Beauty in Chinese Communist Revolutionary Culture." *Modern China* 29/3 (2003), 329-61.

Jackal, Patricia Stranahan. "Changes in Policy for Yanan Women, 1935-1947." *Modern China* 7/1 (1981), 83-112.

Judd, Ellen R. "Prelude to the 'Yan'an Talks': Problems in Transforming a Literary Intelligentsia." *Modern China* 11/3 (1985), 377-408.

Selden, Mark. "Yan'an Communism Reconsidered." *Modern China* 21/1 (1995), 8-44.

Seybolt, Peter J. "Terror and Conformity: Counterespionage Campaigns, Rectification, and Mass Movements, 1942-1943." *Modern China* 12/1 (1986), 39-73.

Wylie, Raymond F. *The Emergence of Maoism*. Stanford: Stanford University Press, 1980.

三八节有感
丁玲

"妇女"这两个字，将在什么时代才不被重视，不需要特别的被提出呢？ 年年都有这一天。每年在这一天的时候，几乎是全世界的地方都开着会，<u>检阅</u>着她们的队伍。延安虽说这两年不如前年热闹，但似乎总有几个人在那里忙着。而且一定有大会，有演说的，有通电，有文章发表。

延安的妇女是比中国其它地方的妇女幸福的。甚至有很多人都在<u>嫉羡</u>的说："为什么<u>小米</u>把女同志吃得那么红胖？"女同志在医院，在<u>休养所</u>，在门诊部都占着很大的比例，却似乎并没有使人惊奇，然而延安的女同志却仍不能免除那种幸运：不管在什么场合都最能作为有兴趣的问题被谈起。而且各种各样的女同志都可以得到她应得的<u>诽议</u>。这些责难似乎都是严重而确当的。

女同志的结婚永远使人注意，而不会使人满意的。她们不能同一个男同志比较接近，更不能同几个都接近。她们被画家们讽刺："一个<u>科长</u>也嫁了么？"诗人们也说："延安只有骑马的<u>首长</u>，没有艺术家的首长，艺术家在延安是找不到漂亮的情人的。"然而她们也在某种场合<u>聆听</u>着这样的<u>训词</u>："他妈的，瞧不起我们老干部，说是 <u>土包子</u>，要不是我们土包子，你想来延安吃小米！"但女人总是要结婚的。（不结婚更有罪恶，她将更多的被作为制造谣言的对象，永远被<u>污蔑</u>。） 不是骑马的就是穿草鞋的，不是艺术家就是总务科长。她们都得生小孩。小孩也有各自的命运：

检阅	jiǎnyuè	review (troops)
嫉羡	jíxiàn	envious
小米	xiǎomǐ	millet
休养所	xiūyǎngsuǒ	sanitorium; rest home
诽议	fěiyì	slander
科长	kēzhǎng	section chief
首长	shǒuzhǎng	leading cadre; chief
聆听	língtīng	listen respectfully
训词	xùncí	lecture; admonition
土包子	tǔbāozi	country bumpkin
污蔑	wūmiè	slander; smear

有的被细羊毛线和花绒布包着，抱在保姆的怀里，有的被没有洗净的布片
包着，扔在床头啼哭，而妈妈和爸爸都在大嚼着孩子的<u>津贴</u>，（每月２５
元，价值二斤半猪肉）要是没有这笔津贴，也许他们根本就尝不到肉味。
然而女同志究竟应该嫁谁呢，事实是这样，被逼着带孩子的一定可以得到
公开的<u>讥讽</u>："回到家庭了的<u>娜拉</u>。"而有着保姆的女同志，每一个星期可以
有一天最卫生的<u>交际舞</u>。虽说在背地里也会有难比的<u>诽语悄声</u>的传播着，
然而只要她走到那里，那里就会热闹，不管骑马的，穿草鞋的，总务科
长，艺术家们的眼睛都会望着她。这同一切的理论都无关，同一切主义思
想也无关，同一切开会演说也无关。然而这都是人人知道，人人不说，而
且在做着的现实。

　　离婚的问题也是一样。大抵在结婚的时候，有三个条件是必须注意到
的。一、政治上纯洁不纯洁，二、年龄相貌差不多，三、彼此有无帮助。
虽说这三个条件几乎是人人具备（公开的汉奸这里是没有的。而所谓帮助
也可以说到鞋袜的<u>缝补</u>，甚至女性的安慰），但却一定<u>堂皇</u>的考虑到。而
离婚的<u>口实</u>，一定是女同志的落后。我是最以为一个女人自己不进步而还
要拖住她的丈夫为可耻的，可是让我们看一看她们是如何落后的。她们在
没有结婚前都抱着有<u>凌云</u>的志向，和刻苦的斗争生活，她们在生理的要求
和"彼此帮助"的蜜语之下结婚了，于是她们被逼着做了<u>操劳</u>的回到家

津贴	jīntiē	subsidy; allowance
讥讽	jīfěng	ridicule
娜拉	Nàlā	Nora, from Henrik Ibsen's *The Doll's House*: a reference to Lu Xun's 鲁迅 (1881-1936) essay of 1923, "What Happens after Nora Leaves Home?," in which he speculates about the fate of Chinese Noras once they enter society
交际舞	jiāojìwǔ	dance party
诽语悄声	fěiyǔ qiāoshēng	whispered slander
缝补	féngbǔ	sew and mend
堂皇	tánghuáng	openly and above board
口实	kǒushí	pretext; excuse
凌云	língyún	soaring; to reach the clouds
操劳	cāoláo	work hard

庭的娜拉。她们也唯恐有"落后"的危险，她们四方奔走，<u>厚颜</u>的要求托儿所收留她们的孩子，要求刮子宫，宁肯受一切处分而不得不冒着生命的危险悄悄的去吃着<u>坠胎</u>的药。而她们听着这样的回答："带孩子不是工作吗？你们只贪图舒服，<u>好高骛远</u>，你们到底做过一些什么了不起的政治工作？既然这样怕生孩子，生了又不肯负责，谁叫你们结婚呢？"于是她们不能免除"落后"的命运。一个有了工作能力的女人，而还能牺牲自己的事业去作为一个<u>贤妻良母</u>的时候，未始不被人所<u>歌颂</u>，但在十多年之后，她必然也逃不出"落后"的悲剧。即使在今天以我一个女人去看，这些"落后"分子，也实在不是一个可爱的女人。她们的皮肤在开始有<u>折绉</u>，头发在稀少，生活的疲惫夺取她们最后的一点爱娇。她们处于这样的悲运，似乎是很自然的，但在旧的社会里，她们或许会被称为可怜，<u>薄命</u>，然而在今天，却是<u>自作孽</u>、活该。不是听说法律上还在争论着离婚只须一方提出，或者必须双方同意的问题么？离婚大约多半都是男子提出的，假如是女人，那一定有更不道德的事，那完全该女人受<u>诅咒</u>。

我自己是女人，我会比别人更懂得女人的缺点，但我却更懂得女人的痛苦。她们不会是超时代的，不会是理想的，她们不是<u>铁打</u>的。她们抵抗不了社会一切的诱惑，和无声的压迫，她们每人都有一部<u>血泪史</u>，都有过崇高的感情，（不管是升起的或沉落的，不管有幸与不幸，不管仍在孤

厚颜	hòuyán	brazen-faced
坠胎	zhuìtāi	induce an abortion
好高骛远	hàogāo wùyuǎn	over-ambitious
贤妻良母	xiánqīliángmǔ	a dutiful wife and a loving mother
歌颂	gēsòng	extol
折绉	zhézhòu	wrinkle
薄命	bómìng	born under an unlucky star
自作孽	zì zuòniè	have only oneself to blame
诅咒	zǔzhòu	curse
铁打	tiědǎ	unshakeable
血泪史	xuèlèishǐ	heart-rending story; a history full of blood and tears

苦奋斗或<u>卷入庸俗</u>,）这在对于来到延安的女同志说来更不冤枉，所以我是拿着很大的宽容来看一切被<u>沦</u>为女犯的人的。而且我更希望男子们尤其是有地位的男子，和女人本身都把这些女人的过错看得与社会有联系些。<u>少发空议论</u>，多谈实际的问题，使理论与实际不脱节，在每个共产党员的<u>修身</u>上都对自己负责些就好了。

然而我们也不能不对女同志们，尤其是在延安的女同志有些小小的企望。而且勉励着自己，勉励着友好。

世界上从没有无能的人，有资格去获取一切的。所以女人要取得平等，得首先强己。我不必说大家都懂的。而且，一定在今天会有人演说的："首先取得我们的政权"的大话，我只说作为一个<u>阵线</u>中的一员（无产阶级也好，抗战也好，妇女也好），每天所必须注意的事项。

第一、不要让自己生病。无<u>节制</u>的生活，有时会觉得浪漫，有诗意，可爱，然而对今天环境不适宜。没有一个人能比你自己还会爱你的生命些。没有什么东西比今天失去健康更不幸些。只有它同你最亲近，好好注意它，爱护它。

第二、使自己愉快。只有愉快里面才有青春，才有活力，才觉得生命饱满，才觉得能担受一切磨难，才有前途，才有享受。这种愉快不是生活的满足，而是生活的战斗和<u>进取</u>。所以必须每天都做点有意义的工作，都必须读点书，都能有东西给别人，<u>游惰</u>只使人感到生命的空白，疲软，<u>枯萎</u>。

第三、用脑子。最好养好成一种习惯。改正不作思索，<u>随波逐流</u>的毛病。每说一句话，每做一件事，最好想想这话是否正确？这事是否处理

卷入庸俗	juǎnrù yōngsú	caught up in the vulgar world
沦为	lúnwéi	sink to the status of
发空议论	fā kōngyìlùn	empty debate
修身	xiūshēn	cultivate moral character
阵线	zhènxiàn	battle line; front
节制	jiézhì	moderate; abstinence
进取	jìnqǔ	keep forging ahead
游惰	yóuduò	mess around doing nothing productive
枯萎	kūwěi	withered
随波逐流	suíbōzhúliú	drift with the tide

的<u>得当</u>，不违背自己作人的原则，是否自己可以负责。只有这样才不会有后悔。这就是叫通过理性，这，才不会<u>上当</u>，被一切甜蜜所<u>蒙蔽</u>，被小利所诱，才不会浪费热情，浪费生命，而免除烦恼。

第四、下吃苦的决心，坚持到底。生为现代的有觉悟的女人，就要有认定牺牲一切<u>蔷薇色</u>的温柔的梦幻。幸福是暴风雨中的搏斗，而不是在月下弹琴，花前吟诗。假如没有最大的决心，一定会在中途停歇下来。不悲苦，即堕落。而这种支持下去的力量却必须在"<u>有恒</u>"中来养成。没有大的抱负的人是难于有这种不<u>贪便宜</u>，不图舒服的坚忍的。而这种抱负只有真正为人类，而非为己的人才会有。

得当	dédàng	proper; appropriate
上当	shàngdàng	be taken in; fooled
蒙蔽	méngbì	hoodwink
蔷薇色	qiángwēisè	rose-colored
有恒	yǒuhéng	perseverance
贪便宜	tān piányi	seek petty advantages

野百合花

王實

前记

在河边独步时，一位同志脚上的旧式棉鞋，使我又想起了曾穿过这种棉鞋的李芬同志——我所最敬爱的<u>生平</u>第一个朋友。

　　想起她，心脏照例震动一下。照例我觉到血液循环得更有力。

李芬同志是北大1926年级文<u>预科</u>学生，同年入党，1928年春牺牲于她底故乡--湖南宝庆。她底死不是由于被捕，而是被她底亲<u>舅父</u>缚送给当地<u>驻军</u>的。这说明旧中国底代表者是如何残忍。同时，在赴死之前，她曾把所有的三套衬衣裤都穿在身上，用<u>针线</u>上下密密缝在一起：因为，当时宝庆青年女共产党员被捕<u>枪决</u>后，常由军队纵使流氓去<u>奸</u>尸！这又说明着旧中国是怎样一具血腥，丑恶，肮脏，黑暗的社会！从听到她底<u>噩耗</u>时起，我底血管里便一直燃烧着最狂烈的热爱与毒恨。每一想到她，我眼前便浮出她那圣洁的女<u>殉道者</u>底影子，穿着三套密密缝在一起的衬衣裤，由自己的亲舅父缚送去<u>从容就义</u>！每一想到她，我便心脏震动，血液循环的更有力！

（在这<u>歌啭玉堂春、舞回金莲步</u>的升平气象中，提到这样的故事，似乎不太和谐，但当前的现实——请闭上眼睛想一想吧，每一分钟都有我们亲爱的同志在血泊中倒下——似乎与这气象也不太和谐！）

生平	shēngpíng	lifelong
预科	yùkē	preparatory course
舅父	jiùfù	maternal uncle
驻军	zhùjūn	garrison
针线	zhēnxiàn	needle and thread
枪决	qiāngjué	execute by shooting
奸	jiān	rape
噩耗	èhào	the sad news of the death of one's beloved
殉道者	xùndàozhě	martyr
从容就义	cōngróngjiùyì	meet one's death like a hero
歌啭玉堂春、舞回金莲步	gē zhuàn yùtángchūn wǔ huí jīnlián bù	poetic phrases used to describe a time of tranquillity, used ironically of Yan'an in this context

为了民族底利益，我们并不愿再算阶级仇恨的旧账。我们是真正大公无私的。我们甚至尽一切力量拖曳着旧中国底代表者同我们一路走向光明。可是，在拖曳的过程中，旧中国底肮脏污秽也就沾染了我们自己，散布细菌，传染疾病。

我曾不止十次二十次地从李芬同志底影子汲取力量，生活的力量和战斗的力量。这次偶然想到她，使我决心要写一些杂文。野百合花就是它们的总标题。这有两方面的含义：第一，这种花是延安山野间最美丽的野花，用以献给那圣洁的影子；其次，据说这花与一般百合花同样有着鳞状球茎，吃起来味虽略带苦涩，不似一般百合花那样香甜可口，但却有更大的药用价值——未知确否。

1942 年 2 月 26 日

一　我们生活里缺少什么？

延安青年近来似乎生活得有些不起劲，而且似乎肚子里装得有不舒服。

为什么呢？我们生活里缺少什么呢？有人会回答说：我们营养不良，我们缺少维他命，所以……。另有人会回答说：延安男女的比例是"十八比一"，许多青年找不到爱人，所以……。还有人会回答说：延安生活太单调，太枯燥，缺少娱乐，所以……。

这些回答都不是没有道理的。要吃得好一点，要有异性配偶，要生活得有趣，这些都是天经地义。但谁也不能不承认：延安的青年，都是抱定牺牲精神来从事革命，并不是来追求食色的满足和生活的快乐。说他们不起劲，甚至肚子里装着不舒服，就是为了这些问题不能圆满解决，我不敢轻于同意。

污秽	wūhuì	filth
鳞状球茎	línzhuàng qiújīng	scaly bulb
未知确否	weìzhīquèfǒu	uncertain about something
枯燥	kūzào	dull and dry
天经地义	tiānjīngdìyì	perfectly justified
食色	shísè	food and sex

那么，我们生活里到底缺些什么呢？下面一段谈话可能透露一些消息。

新年假期中，一天晚上从友人处归来，昏黑里，前面有两个青年女同志在低声而兴奋地谈着话。我们相距丈多远，我放轻脚步<u>凝神谛听</u>着：

"……<u>动不动</u>，就说人家小资产阶级<u>平均主义</u>；其实，他自己倒真有点特殊主义。事事都只顾自己特殊化，对下面同志，身体好也罢坏也罢，病也罢，死也罢，差不多漠不关心！"

"哼，到处乌鸦一般黑，我们底××同志还不也是这样！"

"说得好听！阶级友爱呀，什么呀——屁！好像连人对人的同情心都没有！平常见人装得笑嘻嘻，其实是<u>皮笑肉不笑</u>，肉笑心不笑。稍不<u>如意</u>，就瞪起眼睛，<u>搭</u>出首长<u>架子</u>来训人。"

"大头子是这样，小头子也是这样。我们底科长，×××，对上是<u>毕恭毕敬</u>的，对我们，却是<u>神气活现</u>，好几次同志病了，他连看都不伸头看一下。可是，一次老鹰抓了他一只小鸡，你看他多么关心这件大事呀！以后每次看见老鹰飞来，他却嚎嚎的叫，扔土块去打它——自私自利的家伙！

她们还继续低声兴奋地谈着。因为要分路，我就只听到这里为止，这段谈话也许有偏颇，有夸张，其中的"形象"也许没有太大的普遍性：但我们决不能否认它有镜子底作用。我们生活里到底缺少什么呢？镜子里看吧。

沉默了一下。我一方面佩服这位女同志<u>口齿</u>尖利，一方面惘然<u>若有所失</u>。

凝神谛听	níngshén dìtīng	listen attentively
动不动	dòngbudòng	at the slightest provocation; at every turn
平均主义	píngjūnzhǔyì	egalitarianism
皮笑肉不笑	píxiào ròubúxiào	put on a false smile
如意	rúyì	as one wishes
搭架子	dā jiàzi	put on airs
毕恭毕敬	bìgōngbìjìng	extremely deferential
神气活现	shénqì huóxiàn	very cocky
口齿	kǒuchǐ	ability to talk
若有所失	ruòyǒusuǒshī	feel as if something is missing

"害病的同志真太多了，想起来叫人难过。其实，害病，倒并不希望那类人来看你。他只能给你添难受。他底声音、表情、态度，都不使你感觉他对你有什么关怀、爱护。"

"我两年来换了三四个工作机关，那些首长以及科长、主任之类，真正关心干部爱护干部的，实在太少了。"

"是呀，一点不也错！他对别人没有一点爱，别人自然也一点不爱他。要是做群众工作，非<u>垮台</u>不可……。"

二　碰"碰壁"

在本报"青年之页"第12期上，读到一位同志底标题为"碰壁"的文章，不禁有感。

先抄两段原文：

新从<u>大后方</u>来的一位中年朋友，看到延安青年忍不
住些微<u>拂意</u>的事；<u>牢骚</u>满腹，到处发泄的情形，深以为
不然地说："这算得什么！我们在外面不知碰了多少壁，
<u>受人多少气</u>……"
他的话是对的。延安虽也有着令人生气的"脸色"，
和一<u>些</u>不能<u>尽如人意</u>的事物；可是在一个碰壁多少次，尝
够人生冷暖的人看来，却是<u>微乎其微</u>，算不得什么的。至
於在<u>入世未深</u>的青年，尤其是学生出身的，那就<u>迥乎不
同</u>了。家庭和学校<u>哺乳</u>他们成人，爱和热向他们<u>细语</u>着

垮台	kuǎtái	come to grief
大后方	dàhòufāng	Nationalist rear areas
拂意	fúyì	thwarted
牢骚	láosāo	discontent; complaint
受气	shòuqì	bullied
尽如人意	jìnrúrényì	to have things go as one would wish
微乎其微	wēihūqíwēi	next to nothing; insignificant
入世未深	rùshìwèishēn	lack experience of life
迥乎不同	jiǒnghū bùtóng	utterly different
哺乳	bǔrǔ	suckle; nurse
细语	xìyǔ	talk to tenderly

人生，教他们<u>描摹</u>单纯和美丽的憧憬；现实的丑恶和冷
淡于他们是陌生的，无怪乎他们一遇到小小的风浪就要
叫嚷，感到从来未有过的不安。

我不知道作者这位"中年朋友"是怎样的一个人，但我认为他底这种<u>知足</u>
<u>者长乐</u>的人生哲学，不但不是"对的"，而是有害的。青年的可贵，在于他们
纯洁，敏感，热情，勇敢，他们充满着生命底新锐的力。别人没有感觉的
黑暗，他们先感觉；别人没有看到的肮脏，他们先看到；别人不愿说不敢
说的话，他们大胆地说，因此，他们意见多一些，但不见得就是"牢骚"；他
们的话或许说得不够<u>四平八稳</u>，但也不见得就是"叫嚷"。我们应该从这些所
谓"牢骚""叫嚷"和"不安"的现象里，去探求那产生这些现象的问题底本质，
合理地（注意：合理地！青年不见得总是"盲目的<u>叫嚣</u>"。）消除这些现象
的根源。说延安比"外面"好得多，教导青年不发"牢骚"，说延安的黑暗方面
只是"些微拂意的事"，"算不得什么"，这丝毫不能解决问题。是的，延安比
"外面"好得多，但延安可能而且必须更好一点。

(Cont.)

描摹	miáomó	describe; portray
知足者长乐	zhīzúzhěchánglè	content with one's lot
四平八稳	sìpíngbāwěn	well-organized
叫嚣	jiàoxiāo	clamor

5. CULTURAL POLICY IN THE PEOPLE'S REPUBLIC

Talks at the Yan'an Forum on Art and Literature
Mao Zedong

Mao Zedong gave two keynote speeches at the Yan'an Forum on Art and Literature in the Chinese Communist Party (CCP) stronghold, or base area, in May 1942. The first speech opened the conference, and the second concluded it. The conference itself called for "an exchange of opinions" among party members and intellectuals living in the base area on the relationships between literature, art, and revolution. Its stated aims were to promote the correct development of art and literature, to safeguard the revolutionary work, and to ensure national liberation. (The threat of Japanese invasion had temporarily produced an *entente* between the Nationalists and the Communists, and cultural production was one area of mutual acceptance.) Mao spoke in his *Talks* of the cultural army which worked alongside the military army in the revolution: both of these "two fraternal armies" were needed to carry out the revolution. In the short period between his opening and closing speeches, however, Mao's line on the exchange of opinions hardened, and in the second speech he laid out his own vision of the role of culture within a communist state, a position which was to be elevated from theory to policy over the next few years. The months that led up to the publication of the *Talks* in October 1943 saw further changes take place. Mao was elected chairperson of the Politburo of the CCP and of its three-person Secretariat. The Rectification Campaign (整风运动 *Zhengfeng yundong*), designed to root out unorthodox thought and to discipline Party members, changed gear and was directed against those writers whose criticisms had led to the *Talks*. Those artists and writers who had thought it within their remit to criticize Party privileges, excesses, or gender inequalities in the base areas were soon to discover the effects of Mao's *Talks*.

It may seem strange for the leader of a guerrilla army, threatened by external forces and civil war, to formulate a cultural policy with such determination, but Mao Zedong believed that political and propaganda control were necessary precursors to power. Mao's own personality incorporated many of the tensions that framed the Chinese revolutions of the early twentieth century: as peasant and intellectual, as revolutionary and classical scholar. He may have moved a long way from the Mao of 1917—who wrote an article in *Xin qingnian* full of concern for the failing state, and replete with allusions to the Confucian canon, Daoist philosophers, and Neo-Confucian intellectuals[1]—but Mao never lost sight of the power of the written word in China. His own literary credentials (he

---

1. Cf. Stuart Schram, *The Thought of Mao Tse-Tung*, 15.

wrote good quality regulated verse in classical Chinese) gave him a certain authority on artistic matters, even while they led him to formulate policies which valorized the old-style writing denounced by the May Fourth iconoclasts. Mao's position on the New Culture movement remained complex. On its twentieth anniversary in 1939, he maintained that "the whole of the revolutionary movement found its origins in the actions of young students and intellectuals who had been awakened."[2] Yet at the same time, he criticized both the literature they produced and their ineffectual struggles. If Mao himself was a small player in this earlier cultural movement, he certainly became the most influential figure in the rural and social revolution that succeeded it. The unity Mao called for between the intellectual army and the military fighters signaled his ongoing view that cultural work was subordinate to politics, but still "an indispensable part of revolutionary work as a whole'."[3] The *Talks at the Yan'an Forum* were precisely about realizing this vision of a new revolutionary culture.

The immediate background to the *Talks* in 1942 was an invitation to voice criticism, but those revolutionary writers who had heeded the Party's call to come to Yan'an and serve—such as Ding Ling and Wang Shiwei—used the opportunity to criticize not themselves but their leaders, and cadres in particular.[4] Tension between those who had made the Long March and new arrivals was bubbling over, and fractious arguments over war strategies preoccupied the participants. The conference was convened, after several weeks of attacks and dissent in order, to reassert leadership and remind members of pressing external threats.

Two main texts of the Talks exist: the 1943 imprint, and a later version which Mao revised and published in 1953. Over eighty editions of the 1943 text were in circulation; after 1953, all subsequent editions were based on the revised version. Both texts are important, and detailed comparison between them is fruitful in documenting changing attitudes. The later edition was more than just a polished version of the original, and it included substantive changes, making it "more rigid in its dialectical materialist analysis and yet broader in its ability to appreciate popular culture."[5] It was this edition which was to influence the literary policies of the Cultural Revolution period. A clear Leninist line is visible in the text, which stresses the use of art as a political weapon and pays homage to the

---

2. Schram, *The Thought of Mao Tse-Tung*, 4. The passage was later removed from the speech.

3. Translation from Bonnie S. McDougall, *Mao Zedong's "Talks at the Yan'an Conference on Literature and Art,"* 75.

4. For an account of the brutal psychological techniques of the Rectification Campaign of the early 1940s, the personalities involved in the criticisms, and the Party's response, see Merle Goldman, *Literary Dissent in Communist China*, 18-50.

5. McDougall, *Mao Zedong's "Talks at the Yan'an Conference on Literature and Art,"* 8.

socialist realism of Soviet literature, although the theories on mass literature espoused by Qu Qiubai and Zhou Yang are also on display. Mao's Talks at Yan'an have been studied from political and literary angles, and their later legacy is no less important than the impact they had on Yan'an itself.

Mao's starting premise in the *Talks* is that literature and art are a component part of the revolution, a weapon in the struggle to unite the people and crush the enemy. Writers must first identify themselves with the Party in this aim, and then with the masses in order to fulfill the task. The masses were to be praised, educated, and supported in their process of reform. Literary workers needed to get to know and become one with the workers, peasants, and soldiers in order to understand them and guide them. They should study the language of the masses, engage in self-transformation, rid themselves of their bourgeois habits, and improve their knowledge of Marxism-Leninism. Mao reiterated the importance of the audience, the masses, in his concluding talk on May 23. Feudal literature serves the exploiters and oppressors, slave literature serves imperialists, but the new literature and art is revolutionary, and it serves the people. The new art, it should be noted, may take and reconstruct old forms to make them revolutionary, so long as it is under the leadership of the masses. A concentration on this fundamental principle, the question of whom art serves, enabled Mao to find a place for traditional forms of literature, and to uphold his critique of May Fourth writings on both literary and political grounds.

In his second *Talk*, Mao set the parameters of the task. How could Party members raise standards and reach a wider audience? The answer was straightforward: learn from the masses. Mao's rhetoric here develops Lu Xun's theories on revolutionary art by setting out in detail its goals, meaning, and purpose. If popular life is the source for literary material, then the task for the revolutionary mind was to process this life of the masses, to distil it in concentrated form so that it could awaken minds and souls to the struggle. Art was indeed to be didactic, since the audience had to be guided in their own journey to self-awareness. For Mao, art was a craft, a skill which all could hone, rather than a gift of the muses. All art was class-based, just like humanity itself; no art existed for its own sake. Revolutionary art exposes the dark forces in society, and heralds the bright ones (a direct rebuttal of the criticism Wang Shiwei expresses in his essay "Wild Lilies"). Marxism-Leninism will destroy feudal, bourgeois, decadent or nihilistic forms of creativity, and help overcome shortcomings among artists such as idealism or foreign dogmatism. The standards for literary criticism were both political and artistic, and the aim in producing works should be to meet both these criteria. Yet while art was to be judged by aesthetic standards, the criteria for its political aspects were far more tendentious. Indeed, for Mao, the effects of a work were as important as its motives. The dangerous nature of literary and artistic work became apparent in the years after the Yan'an talks, as the notion that cultural producers should be judged by outcomes, not intentions, took hold. Just as politicians were judged on the basis of outcomes, so too could artists give up any hope that good intentions would exculpate them if their work failed to serve the revolutionary cause.

The base camps were fundamental to Mao's developing thought on the relations between the arts and revolution. Yan'an was a geopolitical entity, the crucible for ideological struggle and the testing ground for Chinese models of communism. As a phase in CCP history, the Yan'an period defined a "'Chinese road' to the conquest of power,"[6] with the years 1936-47 representing a major phase in the evolution of Mao's political thought. Base camps were the places where communism could be enacted in daily life, where writers could learn directly from the masses, and where they could produce true revolutionary literature. There professional dramatists could go among the people and study village and army theater groups, professional writers could study the reportage literature and wall newspapers of the villages, and professional musicians could study the songs of the masses. There Mao's policies in literature and literary theory could be implemented, as Yan'an led the way for the rest of the country. Proletarian realism, as in the Soviet Union, was the label of choice, and utilitarian art ruled. Since art was to be for the masses, it had to appeal to the masses, including the illiterate. Indeed, while the *Talks* led to the silencing of certain Yan'an writers, and later, indirectly, to the Anti-Rightest struggle and to the brutal treatment meted out to intellectuals during the Cultural Revolution, they also encouraged a new interest in popular literature and theater, in local dance and drama forms, and in oral narratives, such as those delivered to clapper beat accompaniment that had captivated audiences since the Song dynasty.[7]

Excerpted from Mao Zedong, *Mao Zedong xuanji,* vol. 3 (Beijing: Renmin Chubanshe, 1966), 809-819.

Further Reading

Apter, David E., and Tony Saich. *Revolutionary Discourse in Mao's Republic*. Cambridge, Mass.: Harvard University Press, 1994.
Cheek, Timothy. *Propaganda and Culture in Mao's China: Deng Tuo and the Intelligentsia*. Oxford: Oxford University Press, 1997.

---

6. Schram, *The Thought of Mao Tse-Tung*, 12.
7. McDougall, *Mao Zedong's "Talks at the Yan'an Conference on Literature and Art,"* 37.

―――――. *Mao Zedong and China's Revolutions: A Brief History with Documents*. New York: Palgrave Macmillan. 2002.

Chung, Hilary, ed. *In the Party Spirit: Socialist Realism and Literary Practice in the Soviet Union, East Germany and China*. Rodopi, 1996.

Denton, Kirk. *The Problematic of Self in Modern Chinese Literature: Hu Feng and Lu Ling*. Stanford: Stanford University Press, 1998.

Feuerwerker, Yi-Tsi Mei. *Ideology, Power, Text: Self-Representation and the Peasant "Other" in Modern Chinese Literature*. Stanford: Stanford University Press, 1998.

Goldman, Merle. *Literary Dissent in Communist China*. Cambridge, Mass.: Harvard University Press, 1967.

Hsia, C. T. *A History of Modern Chinese Fiction*. New Haven: Yale University Press, 1971.

Ip, Hung-yok. *Intellectuals in Revolutionary China 1921-1949*. London: Routledge, 2005.

McDougall, Bonnie S. *Mao Zedong's "Talks at the Yan'an Conference on Literature and Art": A Translation of the 1943 Text with Commentary*. Ann Arbor: University of Michigan Center for Chinese Studies, 1980.

―――――, and Kam Louie. *The Literature of China in the Twentieth Century*. London: C. Hurst and Co., 1997.

Schram, Stuart. *The Thought of Mao Tse-Tung*. Cambridge: Cambridge University Press, 1989.

Shen, Vivian. *The Origins of Left-Wing Cinema in China 1932-37*. London: Routledge, 2005.

在延安文艺座谈会上的讲话·结论（一九四二年五月二十三日）

同志们！我们这个会在一个月里开了三次。大家为了追求真理，进行了热烈的争论，有党的和非党的同志几十个人讲了话，把问题展开了，并且具体化了。我认为这是对整个文学艺术运动很有益处的。

我们讨论问题，应当从实际出发，不是从<u>定义</u>出发。如果我们按照教科书，找到什么是文学、什么是艺术的定义，然后按照它们来规定今天文艺运动的<u>方针</u>，来评判今天所发生的各种见解和争论，这种方法是不正确的。我们是<u>马克思主义者</u>，马克思主义叫我们看问题不要从<u>抽象</u>的定义出发，而要从客观存在的事实出发，从分析这些事实中找出方针、政策、办法来。我们现在讨论文艺工作，也应该这样做。

现在的事实是什么呢？事实就是：中国的已经进行了五年的<u>抗日战争</u>；全世界的反<u>法西斯</u>战争；中国大地主<u>大资产阶级</u>在抗日战争中的动摇和对于人民的高压政策；"五四"以来的革命文艺运动，这个运动在二十三年中对于革命的伟大贡献以及它的许多缺点；八路军新四军的抗日民主<u>根据地</u>，在这些根据地里面大批文艺工作者和八路军新四军以及工人农民的结合；根据地的文艺工作者和国民党统治区的文艺工作者的环境和任务的区别；目前在延安和各抗日根据地的文艺工作中已经发生的争论问题。这些就是实际存在的不可否认的事实，我们就要在这些事实的基础上考虑我们的问题。

定义	dìngyì	definition
方针	fāngzhēn	policy; guiding principle
马克思主义者	Mǎkèsīzhǔyìzhě	Marxist(s)
抽象	chōuxiàng	abstract; general
抗日战争	Kàng-Rì Zhànzhēng	War of Resistance against Japanese Aggression
法西斯	fǎxīsī	fascist
大资产阶级	dàzīchǎnjiējí	the big bourgeoisie
根据地	gēnjùdì	base area

那末，什么是我们的问题的中心呢？我以为，我们的问题基本上是一个为群众的问题和一个如何为群众的问题。不解决这两个问题，或这两个问题解决得不适当，就会使得我们的文艺工作者和自己的环境、任务不<u>协调</u>，就使得我们的文艺工作者从外部从内部碰到<u>一连串</u>的问题。我的结论，就以这两个问题为中心，同时也讲到一些与此有关的其他问题。

一

第一个问题：我们的文艺是为什么人的？

这个问题，本来是马克思主义者特别是列宁所早已解决了的。列宁还在一九〇五年就已<u>着重</u>指出过，我们的文艺应当"为千千万万劳动人民服务"。在我们各个抗日根据地从事文学艺术工作的同志中，这个问题似乎是已经解决了，不需要再讲的了。其实不然。很多同志对这个问题并没有得到明确的解决。因此，在他们的情绪中，在他们的作品中，在他们的行动中，在他们对于文艺方针问题的意见中，就不免或多或少地发生和群众的需要不相符合，和实际斗争的需要不相符合的情形。当然，现在和共产党、<u>八路军</u>、<u>新四军</u>在一起从事于伟大解放斗争的大批的文化人、文学家、艺术家以及一般文艺工作者，虽然其中也可能有些人是暂时的<u>投机分子</u>，但是绝大多数却都是在为着共同事业努力工作着。依靠这些同志，我们的整个文学工作，戏剧工作，音乐工作，美术工作，都有了很大的成绩。这些文艺工作者，有许多是抗战以后开始工作的；有许多在抗战以前就做了多时的革命工作，经历过许多辛苦，并用他们的工作和作品影响了广大群众的。但是为什么还说即使这些同志中也有对于文艺是为什么人的问题没有明确解决的呢？难道他们还有主张革命文艺不是为着人民大众

协调	xiétiáo	in harmony; coordinated
一连串	yìliánchuàn	a succession of; series of
着重	zhuózhòng	emphasize; stress
八路军	Bālùjūn	Eighth Route Army (led by CCP in War of Resistance)
新四军	Xīnsìjūn	New Fourth Army
投机分子	tóujīfènzǐ	opportunists

而是为着<u>剥削</u>者压迫者的吗？

诚然，为着剥削者压迫者的文艺是有的。文艺是为地主阶级的，这是封建主义的文艺。中国封建时代统治阶级的文学艺术，就是这种东西。直到今天，这种文艺在中国还有颇大的势力。文艺是为资产阶级的，这是资产阶级的文艺。像鲁迅所批评的<u>梁实秋</u>一类人，他们虽然在口头上提出什么文艺是超阶级的，但是他们在实际上是主张资产阶级的文艺，反对无产阶级的文艺的。文艺是为帝国主义者的，<u>周作人</u>、<u>张资平</u>这批人就是这样，这叫做<u>汉奸</u>文艺。在我们，文艺不是为上述种种人，而是为人民的。我们曾说，现阶段的中国新文化，是无产阶级领导的人民大众的<u>反帝反封建</u>的文化。真正人民大众的东西，现在一定是无产阶级领导的。资产阶级领导的东西，不可能属于人民大众。新文化中的新文学新艺术，自然也是这样。对于中国和外国过去时代所遗留下来的丰富的文学艺术遗产和优良的文学艺术传统，我们是要继承的，但是目的仍然是为了人民大众。对于过去时代的文艺形式，我们也并不拒绝利用，但这些旧形式到了我们手里，给了改造，加进了新内容，也就变成革命的为人民服务的东西了。

那末，什么是人民大众呢？最广大的人民，占全人口百分之九十以上的人民，是工人、农民、兵士和<u>城市小资产阶级</u>。所以我们的文艺，第一

剥削	bōxuē	exploit
梁实秋	Liáng Shíqiū	academic and writer (1903-87), member of the literary circle that grew up around Xu Zhimo and Wen Yiduo, left for Taiwan in 1949
周作人	Zhōu Zuòrén	brother of Lu Xun, writer (1885-1967), leading figure of May Fourth Movement, imprisoned for traitorous activities during 1945-49
张资平	Zhāng Zīpíng	writer and literary figure (1853-1959) associated with Creationist group, accused of treachery for serving under the Japanese puppet government
汉奸	hànjiān	traitor (to China)
反帝反封建	fǎndì fǎnfēngjiàn	anti-imperial; anti-feudal
城市 小资产阶级	chéngshì xiǎozīchǎnjiējí	urban petit-bourgeoisie

是为工人的，这是领导革命的阶级。第二是为农民的，他们是革命中最广大最坚决的同盟军。第三是为武装起来了的工人农民即八路军、新四军和其他人民武装队伍的，这是革命战争的主力。第四是为城市小资产阶级劳动群众和知识分子的，他们也是革命的同盟者，他们是能够长期地和我们合作的。这四种人，就是中华民族的最大部分，就是最广大的人民大众。

我们的文艺，应该为着上面说的四种人。我们要为这四种人服务，就必须站在无产阶级的立场上，而不能站在小资产阶级的立场上。在今天，坚持个人主义的小资产阶级立场的作家是不可能真正地为革命的工农兵群众服务的，他们的兴趣，主要是放在少数小资产阶级知识分子上面。而我们现在有一部分同志对于文艺为什么人的问题不能正确解决的关键，正在这里。我这样说，不是说在理论上。在理论上，或者说在口头上，我们队伍中没有一个人把工农兵群众看得比小资产阶级知识分子还不重要的。我是说在实际上，在行动上。在实际上，在行动上，他们是否对小资产阶级知识分子比对工农兵还更看得重要些呢？我以为是这样。有许多同志比较地注重研究小资产阶级知识分子，分析他们的心理，着重地去表现他们，原谅并辩护他们的缺点，而不是引导他们和自己一道去接近工农兵群众，去参加工农兵群众的实际斗争，去表现工农兵群众，去教育工农兵群众。有许多同志，因为他们自己是从小资产阶级出身，自己是知识分子，于是就只在知识分子的队伍中找朋友，把自己的注意力放在研究和描写知识分子上面。这种研究和描写如果是站在无产阶级立场上的，那是应该的。但他们并不是，或者不完全是。他们是站在小资产阶级立场，他们是把自己的作品当作小资产阶级的自我表现来创作的，我们在相当多的文学艺术作品中看见这种东西。他们在许多时候，对于小资产阶级出身的知识分子寄予满腔的同情，连他们的缺点也给以同情甚至鼓吹。对于工农兵群众，则缺乏接近，缺乏了解，缺乏研究，缺乏知心朋友，不善于描写他们；倘若描写，也是衣服是劳动人民，面孔却是小资产阶级知识分子。他们在某些

同盟军	tóngméngjūn	allied forces
关键	guānjiàn	crux; key
口头	kǒutóu	in words; orally
原谅	yuánliàng	forgive; excuse
寄予	jìyǔ	express; show

方面也爱工农兵，也爱工农兵出身的干部，但有些时候不爱，有些地方不
爱，不爱他们的感情，不爱他们的姿态，不爱他们的<u>萌芽状态</u>的文艺（<u>墙
报</u>、<u>壁画</u>、民歌、民间故事等）。他们有时也爱这些东西，那是为着<u>猎
奇</u>，为着<u>装饰</u>自己的品，甚至是为着追求其中落后的东西而爱的。有时就
公开地<u>鄙弃</u>它们，而偏爱小资产阶级知识分子的乃至资产阶级的东西。这
些同志的立足点还是在小资产阶级知识分子方面，或者换句文雅的话说，
他们的<u>灵魂深处</u>还是一个小资产阶级知识分子的王国。这样，为什么人的
问题他们就还是没有解决，或者没有明确地解决。这不光是讲初来延安不
久的人，就是到过前方，在根据地、八路军、新四军做过几年工作的人，
也有许多是没有彻底解决的。要彻底地解决这个问题，非有十年八年的长
时间不可。但是时间无论怎样长，我们却必须解决它，必须明确地彻底地
解决它。我们的文艺工作者一定要完成这个任务，一定要把立足点移过
来，一定要在深入工农兵群众、深入实际斗争的过程中，在学习马克思主
义和学习社会的过程中，逐渐地移过来，移到工农兵这方面来，移到无产阶
级这方面来。只有这样，我们才能有真正为工农兵的文艺，真正无产阶
级的文艺。

为什么人的问题，是一个根本的问题，原则的问题。过去有些同志间
的争论、分歧、对立和不团结，并不是在这个根本的原则的问题上，而是
在一些比较<u>次要</u>的甚至是无原则的问题上。而对于这个原则问题，争论的
双方倒是没有什么分歧，倒是几乎一致的，都有某种程度的轻视工农兵、
脱离群众的倾向。我说某种程度，因为一般地说，这些同志的轻视工农
兵、脱离群众，和国民党的轻视工农兵、脱离群众，是不同的；但是无论
如何，这个倾向是有的。这个根本问题不解决，其他许多问题也就不易解
决。比如说文艺界的<u>宗派主义</u>吧，这也是原则问题，但是要去掉宗派主

萌芽状态	méngyá zhuàngtài	rudimentary; embryonic
墙报	qiángbào	wall newspapers
壁画	bìhuà	mural; fresco
猎奇	lièqí	seek novelty
装饰	zhuāngshì	adorn; ornament
鄙弃	bǐqì	*v* disdain
灵魂深处	línghún shēnchù	in the depths of the soul
次要	cìyào	secondary
宗派主义	zōngpàizhǔyì	sectarianism; factionalism

义，也只有把为工农，为八路军、新四军，到群众中去的口号提出来，并加以切实的实行，才能达到目的，否则宗派主义问题是断然不能解决的。鲁迅曾说："联合战线是以有共同目的为必要条件的。……我们战线不能统一，就证明我们的目的不能一致，或者只为了小团体，或者还其实只为了个人。如果目的都在工农大众，那当然战线也就统一了。"这个问题那时上海有，现在重庆也有。在那些地方，这个问题很难彻底解决，因为那些地方的统治者压迫革命文艺家，不让他们有到工农兵群众中去的自由。在我们这里，情形就完全两样。我们鼓励革命文艺家积极地亲近工农兵，给他们以到群众中去的完全自由，给他们以创作真正革命文艺的完全自由。所以这个问题在我们这里，是接近于解决的了。接近于解决不等于完全的彻底的解决；我们说要学习马克思主义和学习社会，就是为着完全地彻底地解决这个问题。我们说的马克思主义，是要在群众生活群众斗争里实际发生作用的活的马克思主义，不是口头上的马克思主义。把口头上的马克思主义变成为实际生活里的马克思主义，就不会有宗派主义了。不但宗派主义的问题可以解决，其他的许多问题也都可以解决了。

二

为什么人服务的问题解决了，接着的问题就是如何去服务。用同志们的话来说，就是：努力于提高呢，还是努力于<u>普及</u>呢？

有些同志，在过去，是相当地或是严重地轻视了和忽视了普及，他们不适当地太强调了提高。提高是应该强调的，但是片面地孤立地强调提高，强调到不适当的程度，那就错了。我在前面说的没有明确地解决为什么人的问题的事实，在这一点上也表现出来了。并且，因为没有弄清楚为什么人，他们所说的普及和提高就都没有正确的标准，当然更找不到两者的正确关系。我们的文艺，既然基本上是为工农兵，那末所谓普及，也就是向工农兵普及，所谓提高，也就是从工农兵提高。用什么东西向他们普及呢？用封建地主阶级所需要、所便于接受的东西吗？用资产阶级所需要、所便于接受的东西吗？用小资产阶级知识分子所需要、所便于接受的东西吗？都不行，只有用工农兵自己所需要、所便于接受的东西。因此在

普及	pǔjí	extend; popularize

教育工农兵的任务之前，就先有一个学习工农兵的任务。提高的问题更是如此。提高要有一个基础。比如一桶水，不是从地上去提高，难道是从空中去提高吗？那末所谓文艺的提高，是从什么基础上去提高呢？从封建阶级的基础吗？从资产阶级的基础吗？从小资产阶级知识分子的基础吗？都不是，只能是从工农兵群众的基础上去提高。也不是把工农兵提到封建阶级、资产阶级、小资产阶级知识分子的"高度"去，而是沿着工农兵自己前进的方向去提高，沿着无产阶级前进的方向去提高。而这里也就提出了学习工农兵的任务。只有从工农兵出发，我们对于普及和提高才能有正确的了解，也才能找到普及和提高的正确关系。

一切种类的文学艺术的源泉究竟是从何而来的呢？作为<u>观念形态</u>的文艺作品，都是一定的社会生活在人类头脑中的反映的产物。革命的文艺，则是人民生活在革命作家头脑中的反映的产物。人民生活中本来存在着文学艺术原料的<u>矿藏</u>，这是<u>自然形态</u>的东西，是粗糙的东西，但也是最生动、最丰富、最基本的东西；在这点上说，它们使一切文学艺术<u>相形见绌</u>，它们是一切文学艺术的<u>取之不尽、用之不竭</u>的唯一的源泉。这是唯一的源泉，因为只能有这样的源泉，此外不能有第二个源泉。有人说，书本上的文艺作品，古代的和外国的文艺作品，不也是源泉吗？实际上，过去的文艺作品不是源而是流，是古人和外国人根据他们彼时彼地所得到的人民生活中的文学艺术原料创造出来的东西。我们必须继承一切优秀的文学艺术遗产，批判地吸收其中一切有益的东西，作为我们从此时此地的人民生活中的文学艺术原料创造作品时候的<u>借鉴</u>。有这个借鉴和没有这个借鉴是不同的，这里有文野之分，粗细之分，高低之分，快慢之分。所以我们决不可拒绝继承和借鉴古人和外国人，哪怕是封建阶级和资产阶级的东西。但是继承和借鉴决不可以变成替代自己的创造，这是决不能替代

观念形态	guānniàn xíngtài	ideology
矿藏	kuàngcáng	(mineral) resource; reserve
自然形态	zìrán xíngtài	natural form
相形见绌	xiāngxíng jiànchù	pale in comparison
取之不尽	qǔ zhī bú jìn	inexhaustible
用之不竭	yòng zhī bù jié	
借鉴	jièjiàn	reference tool; to draw on

69

的。文学艺术中对于古人和外国人的毫无批判的<u>硬搬</u>和模仿，乃是最没有出息的最害人的文学教条主义和艺术教条主义。中国的革命的文学家艺术家，有出息的文学家艺术家，必须到群众中去，必须长期地无条件地全心全意地到工农兵群众中去，到火热的斗争中去，到唯一的最广大最丰富的源泉中去，观察、体验、研究、分析一切人，一切阶级，一切群众，一切生动的生活形式和斗争形式，一切文学和艺术的原始材料，然后才有可能进入创作过程。否则你的劳动就没有对象，你就只能做鲁迅在他的<u>遗嘱</u>里所<u>谆谆</u>嘱咐他的儿子万不可做的那种空头文学家，或空头艺术家。

人类的社会生活虽是文学艺术的唯一源泉，虽是较之后者有不可比拟的生动丰富的内容，但是人民还是不满足于前者而要求后者。这是为什么呢？因为虽然两者都是美，但是文艺作品中反映出来的生活却可以而且应该比普通的实际生活更高，更强烈，更有集中性，更<u>典型</u>，更理想，因此就更带普遍性。革命的文艺，应当根据实际生活创造出各种各样的人物来，帮助群众推动历史的前进。例如一方面是人们受饿、受冻、受压迫，一方面是人剥削人、人压迫人，这个事实到处存在着，人们也看得很<u>平淡</u>；文艺就把这种日常的现象集中起来，把其中的矛盾和斗争典型化，造成文学作品或艺术作品，就能使人民群众惊醒起来，感奋起来，推动人民群众走向团结和斗争，实行改造自己的环境。如果没有这样的文艺，那末这个任务就不能完成，或者不能有力地迅速地完成。

什么是文艺工作中的普及和提高呢？这两种任务的关系是怎样的呢？普及的东西比较简单<u>浅显</u>，因此也比较容易为目前广大人民群众所迅速接受。高知识和文艺作品，去提高他们的斗争热情和胜利信心，加强他

硬搬	yìngbān	copy everything mechanically
遗嘱	yízhǔ	will; testament
谆谆	zhūnzhūn	earnestly; ceaselessly
典型	diǎnxíng	typical; representative
平淡	píngdàn	dull
浅显	qiǎnxiǎn	easy to understand

们的团结，便于他们同心同德地去和敌人作斗争。对于他们，第一步需要还不是"<u>锦上添花</u>"，级的作品比较细致，因此也比较难于生产，并且往往比较难于在目前广大人民群众中迅速流传。现在工农兵面前的问题，是他们正在和敌人作残酷的流血斗争，而他们由于长时期的封建阶级和资产阶级的统治，不识字，无文化，所以他们迫切要求一个普遍的<u>启蒙运动</u>，迫切要求得到他们所急需的和容易接受的文化而是"<u>雪中送炭</u>"。所以在目前条件下，普及工作的任务更为迫切。轻视和忽视普及工作的态度是错误的。

锦上添花	jǐnshàng tiānhuā	add flowers to brocade; make the good even better
启蒙运动	qǐméng yùndòng	the Enlightenment; impart elementary knowledge
雪中送炭	xuězhōng sòngtàn	send charcoal in snowy weather; provide help at the right time

6. TOTAL REFORM

Excerpts from *Red Flag*

The Great Proletarian Cultural Revolution (文化大革命 Wenhua Da Geming, 文革 Wenge) provokes some of the strongest images and feelings of any period in twentieth-century Chinese history: the hysterical enthusiasm of thousands of students in army green at mass rallies in Tiananmen Square, young people brandishing the *Little Red Book* of Mao Zedong Thought, revulsion at the humiliations and beatings of teachers and intellectuals, the specter of urban youth exiled to the countryside for re-education, the intrigue of the plane crash that killed Lin Biao as he fled to the Soviet Union, and the eventual trial of the Gang of Four who instigated and supported the hard left policies of the revolution. Intended to refocus China on communist ideals, the Cultural Revolution can be seen as a parody of traditional China. Instead of revering the elderly, young people were incited to mock and denounce them; instead of treating texts with thoughtful reverence, people waved Mao's writings around as a symbol of blind loyalty; instead of genuine self-scrutiny, wild self-criticism was encouraged.

The Cultural Revolution, which lasted from 1966 to 1976, remains a complex and much-debated phenomenon. Commentators refer to it as a watershed in history, the "defining decade of half a century of communist rule in China."[1] While an extended analysis is beyond our scope here, its progress can be documented via a specific chain of events and via a set of social movements. The chain of events began in 1966 with literary criticism by Yao Wenyuan; the social movements had a two-decade lead-in time and would reverberate throughout China until the late 1970s. The Cultural Revolution encompassed wide-scale social disruption and economic turmoil as well as personal power politics. There was nothing very cultured about the Cultural Revolution, which at its high tide in 1966-67 promoted the destruction of anything to do with traditional China or intellectual society, as part of its goal to root out revisionism and ensure ongoing revolution. Books, art, and artifacts were destroyed in a frenzy of political correctness. The human costs were even greater, as tens of thousands died and millions were separated from their families for years. The legacy of the Cultural Revolution is still contested. Few could argue that it did not fundamentally alter China's relations with the rest of the world, while in China itself the sheer violence of the protracted experience forced a rethink of the national psyche for some, and a defensive patriotism for others. The genre of "scar literature" (伤痕文学 *shanghen wenxue*) from the 1980s testifies to the level of trauma, and to the need for catharsis

---

1. Roderick MacFarquhar and Michael Schoenhals, *Mao's Last Revolution*, 1.

that its victims felt. Scholars also argue, however, that without the Cultural Revolution there would have been no economic revolution in China, no reform and opening up, and no rise of a new superpower.[2]

Historians such as Philip Huang have argued that the Cultural Revolution should be seen as part of the wider Chinese revolution, which charts not just the rise to power of the Communist Party and the establishment of the People's Republic in 1949, but also the various large-scale changes that occurred in the decades after 1949. In this sense, the Cultural Revolution can be seen as the third stage of the big sea change of the post-Liberation era, following land redistribution and the associated dismantling of the landlord class, and the socialist reconstruction of the mid-1950s which collectivized private property and was "in so many ways the climax of three decades of revolution making."[3] Deep belief in each of these projects became a test of revolutionary commitment. In describing a similar "processual" model for revolution, Joseph Esherick has highlighted the impact of the Yan'an period on the later Cultural Revolution. In particular, the Rectification Campaign of 1942-44 (see chapter 4) had two lasting effects: it united a revolutionary leadership around Mao himself, and it showed how dissenting voices (here, intellectuals) could either be suppressed or persuaded into a deeper commitment to the Party's aims through criticism and self-criticism.

The immediate ideological backdrop, meanwhile, was the Great Leap Forward. The disastrous outcomes of this campaign are well known. Mao's attempt to speed up economic growth through unrealistic steel and grain targets—which in practice meant feeding steel furnaces with scrap metals and drawing swathes of peasants away from the fields—resulted not in communist utopia but in the worst famines of the twentieth century. Floods and drought exacerbated human folly, and recent demographic analyses undertaken in the West show that there were around 30 million excess deaths in the period 1958-61.[4] As different regions strove to outdo each other in attaining their targets and demonstrating their commitment to the nation, misreporting became rife, and the scale of the unfolding tragedy was played down. Remedial measures which might have benefited the country were delayed as Mao rejected criticisms from politicians such as army commander Peng Dehuai. Mao himself attributed the failure of the project to the fact that the people were not ideologically ready for the next stage on the road to communism. And, since the failure resulted from insufficient commitment, the answer was not retreat, but the redoubling of revolutionary efforts.

---

2. See, for example, Lucian Pye, "Reassessing the Cultural Revolution," 610.
3. Philip C. C. Huang, "Rural Class Struggle in the Chinese Revolution,"107.
4. Roderick MacFarquhar, *The Origins of the Cultural Revolution, Volume Three*, 4.

Although communization—the division of the people into communes, for labor and living purposes—was to continue for many more years, by the early 1960s the moderates, headed by Zhou Enlai, had won out and political effort was once again channeled toward agriculture and the stabilizing of economic policies. Retrenchment was signaled by a greater focus on the brigade than on the commune, by tacit acceptance of some private production, by less stringent egalitarianism, and by the abolition of unpopular mess halls and communal dining. In order to minimize grain shortages, the state planned to reduce the urban population by 10 million in three years, and many new town-dwellers were rusticated to their previous home districts.[5] Quality was once again seen as desirable in areas such as higher education. Mao voluntarily removed himself from active politics, retiring to a "second front" after acknowledging certain mistakes. He was not to remain there for long.

Deprivation in the countryside was not the only issue dividing Chinese leaders. A further factor that troubled Mao remained critical throughout the 1960s: the direction of Soviet communism. Mao increasingly believed that Khruschev was diverging from true Marxism-Leninism, and betraying the revolution. Khrushchev's attacks on Stalin did not help, since criticizing a personality cult threatened Mao's own deified position. And when it began to look as if the Russian leaders were moving toward some form of dialogue with the United States, a Sino-Soviet split became inevitable. Mao accused the Soviets of revisionism, the same charge later laid against members of his own party who sought to put reality over ideology. Along with worries over Vietnam and India, the loss of a sense of worldwide support for the true communist cause was a serious blow, coming as it did at a time of deep demoralization within China. According to MacFarquhar, without the strains and finally the "open rift" between Moscow and Beijing, "it would have been far less likely, if not inconceivable, that Mao would have developed the theories that underlay the Cultural Revolution."[6] China's alienation from the international community led Mao to believe that he needed to press ahead with radical domestic overhaul. Contradictions between socialism and capitalism, between communism and capitalism, and between true Marxism-Leninism and the deviant path of revisionism began to be theorized. Socialist art and writing was singled out as a neglected area that required attention. Mao created a small group under Peng Zhen to oversee the revolutionizing of culture, and as a new rectification campaign began, most of the elements which would characterize the Cultural Revolution were in place.

The text excerpted below dates from 1966, the height of the Red Guard phase of the Cultural Revolution. After the 11th Plenum of the Communist Party had endorsed Mao's line on revisionism, the Cultural Revolution

---

5. MacFarquhar, *The Origins, Volume Three*, 30.
6. Ibid., 375.

Group (including Mao's wife, Jiang Qing) urged the criticism of all in authority who were "taking the capitalist road." Mao wanted power wrested back from "corrupt" party officials and reassigned to the real bearers of revolution: mass organizations, the army, and those good cadres who remained. He was increasingly convinced that the blame for the revolution's failings lay within the Party; and a document titled "The Twenty-Three Articles" made it clear that cadres who had taken the capitalist road could expect thorough reform. Teams of Red Guards formed, with Mao's encouragement, to resist the work teams that his deputy Liu Shaoqi had sent to purge corrupt cadres. The forces of idealistic youth and of the army were unleashed to act as a revolutionary corrective from within. "Big character" posters were used as campaigning tools to denounce liberals. "Spontaneous" mass protests were officially authorized. School and college teaching was suspended as disorder increased. Free travel to Beijing permitted young people to engage in revolution, to "exchange experiences," and to attend mass rallies. The "four olds" (ideas, customs, culture, and habits) were to be struggled against, as were misguided officials, including Liu Shaoqi and Deng Xiaoping. As society was mobilized and polarized, some provincial authorities came near to collapse.

During the high tide of the Cultural Revolution, appearances mattered much more than substance, and symbolic representations counted at least as much as the reality of social structures.[7] Mao had failed to enact the wide-scale material changes he sought in the Great Leap Forward, and so he moved the core debate to the metaphysical. The mood was one of extreme uncertainty, heightened by the use of intense, inflammatory language. The distinction between a revolutionary and a counter-revolutionary, between a leftist and a rightist, could shift at any moment. Propaganda became an industry, as Mao used his power both to authorize official party documents and to encourage polemics from others. *Red Flag* (红旗 Hongqi) was the journal that proclaimed Communist Party theory, and it operated for most of the Cultural Revolution period under the editorship of Chen Boda, one of the Cultural Revolution Group and a longterm member of Mao's inner circle. Its editorials often set policy direction, and its tone and diction helped to whip up political fervor.[8] The language of the articles in *Red Flag* was itself revolutionary: it created a new style, introduced new phraseology, and even minted new vocabulary. Self-aggrandizing rhetorical flourishes are offset by crude insults dismissing enemies. Its oratorical style is infused with earthy language as writers sought to use the lexicon of the peasants to demonstrate their

---

7. As Philip Huang writes, the Cultural Revolution "stands out in human history for the extreme disjunction between representational reality and objective reality." See Huang, "Rural Class Struggle in the Chinese Revolution," 111.

8. That said, *Red Flag* was just as subject to the vagaries of power as was the rest of society, and the journal was shut down briefly in August 1967 when several radical members of the Cultural Revolution Group were dismissed.

political correctness. Color codes (black and red), binary oppositions, and cataclysmic metaphors lend the symbolic language force. As the extract below makes clear, language was as key to China's revolution as it is to culture itself, and the Maoists exploited this connection for all it was worth.

Excerpted from the editorial "Wuchan jieji wenhua da geming wansui," *Hongqi* 8 (1966), 4-11.

Further Reading

Dittmer, Lowell. *China's Continuous Revolution*. Berkeley: University of California Press, 1987.

————, and Chen Ruoxi. *Ethics and Rhetoric of the Chinese Cultural Revolution*. Berkeley: University of California Press, 1981.

Esherick, Joseph. "Ten Theses on the Chinese Revolution." *Modern China* 21/1 (1995), 45-76.

Fokkema, D. W. *Literary Doctrine in China and Soviet Influence 1956-1960*. London: Mouton and Co., 1965.

Guo Jian. "Resisting Modernity in Contemporary China: The Cultural Revolution and Postmodernism," *Modern China* 25/3 (1999), 343-76.

Harding, Harry. "The Chinese State in Crisis, 1966-9." In Roderick MacFarquhar, ed., *The Politics of China: The Eras of Mao and Deng*, 148-247. Cambridge: Cambridge University Press, 1997.

Huang, Philip C. C. "Rural Class Struggle in the Chinese Revolution." *Modern China* 1 (1995), 105-43.

MacFarquhar, Roderick, *The Origins of the Cultural Revolution, Volume 3: The Coming of the Cataclysm 1961-1966*. Oxford: Oxford University Press, 1997.

————, ed. *The Politics of China: The Eras of Mao and Deng*. Cambridge: Cambridge University Press, 1997.

————, and Michael Schoenhals. *Mao's Last Revolution*. Cambridge, Mass.: Harvard University Press, 2006.

Pye, Lucian W. "Reassessing the Cultural Revolution." *China Quarterly* 108 (1986), 597-612.

无产阶级文化大革命万岁

《红旗》社论 一九六六年 8 期（6 月 8 日出版）

毛主席的<u>党中央</u>直接领导的一个史无前例的、群众性的<u>无产阶级文化大革命</u>迅速地猛烈地开展，其势如<u>排山倒海</u>，锐不可当。

广大的工农兵、广大的革命干部和广大的革命知识分子，高举着毛泽东思想伟大红旗，正在横扫钻进党内的资产阶级代表人物，横扫一切<u>牛鬼蛇神</u>，横扫一切腐朽的资产阶级意识形态和封建的<u>意识形态</u>。在政治战线和思想文化战线上，出现了一个空前未有的大好形势。

这是在上层建筑中，在意识形态领域里的一场"<u>兴无灭资</u>"的极其尖锐复杂的阶级斗争。这是一场资产阶级<u>复辟</u>和无产阶级反复辟的你死我活的斗争。这场斗争，关系到我国无产阶级专政和社会主义经济基础能否巩固和向前发展，关系到我们党和国家变不变颜色，关系到我们党和国家的命运和前途，也关系到世界革命的命运和前途。对这场斗争，切切不可等闲视之。 为什么必须进行无产阶级文化革命？为什么无产阶级文化革命这样重要？

毛泽东同志科学地总结了国际无产阶级专政的历史经验，提出了社会主义社会的矛盾、阶级和阶级斗争的学说。他经常提醒我们千万不要忘记阶级斗争，千万不要忘记突出政治，千万不要忘记巩固无产阶级专政，

党中央	Dǎngzhōngyāng	Communist Party Central Committee
无产阶级 文化大革命	wúchǎnjiējí Wénhuà Dàgémìng	Great Proletarian Cultural Revolution
排山倒海	páishān dǎohǎi	great force; momentum
牛鬼蛇神	niúguǐ shéshén	ox ghosts and snake demons; forces of evil
意识形态	yìshì xíngtaì	social ideology; ways of thinking
战线	zhànxiàn	(war) front
兴无灭资	xīngwúmièzī	to foster what is proletarian and eliminate what is bourgeois— abbr. of 兴无(产阶级)灭资(产阶级)
复辟	fùbì	restore the old order; restore a dethroned emperor

必须采取各种措施防止修正主义篡夺领导，防止资本主义复辟。他指出：要推翻一个政权，必须先抓上层建筑，先抓意识形态，做好舆论准备，革命的阶级是这样，反革命的阶级也是这样。毛泽东同志正是从这样一个基本观点出发，号召我们在意识形态领域里开展"兴无灭资"的阶级斗争。这是一个伟大的真理，这是对于马克思列宁主义的一个伟大发展。在历史上，资产阶级从封建地主阶级手里夺取政权，就是先抓意识形态，先作舆论准备。欧洲资产阶级，从"文艺复兴"起，就不断地批判封建的意识形态，宣传资产阶级的意识形态。经过了好几个世纪的舆论难备，欧洲各国的资产阶级才先后在十七、十八世纪夺取了政权，建立了资产阶级专政。

在一百多年以前，马克思和恩格斯开始宣传共产主义学说，就是为无产阶级夺取政权作舆论准备的。俄国无产阶级革命，经过了几十年的舆论准备，才夺取了政权。我们自己的切身经验，更是记忆犹新的。当中国无产阶级开始登上政治舞台的时候，力量薄弱，手无寸铁。干革命，从那里开始？宣传马克思列宁主义，揭露帝国主义和它在中国的走狗。中国无产阶级夺取政权的斗争，就是从五四文化革命开始的。

中国无产阶级夺取政权的历史，从根本上说来，就是毛泽东思想掌握工农兵群众的历史。群众说得好："没有毛泽东思想，就没有新中国。"伟大的革命旗手毛泽东同志，把马克思列宁主义同中国革命实践结合起来，使得中国革命的面目为之一新。历史经验告诉我们，有了毛泽东思想，就能日益得到群众的拥护，就有了军队、有了枪，就能一块一块地建立革命根据地，一部分一部分地夺取政权，而终于夺取了全国政权。

修正主义	xiūzhèngzhǔyì	revisionism
封建地主阶级	fēngjiàn dìzhǔ jiējí	feudal landlord classes
文艺复兴	Wényìfùxīng	Renaissance
恩格斯	Ēngésī	Friedrich Engels
记忆犹新	jìyìyóuxīn	still fresh in the memory
手无寸铁	shǒu wú cùntiě	unarmed
马克思列宁主义	Mǎkèsī-Lièníngzhǔyì	Marxism-Leninism
走狗	zǒugǒu	running dogs; lackeys; stooges

无产阶级取得了政权，就成了统治的阶级，地主资产阶级成了被统治的阶级。地主阶级和反动资产阶级绝不甘心被统治，绝不甘心死亡，他们时时刻刻梦想复辟，颠覆无产阶级专政，企图重新骑在劳动人民的头上。他们还有很强大的力量，他们有金钱，有广泛的社会联系和国际联系，有反革命的经验，特别是<u>剥削阶级</u>的意识形态还有很大的市场。革命队伍中的一些不坚定的分子，会被剥削阶级的思想腐蚀，以至变成反革命。而且，小资产阶级自发势力还每时每刻产生资本主义。无产阶级夺取了政权，还存在丧失政权的危险，社会主义制度建立以后，还存在资本主义复辟的危险。如果不严重地注意这一点，采取必要的措施，那就要使我们党和国家变颜色，那就要千百万人头落地。

在生产资料所有制方面实现了社会主义改造之后，被打倒了的地主资产阶级，他们最重要的一个阵地，就是资产阶级的和封建主义的意识形态。他们的复辟活动，首先就是要抓意识形态，千方百计地用他们那一套<u>腐朽</u>的思想，欺骗群众。抓意识形态，制造舆论，这是资产阶级颠覆无产阶级专政的准备。一旦时机成熟，他们就要用这种方式或那种方式举行政变，夺取政权。

苏联在建立了<u>社会主义生产关系</u>之后，没有认真地进行无产阶级文化革命。资产阶级意识形态日益<u>泛滥</u>，腐蚀着人们的头脑，并且以一种令人不易察觉的方式，瓦解着社会主义生产关系。<u>斯大林</u>逝世之后，<u>赫鲁晓夫</u>修正主义集团更加明目张胆地制造反准命舆论，不久，他们就举行了颠覆无产阶级专政的"<u>宫廷</u>"政变，篡夺了党权、军权、政权。

剥削阶级	bōxuē jiējí	exploiting classes
腐朽	fǔxiǔ	rotten; decadent
社会主义生产关系	shèhuìzhǔyì shēngchǎn guānxi	socialist relations of production
泛滥	fànlàn	spread unchecked
斯大林	Sīdàlín	Joseph Stalin, whose forced collectivization of agriculture, rapid industrialization, and purges of leaders in the 1930s provided a model for Mao
赫鲁晓夫	Hèlǔxiǎofū	Nikita Khruschev
宫廷政变	gōngtíng zhèngbiàn	palace coup

一九五六年匈牙利反革命事件，反革命分子也是先作舆论准备，然后上街闹事，举行暴乱。这个反革命事件就是在帝国主义策划下，由裴多菲俱乐部一群反共知识分子发动的。当时还挂着共产党员牌子的纳吉，"黄袍加身"，做了反革命的头目。国际无产阶级专政的历史经验告诉我们：不进行无产阶级文化革命，不坚持消灭资产阶级意识形态，无产阶级专政就不能巩固，社会主义制度就不能巩固。资产阶级思想自由泛滥的结果，必然是无产阶级专政被颠覆，必然出现像赫鲁晓夫那样的资产阶级代表人物，采取"宫廷"政变的形式，或者采取武装政变的形式，或者两种形式相结合，来夺取政权。要巩固无产阶级专政，要使无产阶级专政的国家沿着社会主义、共产主义的方向发展，就必须进行无产阶级文化革命，兴无产阶级的意识形态，灭资产阶级的意识形态，彻底地拔掉修正主义的思想根子，牢牢地扎下马克思列宁主义、毛泽东思想的根子。

社会主义革命和社会主义建设，需要努力去做多方面的工作。在这些工作中，必须贯串一条红线，这条红线就是无产阶级和资产阶级之间的阶级斗争，就是社会主义和资本主义两条道路的斗争，就是无产阶级和资产阶级之间在意识形态方面的阶级斗争。

匈牙利反革命事件	Xiōngyálì fǎngémìng shìjiàn	the Hungarian uprising or revolution of October/ November 1956, in which student demonstrations against the Hungarian Communist government led to a popular revolt, suppressed by Soviet troops. Mao advised Khruschev to crush the "rebellion."
裴多菲俱乐部	Péiduōfēi jùlèbù	Petofi Club (named after the famed Hungarian poet), group of intellectuals whose meetings and influence fomented the 1956 uprising
黄袍加身	huángpáo jiāshēn	be acclaimed emperor (Mao used this expression of Deng)

毛泽东同志教导我们："无产阶级和资产阶级之间的阶级斗争，各派政治力量之间的阶级斗争，无产阶级和资产阶级之间在意识形态方面的阶级斗争，还是长时期的，曲折的，有时甚至是很激烈的。无产阶级要按照自己的世界观改造世界，资产阶级也要按照自己的世界观改造世界。在这一方面，社会主义和资本主义之间谁胜谁负的问题还没有真正解决。"（《关于正确处理人民内部矛盾的问题》）

无产阶级文化革命，就是要解决无产阶级和资产阶级之间在意识形态方面"谁胜谁负"的问题。这是一个长期的、艰巨的、贯串在一切工作中的历史任务。

有些同志，把无产阶级和反动资产阶级在报刊上的争论，看作是文人"打笔墨官司，无足轻重"。有些同志，埋头业务，不关心思想文化战线上的斗争，不注意意识形态领域里的阶级斗争。这是完全错误的，极端危险的。如果听任资产阶级的意识形态自由泛滥，其结果就会是无产阶级专政变为资产阶级专政，社会主义制度变为资本主义制度，变为半殖民地半封建的制度。对于这些同志，要大喝一声：同志！敌人磨刀霍霍，要杀我们的头，要推翻我们的政权，你怎么视而不见、听而不闻呢？

夺取政权要靠枪杆子、笔杆子，巩固政权也要靠这两杆子。我们要保卫和发展革命事业，不仅要牢牢地抓住我们的枪杆子，而且必须拿起无产阶级的笔杆子，横扫资产阶级的笔杆子。消除资产阶级的意识形态，才能巩固无产阶级政权，才能更加牢固地抓住无产阶级的枪杆子。

看看思想文化战线上的阶级斗争，令人惊心动魄。

艰巨的	jiānjùde	arduous; formidable
打笔墨官司	dǎbǐmòguānsi	engage in a polemic with someone
无足轻重	wúzúqīngzhòng	insignificant; of no consequence
专政	zhuānzhèng	dictatorship
磨刀霍霍	módāohuòhuò	sharpening swords; sabre-rattling
枪杆子	qiāng gǎnzi	the barrel of a gun
惊心动魄	jīngxīndòngpò	be terrified, profoundly affected

建国以来，在思想文化战线上，无产阶级同资产阶级的斗争，马克思主义同反马克思主义的斗争，从来没有停止过。在建立了社会主义的生产关系之后，这种意识形态领域里的阶级斗争，更加深入，更加复杂，更加激烈。

一九五七年资产阶级右派向党向社会主义发动了<u>猖狂进攻</u>。在这次进攻中，<u>章罗联盟</u>反动政客集团公开出台以前，资产阶级右派的知识分子，就放出了大量的<u>毒草</u>，一批反革命的观点、反革命的政纲和反革命的电影、小说，纷纷出笼了。很显然，这一套东西，都是为资产阶级右派夺取政权作舆论准备的。中国人民在党中央和毛主席的英明领导下，打退了资产阶级右派的猖狂进攻，在政治战线和思想战线上取得了重大胜利。

一九五八年，中国人民在社会主义建设总路线的伟大红旗照耀下，意气风发，干劲冲天，在各条战线上展开了<u>大跃进</u>，大办人民公社。同时，工农兵群众热情地活学活用毛主席著作。思想文化战线上也开始了革命。一九五九年到一九六二年这个期间，由于苏联修正主义者的破坏和连续三年的严重自然灾害，我国遭受了暂时经济困难。困难，吓不倒革命的中国人民。中国人民在党中央和毛主席的英明领导下，埋头苦干，奋发图强。经过了几年，就克服了困难，出现了大好形势。可是在经济困难的几年里，牛鬼蛇神纷纷出笼，反动资产阶级向党向社会主义的进攻，达到了极其猖獗的程度。

猖狂进攻	chāngkuáng jìngōng	savage onslaught
章罗联盟	Zhāng-Luó liánméng	the union of "reactionaries" Zhang Bojun and Luo Longji, famous rightists of the era
毒草	dúcǎo	poisonous weeds; harmful writings
大跃进	Dàyuèjìn	Great Leap Forward, the disastrous production campaign of 1957-59

在哲学界，<u>杨献珍大肆宣传</u>否认意识和存在具有同一性的谬论，来打击工农兵群众发挥主观能动性，来反对大跃进。接着杨献珍又抛出了"<u>合二而一</u>"论，为"<u>三和一少</u>"、"<u>三自一包</u>"的极端反动政治路线，提供哲学"根据"。钻近党内的那些 代表资产阶级的所谓"权威"人物，猖狂地挥舞起"庸俗化"、"简单化"、"实用主义"这三根棍子，反对工农兵活学活用毛主席著作。他们还利用职权，禁止报刊发表工农兵的哲学论文。同时，某些资产阶级"专家"，借研究哲学史为名，大肆宣扬"自由、平等、博爱"，大肆吹捧孔子，利用孔子这具<u>僵尸</u>，宣扬他们一整套的资产阶级观点。

杨献珍	Yáng Xiànzhēn	an alternate member of the 8th Central Committee and Marxist philosopher who encouraged the study of dialectics
大肆宣传	dàsìxuānchuán	proclaim noisily; give much publicity to
合二而一论	héèréryīlùn	"combining two into one": during the Cultural Revolution the slogan "one divides into two" became an important political issue, as Mao's opponents were accused of betraying Marxism-Leninism by misstating the principle of contradiction. They were charged with putting unity first and class struggle second, or "combining two into one"
三和一少	sānhéyīshǎo	those who unite the three facets of imperialism, revisionism, and reactionism but who lack the one facet of aiding the revolution
三自一包	sānzìyībāo	Liu Shaoqi's program for economic regeneration in the aftermath of the Great Leap Forward. It permitted a degree of private landholding, free markets, and individual responsibility for profit (the "three selfs"), together with production contract quotas at a household level (the "one taking charge")
僵尸	jiāngshī	corpse

在经济学界，<u>孙冶方</u>等人提出一整套修正主义谬论。他们反对毛泽东思想挂帅、政治挂帅，主张利润技帅、钞票挂帅。他们妄图改变社会主义的生产关系，把社会主义企业变成资本主义的企业。

在史学界，一批资产阶级"权威"，对一九五八年开始的史学革命，大肆攻击。他们反对史学研究工作要以马克思列宁主义、毛泽东思想挂帅，宣扬史料就是一切。他们用所谓"历史主义"，反对马克思列宁主义的阶级斗争学说。他们对革命的史学工作者批判帝王将相，突出农民和农民战争，十分仇恨。他们对帝王将相歌颂到无以复加的程度，对农民和农民战争则尽情污蔑。他们是史学界里的资产阶级"保皇党"。其中，有些人是反共老手。<u>吴晗</u>、<u>翦伯赞</u>就是这样的人物。在文艺界，资产阶级代表人物极力宣扬对抗毛主席文艺路线的一整套修正主义文艺路线，卖力地宣扬他们的所谓三十年代传统。"写真实"论，"<u>现实主义</u>广阔的道路"论，"现实主义深化"论，反"<u>题材决定</u>"论，"<u>中间人</u>

孙冶方	Sūn Yěfāng	leading Marxist economist (1908-83), who was punished for his links to Liu Shaoqi and modernizing theories, later became advisor to Zhao Ziyang
吴晗	Wú Hán	author of the article on Hai Rui that became a trigger for the launching of of the Cultural Revolution (1909-69)
翦伯赞	Jiǎn Bózàn	historian and vice-president of Beijing University (1898-1968) criticized for his historical methodology; died by suicide
现实主义	xiànshí zhǔyì	realism; the eight –isms listed are the so-called "eight black discourses" that Jiang Qing *et al.* railed against during the Cultural Revolution
题材决定	tícáijuédìng	set topics; pre-determined literary themes
中间人物	zhōngjiānrénwù	"middle characters"; theory promoted by Shao Quanlin and Zhao Shuli, which questioned whether all lit erary characters need be happy, noble heroes

物”论，反“火药味”论，“时代精神汇合”论，“离经叛道”论，等等，就是他们的代表性论点。在这些论点“指导”下，出了一批反党反社会主义的坏戏、坏电影、坏小说、坏电影史、坏文学史。在教育界，资产阶级代表人物，极力反对毛主席提出的使受教育者在德育、智育、体育几方面都得到发展，成为有社会主义觉悟的有文化的劳动者这个教育方针，极力反对半工半读教育制度，宣扬苏联修正主义的一套教育“理论”和制度。他们拼死命地和我们争夺青年一代，妄图把青年一代培养成资产阶级的接班人.

在新闻界，资产阶级代表人物极力反对新闻要有指导性，提倡资产阶级的所谓“知识性”。他们妄图扼杀马克思列宁主义、毛泽东思想对新闻工作的领导，妄图让资产阶级的货色自由泛滥，妄图夺取我们的新闻阵地。

在这股逆流中，最反动、最猖狂的是“三家村”反党集团。他们的阵地很多，有报纸，有刊物，有讲坛，有出版机关。他们的手特别长，伸到了文

火药味	huǒyàowèi	"smell of gunpowder"; be bellicose
时代精神汇合	shídàijīngshénhuìhé	"uniting with the spirit of the times"; theory propounded by Zhou Gucheng, which was initially allowed by Mao as as an example of healthy literary discourse, but was later criticized during the Cultural Revolution
离经叛道	líjīng pàndào	depart from the classics and rebel against orthodoxy; deviate from (communist) doctrine
半工半读	bàngōng bàndú	system where students worked part-time and studied part-t time, lauded by Mao at this p point, disliked by moderates and students
三家村	Sānjiācūn	here refers to the Beijing officials Deng Tuo, Wu Han, and Liao Mosha, and their letters on society and the arts published serially in 1961

化领域的各界里，篡夺了部分的领导权。他们的反动政治嗅觉最灵敏，他们的作品配合反动政治气候最及时。他们是有指挥、有组织、有计划、有目的地为复辟资本主义、推翻无产阶级专政作舆论准备的。

在这股逆流中，钻进党内的资产阶级代表人物起了主要作用。他们打着"红旗"反红旗，披着马克思列宁主义、毛泽东思想的外衣反对马克思列宁主义、毛泽东思想。他们把自己打扮成马克思主义的"权威"，打扮成解释党的政策的"权威"，大肆放毒，欺骗群众。他们利用职权，一方面让牛鬼蛇神大批出笼，一方面压倒无产阶级左派进行反击。这是一撮挂着共产主义羊头、卖反党反社会主义狗肉的阴谋家。这是一些最危险的人物。

篡夺　　　　　cuànduó　　　　　usurp; seize illegally

7. THE UNREFORMED

On Family Background
Yu Luoke

Commonly circulated clichés have it that the Cultural Revolution was a period of rigid intellectual orthodoxy. Millions were entranced by the dogma of the day; and for those who were not, dissent was simply too dangerous to countenance. Recent research, however, suggests that thinking against the grain was far more plentiful than was once acknowledged. Pioneered by scholars such as Song Yongyi and Sun Dajin, the inquiry into heterodox thought during the Cultural Revolution has cast new light on the "ten years of chaos" and revealed that this very chaos provided a cover for all kinds of illicit ideological activities. As "educated youths" (知青 *zhiqing*) were rusticated *en masse* to some of the nation's most far-flung and forbidding regions, hundreds of study groups sprang up, giving young people a forum in which to share their experiences of revolution. Cut loose from the familiar moorings of family and school, many acquired a new independence of thought, and a new desire to express it. For others, the spur to rebel came earlier, as they heeded Mao's call to nurture "independent thinking" during the first heady days of the mass movement, only to realize when it was far too late just how expedient his motives had been. Either way, the Cultural Revolution—for all its mass lines, little red books, and giant rallies—created many of the material conditions in which dissidence might thrive, and thrive it did. Indeed, Song goes so far as to suggest that the democratic movements of the post-Mao period were spawned, ironically enough, during the high tide of ultra-Maoism.

Yet a closer inspection of these ideological counter-currents reveals that this irony is not quite as rich as it might first appear. Much of the dissent revolved around the notion of a socialism which had been derailed in the direction of social injustice, and required resetting along more egalitarian lines. Altogether, several dozen "poisonous weeds" (heterodox writings) were targeted for uprooting during the period; and although the text under analysis in this chapter—Yu Luoke's "On Family Background" (Chushen lun)—is the most celebrated, many others caused ripples with their condemnation of the blighted Party ethos. As a rule, these "new trends of thought" (新思潮 *xin sichao*) traced their ideological origins back to the overtly humanist, quasi-democratic strains within classical Marxism. As early as 1966, two Beijing high school students used the pseudonym Yilin-Dixi to publish an open letter to party chief Lin Biao, in which they claimed that the "People's Republic based upon the principle of the people's democratic dictatorship has become obsolete."[1] They called for a return to the spirit, rather than the warped letter, of Marxism, and demanded a new Chinese society modeled on the Paris Commune of 1871. The students soon found themselves in jail, but their critique, as Shaoguang Wang observes,[2] had set the tone for protest to come. As the Cultural Revolution continued its violent, power-grabbing progress, and the dream of a new Paris Commune slipped from view, independent study groups sprang up across the country with the aim of getting these utopian ideals back on track. Most conspicuous, and most daring, were the Sheng-wu-lian group in Changsha and the Bei-jue-yang group in Wuhan, though many others also flourished.

At the core of their dissent was the notion of class—and its use and abuse as a category of socio-political differentiation. For many young dissidents, class relations in China had sedimented into a depressingly familiar pattern, in which the players had changed, but the basic law of inequity remained. This law was enshrined in the policy of "class line" (阶级路线 *jieji luxian*), which drew its rationale from the family origin (出身 *chushen*) system. According to this new taxonomy of class, all families were assigned a designation based on the status of the family head between 1946 and 1949. These class designations were inherited patrilineally, either as bane or blessing, during the first three decades which followed 1949. Embraced within the circle of virtue were workers, poor and lower-middle peasants, revolutionary cadres, soldiers, and martyrs, who together comprised approximately nine-tenths of the population. Being "born red" vouchsafed this majority various advantages. Indeed, just as the *gong-nong-bing* (工农兵 workers, farmers, soldiers) of pre-revolutionary China had been oppressed by the landed classes, so were they now acclaimed as the new overlords in an ideological economy which made a fetish of "redness." Meanwhile, those who belonged by nothing other than birthright to "bad" family backgrounds were left disenfranchised, denied opportunities and forced to bear the stigma of their parents' status in the old China. Social exclusion of this kind was suffered by descendants of the former exploiting classes, the politically hostile and their children, those who had been labeled rightists in the Anti-Rightist Campaign of 1957, and others whose communist credentials did not stand up to close enough inspection. As the Cultural Revolution turned more vicious, this minority became the target of extreme violence and persecution. And all the while, pulling the real strings and commandeering the real privilege were the so-called "red capitalists": the senior party officials and their rapacious offspring (the so-called "sons of high cadres," 高干子弟 *gaoganzidi*) who constituted the true elite of revolutionary China.

---

1. Quoted in Shaoguang Wang, "'New Trends of Thought' on the Cultural Revolution," 199.

2. Ibid., 200.

Most of the young dissidents who pushed so earnestly for a "real" Cultural Revolution hailed from the ranks of the politically disadvantaged. For them, the mass movement was a much-craved chance to redistribute property, power, and status of various kinds, and they jumped at it with more zeal than common sense. Yu Luoke was perhaps the boldest of them all, and his critique of China's new caste system was arguably the most stringent. Much of Yu's passion was doubtless born of his own experiences of class discrimination. Both his parents had been labeled rightists in 1957 and, as Yihong Pan notes, Yu's dedication to the Party gave him no choice but "to draw a 'class' line with his parents."[3] Little good this did him. Despite being a talented student, he was twice refused university admission on account of his bad class background, and after volunteering for rural work in 1961, he found himself back in Beijing on the eve of the Cultural Revolution working as a factory apprentice. The new mass movement stepped up Yu's suffering, as he and his family were picked out for persecution by Red Guards on account of their class origins. Many of his frustrations found eloquent outlet in his diary of 1966, which lampooned the powers-that-be and was later confiscated. Around the same time, Yu began work on the essay which would seal both his fate and his iconoclastic status: "On Family Background."

First printed in the rebel newspaper *Journal of Middle School Cultural Revolution* (中学文革报 Zhongxue Wenge Bao) in January 1967, the essay's impact was immediate. Sixty thousand copies of the essay were sold within a week of its publication in Beijing, and over a million were reprinted across the country in the days which followed. Large-scale public debates ensued, in which Yu and his supporters routed the illogicality of their opponents. The sheer resonance of the chord the essay struck came in part from the transparency of its writing: it exposed the injustices of the day—and, in particular, the "bloodline theory" (血统论 *xuetong lun*) which made them possible—with a clear-toned logic which revolutionary discourse had long lost. Moreover, its critique of lineage theory chimed with the fears and feelings of millions across the country. Bloodline theory, as Song Yongyi describes it, was a "radicalized version"[4] of class line policy. It proceeded from the premise that those "born red" (自来红 *zilai hong*) should enjoy inalienable rights and privileges, at the same time as making this "redness" the *de facto* preserve of the *gaoganzidi* and their ilk. In practice, it gave the first cohorts of Red Guards, many of whom hailed from precisely this kind of stock, a mandate for shoring up their status and waging red terror against their rivals. In particular, they sought to transform blood lineage into the decisive criterion for access to further education, an area where they were still outperformed by the so-called

---

3. Yihong Pan, *Tempered in the Revolutionary Furnace*, 72.
4. Song Yongyi, "The Enduring Legacy of Blood Lineage Theory."

"seven black categories" (黑七类 *hei qi lei*). Unsurprisingly, perhaps, university campuses became the arenas for a sometimes intense violence, as the Red Guards menaced and murdered those less red by birth, if not behavior, than themselves. The ferocity of the Red Guards, and the support from on high which they enjoyed, kept opposition to bloodline theory muted throughout most of 1966. But as it became clear that the real targets of Mao's purge were not the "born blacks" so much as the parents of "born reds" within the Party itself whose influence threatened Mao, a new wave of Rebel Red Guards surged up which turned the violence back on their precursors. "On Family Background" appeared amid this mayhem. Yet rather than taking its cues from the power struggle racking the Party elite, the essay's heart is with the Chinese people at a time when, as Lu Xiuyuan puts it, "the absurdity of the class policy"[5] could no longer be ducked.

Imbued as it may have been with the spirit of just remonstrance, Yu's essay was ultimately an article of sedition which challenged the highest authority in the land. And as such, its writer paid the highest price. On January 5, 1968, Yu was arrested, and his study group was branded a "counterrevolutionary clique." The case against him hardened when his diary—replete with subversive thoughts—was discovered in a public lavatory,[6] and he was eventually executed on March 5, 1970, aged 27. Yet Yu's plea for equality, and his status as a pioneer of human rights in China, still echoes on today. John Gittings observes that he was the "foremost folk hero of Cultural Revolutionary dissent, the subject of many poems and eulogies by activists of the Democracy Wall period."[7] Just as importantly, his disdain for the eugenics of color makes for edgy reading at a time when some of the great and the good in China still owe their positions not to talent so much as the lottery of biological birthright.

Yu Luoke. "Chushen lun." In *Dalu dixia kanwuhuibian*, vol. 8. Taibei: Zhonggong yanjiu zazhishe, 1980, 8-14.

Further Reading

Andreas, Joel. "Battling over Political and Cultural Power during the Chinese Cultural Revolution." *Theory and Society* 31/4 (2002), 463-519.

Dittmer, Lowell, and Chen Ruoxi. *Ethics and Rhetoric of the Chinese Cultural Revolution*. Berkeley: University of California Press, 1981.

---

5. Lu Xiuyuan, "A Step Toward Understanding Popular Violence in China's Cultural Revolution," 559.

6. Yu's sister, Yu Luojin, is the author of a memoir titled *A Winter's Tale* (Dongtian de tonghua, 1980), in which she reproaches herself for the loss of the diary.

7. See John Gittings, *The Changing Face of China*, 147.

Gittings, John. *The Changing Face of China: From Mao to Market.* Oxford: Oxford University Press, 2005.

Kraus, Richard Curt. *Class Conflict in Chinese Socialism.* New York: Columbia University Press, 1981.

Lin Jing. *The Red Guards' Path to Violence: Political, Educational, and Psychological Factors.* New York: Praeger, 1991.

Lu Xiuyuan. "A Step Toward Understanding Popular Violence in China's Cultural Revolution." *Pacific Affairs* 67/4 (1994-1995), 533-63.

Pan, Yihong, *Tempered in the Revolutionary Furnace: China's Youth in the Rustication Movement.* Lanham, M.D.: Lexington Books, 2003.

Song Yongyi. "The Enduring Legacy of Blood Lineage Theory." *China Rights Forum* 4 (2004), http://hrichina.org/public/PDFs/EnduringLegacy4-2004.pdf.

———, and Zhou Zehao. "Guest Editors' Introduction." *Contemporary Chinese Thought* (Special Issue on Heterodox Thoughts during the Cultural Revolution, part 1) 32/4 (2001), 3-16.

Thurston, Anne F. *Enemies of the People: The Ordeal of Intellectuals in China's Great Cultural Revolution.* Cambridge: Harvard University Press, 1988.

Wang Shaoguang. "'New Trends of Thought' on the Cultural Revolution." *Journal of Contemporary China* 8/21 (1999), 197-218.

Yu Luojin. *A Chinese Winter's Tale: An Autobiographical Fragment.* Trans. Rachel May and Zhu Zhiyu. Hong Kong: Research Centre for Translation, Chinese University of Hong Kong, 1986.

出身论

遇罗克

一、社会影响和家庭影响问题

先从一副<u>流毒</u>极广的<u>对联</u>谈起。

"<u>老子</u>英雄儿好汉，老子反动儿混蛋，基本如此。"

辩论这副对联的过程，就是对出身不好的青年侮辱的过程。因为这样辩论的最好结果，也无非他们不算是个混蛋而已。初期敢于正面反驳它的很少见，即使有，也常常是<u>羞羞答答</u>的。其实这副对联的上半联是从封建社会的<u>山大王窦尔敦</u>那里借来的。难道批判窦尔敦还需要多少勇气吗？还有人说这副对联起过好作用。是吗？毛主席说，任何真理都是符合于人民利益的，任何错误都是不符合于人民利益的。它起没起过好作用，要看它是否是真理——是否符合毛泽东思想。

这副对联不是真理，是绝对的错误。

它的错误在于：认为家庭影响超过了社会影响，看不到社会影响的决定性作用。<u>说穿</u>了，它只承认老子的影响，认为老子超过了一切。

实践恰好得出完全相反的结论：社会影响远远超过了家庭影响，家庭影响服从社会影响。从孩子一出世就受到了两种影响。稍一懂事就步入学校大门，老师的话比家长的话更有权威性，集体受教育比单独受教育<u>共鸣性</u>更强，在校时间比在家时间更长，党的<u>雨露</u>和毛泽东思想的阳光滋润着这棵新生的幼芽，社会影响便成了主流。

朋友的<u>琢磨</u>，领导的教导，报纸、书籍、文学、艺术的宣传，习俗

流毒	liúdú	exert a baneful influence
对联	duìlián	antithetical couplet
老子	lǎozi	father (colloquial)
羞羞答答	xiūxiudādā	shy; bashful
山大王	shāndàiwang	leader of mountain outlaws
窦尔敦	Dòu Ěrdūn	Robin Hood–style rebel of the Qing dynasty
说穿	shuōchuān	tell things as they really are
共鸣性	gòngmíngxìng	resonance
雨露	yǔlù	grace; favor
琢磨	zhuómó	reflect; ponder

的<u>熏染</u>，工作的<u>陶冶</u>等等，都会给一个人以不可磨灭的影响，这些<u>统称</u>社会影响。这都是家庭影响无法<u>抗衡</u>的。

　　即使是家庭影响，也是社会影响的一部分。一个人家庭影响的好坏，不能机械地以老子如何而定。英雄的老子，反动的妈妈，影响未必是好的。父母都是英雄，子女却流于<u>放任</u>，有时更糟糕。父母思想好，教育方法如果简单<u>生硬</u>，效果也会适得其反。同样，老子不好，家庭影响未必一定不好，列宁就是例证。总之，一个人的家庭影响是好是坏，是不能机械地以出身判定的。出身只是家庭影响的参考。

总的来说，我们的社会影响是好的。这是因为：我们的社会制度是无比优越的，我们的党是一贯突出政治的，是最重视年轻一代成长的；我们绝大多数人民是热爱新社会的。当然，我们也不能忽视阶级斗争的复杂性和<u>尖锐性</u>，不能忽视我们还处在小资产阶级<u>汪洋大海</u>之中。我们的文化教育制度正待彻底改革。有时社会影响又不全是好的。无论是什么出身的青年，如果接受社会上的坏影响，一般总要服从这种坏影响，犯这样或那样的错误。但是只要引导<u>得法</u>，他很快就会抛掉旧东西，回到正确的立场上来。所以，故意让青年背上历史包袱，故意让青年背上家庭包袱，同属于一种错误路线，<u>二者</u>都是残酷的。由于社会影响是无比强大的，但又不见得全是好的，所以不管是什么出身的青年放弃思想改造，都是错误的。对于改造思想来说，出身好的青年比出身不好的青年并没有任何优越性。

　　家庭影响也罢，社会影响也罢，这都是外因。过多地强调影响，就

熏染	xūnrǎn	influence
陶冶	táoyě	exert a favorable influence; mold
统称	tǒngchēng	general designation
抗衡	kànghéng	contend with
放任	fàngrèn	leave to their own devices
生硬	shēngyìng	rigid; harsh
尖锐性	jiānruìxìng	intensity
汪洋大海	wāngyángdàhǎi	the boundless seas
得法	défǎ	go smoothly; with a proper and effective method
二者	èrzhě	both of them

是不承认主观<u>能动性</u>的<u>机械论</u>的表现。人是能够选择自己的前进方向的。这是因为真理总是更强大，更有<u>号召力</u>。你真的相信马克思列宁主义是无比正确的吗？你真的相信毛泽东思想是战无不胜的思想武器吗？你真的承认<u>内因</u>起决定作用吗？那么，你就不应该认为老子的影响比甚么都强大。否则，只能表明你的思想混乱到<u>无以复加</u>的程度了。

二、重在表现问题

如果你没有理由驳倒社会影响大于家庭影响，也驳不倒现在社会的好影响是主流，也不得不赞同出身和家庭影响没有必然的联系。那么，我们可以一起来研究"<u>重在表现</u>"的几个问题。

无产阶级文化大革命的初期，很多人都说"重在表现"是<u>修正主义</u>观点。后来听说这是毛主席提出来的，才慌忙<u>改口</u>。可见他们对这项政策根本不理解。让他们来解释这项政策，就必然会<u>任意</u>歪曲。<u>限于篇幅</u>，这里只检查三种提法，看是否符合毛泽东思想。

1．出身和<u>成份</u>完全不同

貌似<u>公允</u>的同志常对出身不好的青年这样讲："一我们有成份论，二<u>不唯成份论</u>，三重在政治表现……"这是不看对象。

能动性	néngdòngxìng	dynamic
机械论	jīxièlùn	mechanism
号召力	hàozhàolì	appeal
内因	nèiyīn	internal causes
无以复加	wúyǐfùjiā	in the extreme
重在表现	zhòngzài biǎoxiàn	the "laying stress on behavior" campaign of 1965
修正主义	xiūzhèngzhǔyì	revisionism
改口	gǎikǒu	withdraw a previous remark; eat one's words
任意	rènyì	willfully
限于篇幅	xiànyú piānfú	for reasons of space
成份	chéngfèn	class status
公允	gōngyǔn	just and fair
不唯成份论	bù wéi chéngfènlùn	the notion that class background is not the only way to assess revolutionary fervor

On Family Background

　　江青同志解释过这句话。她说：这是对背叛本阶级的个别份子讲的。江青同志的解释是甚么意思呢？举例说，<u>恩格斯</u>本人是资本家，但他背叛了本阶级，成了共产主义的第一代公民，成了工人阶级杰出的领袖。<u>巴黎公社</u>中也有一些本人是资产阶级份子的委员，但他们是工人阶级公社的代表。我国革命时期也有这样的例证。我们能不能因为他们成份不好而<u>抹煞</u>他们的历史功绩呢？不能！我们要重在政治表现。这就叫"不唯成份论"。我们认为相反的情况也适用于这个公式。对成份是矿工，但背叛了无产阶级，背叛了革命的份子，也要重在表现，也没有一点可以轻恕他的罪恶的理由。小而言之，<u>李鼎铭</u>是地主份子，但他向边区政府提出了"<u>精兵简政</u>"的建议，毛主席赞扬说："不管甚么人……你说的办法对人民有好处，我们就照你的办。"这就是不以人害言，亦即不唯成份论的具体表现。

　　出身和成份是完全不同的两件事。老子的成份是儿子的出身。如果说，在封建家庭是社会的分子，子承父业还是实在情况，那么，到了资本主义社会，这个说法就不完全正确了。家庭的<u>纽带</u>已经松弛了，年轻的一代已经属于社会所有了。而到了社会主义社会，一般的青少年都接受无产阶级教育，准备为无产阶级事业服务了，再把儿子、老子看作<u>一码事</u>，那也太不"适乎潮流"了。

　　毛主席在一九三九年写的《中国革命和中国共产党》一文中说，当时的知识分子属于小资产阶级范畴。在这里并没有<u>分门别类</u>，把哪一个阶级出身的知识分子划归为哪一范畴。

　　毛主席在一九五七年写的《关于正确处理人民内部矛盾的问题》一文中又说："我们的大学生，虽然还有许多人是非劳动人民家庭出身的子

恩格斯	Ēngésī	Friedrich Engels (1820-1895)
巴黎公社	Bālí gōngshè	Paris commune
抹煞	mǒshā	blot out; write off
李鼎铭	Lǐ Dǐngmíng	enlightened gentry landlord of Shaanxi province (1881-1947)
精兵简政	jīngbīngjiǎnzhèng	better troops and simpler administration
纽带	niǔdài	tie; bond
一码事	yì mǎ shì	one and the same
分门别类	fēnménbiélèi	classify; put into categories

女，但是除了少数例外，都是爱国的，都是拥护社会主义的......"这又是一个例证。

由此可知，同一个家庭的成员不见得就是同一个阶级的成员，这一点连阶级敌人都知道得很清楚。例如，运动期间北京中级人民法院的一份<u>判决书</u>上写道，一个反革命富农分子，因为三个儿子<u>检举</u>了他，夜间持凶器砍死、砍伤了他们。又据一份传单，市内某公社工厂书记——一个<u>蜕化的变质分子</u>，临自杀前，亲手溺毙了自己的孩子。他在<u>遗嘱</u>中说，孩子长大也不会为自己报仇了。

出身和成份是不能<u>相提并论</u>的。有一段对话是很耐人寻味的。甲（是个学生）："你什么出身？"乙："你呢？"甲："我<u>红五类</u>，我爸爸是工人。"乙："那我比你强，我就是工人。"

如果说唯成份论都没有道理，那么唯出身论又怎么能够存在？

有些人会引用毛主席的话反驳说："在阶级社会中，每一个人都在一定的阶级地位中生活，各种思想无不打上阶级的烙印。"这是<u>放之四海而皆准</u>的真理。地主、资本家他们长期在剥削阶级地位中生活，他们的思想无不打上剥削阶级的烙印。因此，他们要想重新做人，就必须<u>脱胎换骨</u>地改造，这也就是我们"有成份论"的根据。但是对他们的子女，就不能这样看了。特别是在新社会长大的青年，能说他们是在剥削阶级地位中生活吗？世界上哪有一种没有剥削的剥削阶级呢？没有这样的东西。

判决书	pànjuéshū	court verdict
检举	jiǎnjǔ	inform against someone
蜕化的变质分子	tuìhuà de biànzhì fènzǐ	degenerate element
遗嘱	yízhǔ	*n* will
相提并论	xiāngtíbìnglùn	place on a par
红五类	hóng wǔ lèi	the five red categories: workers, poor and lower-middle peasants, soldiers, cadres, and martyrs
烙印	làoyìn	brand; mark
放之四海而皆准	fàng zhī sìhǎi ér jiē zhǔn	universally applicable
脱胎换骨	tuōtāi huàngǔ	reborn

给一个人的思想打上烙印的，不只是家庭，更重要的是社会。今天的社会是一所毛泽东思想的大学校。青年人的阶级地位，要么是准备做劳动者，要么是已经成了劳动者。这时对他们还强调"成份"，那就是要把他们赶到敌对阶级中去。

我们必须要划清出身和成份这二者之间不容<u>混淆</u>的界限。谁抹煞了这两条界限，虽然样子很"左"，但实际上就是抹煞了阶级界限。

2．出身和表现关系甚小

于是，公允派的同志不谈成份了。他们说："我们既看出身，也看表现（即政治表现）……"

这是"出身即成份论"的<u>翻版</u>。两相比较，也就是<u>五十步笑百步</u>，没多大差别。

出身是死的，表现是活的，用死标准和活标准同时衡量一个人，能得出同一个结论吗？我们在本文第一个问题已经分析过：出身是家庭影响的一个因素，家庭影响是表现的一个因素，而且是一个次要的因素，社会影响才是表现的主要因素。因此，出身和表现根本没有同一性。究竟一个人所受影响是好是坏，只能从实践中检验。这里所说的实践，就是一个人的政治表现。表现好的，影响就好；表现不好的，影响就不好。这和出身毫无牵涉。

退一步说，我们非要既看出身，又看表现不可，那么请问：出身不好，表现好，是不是可以抹煞人家的成绩？出身好，表现不好，是不是可以<u>掩饰</u>人家的缺点？出身不好，表现不好，是不是要<u>罪加一等</u>？出身好，表现好，是不是要夸大优点？难道这样作是有道理的吗？

"既看出身，也看表现"，实际上不免要滑到"只看出身，不看表现"的<u>泥坑</u>里去。出身多么容易看，一翻<u>档案</u>，就<u>完事大吉</u>了。或者在街

混淆	hùnxiáo	confused; mixed-up
翻版	fānbǎn	reprint; reduplication
五十步笑百步	wǔshí bù xiào bǎi bù	equivalent to "the pot calling the kettle black"
掩饰	yǎnshì	gloss over; cover up
罪加一等	zuìjiāyìděng	doubly guilty
泥坑	níkēng	morass
档案	dàng'àn	file; dossier
完事大吉	wánshìdàjí	everything is just fine

上一见面问对方：“你是什么出身？”便了解了一切。真是又简单又省事。要看表现是何等麻烦，特别是对那些莫名其妙的怀疑派来说，绝不相信你平时的表现，也不相信你大风大浪中的表现，既怀疑你过去的表现，也怀疑你现在的表现，并准备怀疑你将来的表现，直怀疑你个<u>死而后已</u>，才给你<u>盖棺论定</u>。终于连他们也怀疑腻了。如果看出身，两秒钟能解决大问题。再说，表现这种东西，对于某些人根本就没有固定的<u>准绳</u>。爱<u>奉承</u>的人，认为拍马屁是最好的表现；爱虚伪的人，认为<u>客套</u>是最好的表现；爱错误路线的人，认为出身不好的青年终日超经验的<u>忏悔</u>是最好的表现。哪里比得上出身？只需“老子英雄儿好汉，老子反动儿混蛋，老子平常儿骑墙”三句话就解决问题了。

看一看毛主席怎样教导我们吧，毛主席说：“革命的或不革命的或反革命的知识分子的最后分界，看其是否愿意并且实行和工农民众相结合。我们在这里提出了一个标准，我认为是唯一的标准。”这唯一的标准是出身吗？

毛主席又说：“什么人站在革命人民方面，他就是革命派...”这里提到出身吗？

毛主席提出的革命接班人的五项条件，有出身这一条吗？

<u>十六条</u>中的第五条是坚决执行党的阶级路线，谈到要依靠什么人，团结什么人，反对什么人，有出身这个根据吗？

革命左派的三个标准，有出身这个标准吗？没有！全没有！出身好坏与本人革命与否又有什么关系？即使出身不好，一样可以是革命左派，

死而后已	sǐ'érhòuyǐ	till one's dying day
盖棺论定	gàiguānlùndìng	final judgment can be passed on a person only after his death
准绳	zhǔnshéng	yardstick; criterion
奉承	fèngchéng	fawn upon
客套	kètào	civilities; polite chit-chat
忏悔	chànhuǐ	penitent
骑墙	qíqiáng	sit on the fence
十六条	shíliù tiáo	the sixteen points: the guiding principles for carrying out the Cultural Revolution, as laid down in August 1966

可以是无产阶级事业的接班人，可以是革命的依靠对象。在表现面前，所有的青年都是平等的。出身不好的青年不需要人家<u>恩赐</u>的团结，不能够只做人家的<u>外围</u>。谁是<u>中坚</u>？娘胎里决定不了。任何通过个人努力所达不到的权利，我们一概不承认。革命最坚决的人，就是那些表现最优秀的人。谁也不能说<u>王杰</u>的光辉程度就不及<u>雷锋</u>。

　　谈到怎样看表现，想到古代思想家的一则寓言。他说<u>千里马</u>常有，但认识千里马的<u>伯乐</u>不常有。一般人相马，总是根据母马、外形、产地、价钱来判断马的好坏，偏忘记了让马跑一跑，试一试，看看它到底能不能日行千里，夜走八百，这样就分不出哪一匹马是千里马。今天有的人不正是这样吗？他们只是着眼于出身啦，社会关系啦，这些死材料，恰恰忘了真正可以做为根据的表现。<u>久而久之</u>，不但糟踏了千里马，就连普通马也要变成"<u>狗崽子</u>"了。

　　我们必须要摆对出身和表现的位置。衡量一个青年是否革命，出身不是标准，只有表现才是唯一的标准。你们真的认为出身好表现就好，尽可以表现上超过出身不好的同志？只有表现糟糕的人才扯起出身这面大旗

恩赐	ēncì	favor; charity
外围	wàiwéi	peripheral figures
中坚	zhōngjiān	nucleus; backbone; hard core
王杰，雷锋	Wáng Jié, Léi Fēng	soldier-heroes of the PLA: Wang (1942-1965) was from an upper-middle peasant family, whereas Lei (1940-1962) hailed from poor peasant stock
千里马	qiānlǐmǎ	"winged steed" (literally, thousand *li* horse)
伯乐	Bó Lè	a man who lived in the reign period of Duke Mu of Qin (659-621 B.C.), who was reputedly a good judge of horse flesh
久而久之	jiǔ'érjiǔzhī	as time passes
狗崽子	gǒuzǎizi	"sons of bitches (dogs)," derogatory term used to describe the offspring of people from bad class backgrounds

当虎皮，拿老子当商标，要人<u>买账</u>。我们说，你表现不好，比如：顽固坚持反动路线，不学不用毛主席著作等等，就是出身于红五类中的前三类（革干、革军、革烈），也一点没有用处。

出身、社会关系这些东西只能算是参考。只要把一个青年的政治表现了解清楚了，它们就连参考的价值也没有了。

(Cont.)

买账　　　　　　　măizhàng　　　　　　　show respect for; defer to

8. TIANANMEN, 1989

June Fourth—the True Story
Zhang Liang

Although the Beijing Olympics went some way to re-brand its image, Tiananmen Square has been synonymous throughout the last two decades with brutal state oppression. Yet the very fact of this oppression remains contested, and the names given to the events of June 1989 reveal much about the standpoints of their speakers: the Tiananmen Incident, the Tiananmen Massacre, a patriotic-democratic movement, a counter-revolutionary uprising. Day-to-day television coverage ensured that millions across the world remember the white Goddess of Democracy statue, the hunger-strikers, the tanks rolling into the square, and the iconic lone protestor who attempted to halt their progress on Chang'an Avenue. The vivid images gave many a sense of being present, or at least being passively involved. The events marked a critical moment in China's recent history, prompting the reassertion of authoritarian political rule, changing the shape of economic transition, and transforming relations with the outside world. Much has been written about the events and their aftermath, but much has also been forgotten, and a younger generation of Chinese has entered the workforce and even the public arena with little sense of the political constraints which demonstrators were fighting against, or of the sacrifices that they made in doing so.

The events of 1989 centered, at one level, on the question of democracy. Linked to Deng Xiaoping's ongoing program of "Reform and Opening Up" (改革开放 *gaige kaifang*) and to the gradual processes of liberalization and Westernization, the student demands for political representation, for a freer press, and for the right to form unions initially received a sympathetic hearing from the government. Indeed, the aims of the state coincided to a large extent with student calls for the eradication of corruption and for stricter checks on inflation. "Democracy" as a term had undergone much rethinking in the Chinese context during the 1980s, as the twin tenets of centralism and "democratic dictatorship of the people" lost force in the post-Mao era. Now centralized power was seen as an obstacle to growth and reform, and class enemies were beginning to merge into the people as a whole.[1] As collectivist culture and centralized decision-making loosened up under economic reforms, many wanted to speed up the growth of non–state sector industries and to expand expressions of social life outside the purview of the government. This protest call for greater "democracy" was linked to China's standing and status in the wider world, as information flows quickened and the first generation of students to

---

1. See Yijiang Ding, *Chinese Democracy after Tiananmen*, 4-9.

return from studying abroad brought first-hand knowledge of conditions outside China to bear on grassroots internal politics.

This international aspect became still more important as the protests gathered pace. The presence of Western media and the reams of resultant newsprint made the protests a world event, commentated on and interpreted globally in foreign terms. And through this prism, it appeared that students were calling for democracy and freedom—values lauded in the West—rather than attacking local problems of corruption and inflation. The initial spur for international attention was the presence of the Russian president, Mikhail Gorbachev, on a state visit to China from May 15 through 18 with his wife, Raisa. It was this summit that the international media were dispatched to cover, a visit which both fed into the students' agenda and eventually forced policy intervention when the government found itself humiliated by scenes of public festivities and disorder. A reformist Soviet leader was witnessing student defiance in Communist China, and a momentous new epoch in world history seemed to be unfurling. Subsequent events confirmed for many the stark choices facing Communist authorities, as the failed uprising spurred on Eastern European attempts to throw off Soviet rule, and peaceful transitions to independent rule occurred throughout the Communist bloc.

The build-up to the events of June Fourth is well known. Several commentators have provided daily chronologies of the Tiananmen events, often taking April 15 as their starting point and concluding with June 24.[2] The sudden death and funeral of the reformist Hu Yaobang was the initial trigger, prompting an outpouring of grief and protest that was at first deemed "legitimate" but soon took on a will of its own. By April 16 students were smashing bottles out of dormitory windows on the Peking University campus, to protest against Deng "Little Bottle" Xiaoping's earlier treatment of Hu. The following day a rally of up to four thousand people gathered to lay wreaths and demonstrate, and by April 22, the date of Hu's funeral, numbers outside the Great Hall of the People had swelled still further. Meanwhile, government rhetoric was hardening. Protests were labeled "chaotic" (动乱 *dongluan*) in a *People's Daily* editorial in late April, signaling a shift toward the ultimate charge of counter-revolutionary action.[3] A huge demonstration to mark the seventieth anniversary of the May Fourth protests accelerated the pace of protest, and by mid-May groups of students were marching in convoy, many singing the "Internationale," to Tiananmen Square and setting up semi-permanent

---

2. See Andrew J. Nathan and Perry Link, eds., *The Tiananmen Papers*; Theodore Han and John Li, *Tiananmen Square, Spring 1989: A Chronology of the Chinese Democracy Movement*; and Harrison E. Salisbury, *Tiananmen Diary: Thirteen Days in June*.

3. Andrew Nathan notes that this raised the stakes for students, who were now forced to remain in the Square until they had proved that the demonstrations were patriotic and democratic. See Andrew J. Nathan and Perry Link, eds., *The Tiananmen Papers*, xlii.

camps, where they waved pro-democracy banners and gave press interviews. As hunger strikes began, intellectuals presented to the government public declarations in support of the students and their aims, and the government entered into dialogue with their interlocutors, promising reforms.

On May 18, Zhao Ziyang and Li Peng visited hospitalized students in a conciliatory move, but the humiliation of derailments to the Sino-Soviet summit—Gorbachev was forced to use the back entrance of the Great Hall of the People—precipitated events. Martial law was declared on May 20, and while power struggles continued within the leaders' compound at Zhongnanhai amid talk of a high-level party split, the army began to mass. Troops were finally sent in to reclaim the square in the early hours of the morning on June 4, and their action was swift and bloody. Corridors were cleared to allow students to exit the square, but, according to eye-witnesses, troops began firing on those leaving. More died from gunshot wounds on streets off the square, and in stand-offs with the army at flashpoints across the city such as Muxidi. Government figures put the number of deaths around three hundred; other sources claim figures closer to seven thousand. The Red Cross put out a statement, later disputed, claiming 2,600 deaths and sixty thousand wounded that night.[4] The military intervention was critical: the threat of a *coup d'état* was real, and some feared that infighting within the military leadership—in particular stand-offs between the 27th and 38th Armies—would decisively affect the outcome of the events.

That the protestors were students was central to the sense of outrage at their violent suppression: these were young, defenseless, and, to a degree, naïve, activists. Moreover, their status as students tied the demonstrators to longer Chinese traditions, right back to the May Fourth patriots who had sought to modernize China and improve its standing *vis-à-vis* the West through building up its economic and military strength and by language and literary reforms. Echoes of the Cultural Revolution sounded, too. The student democracy movement began with the establishment of student unions in Beijing and elsewhere (later banned by the CCP), with "big character posters" pasted to campus notice-boards, boycotts of classes, and later the hunger strikes in the Square itself. But for a generation of students after June Fourth, Tiananmen became unmentionable. It took courage even to name June Fourth (六四 *Liusi*), let alone commemorate the date. On university campuses, security was exceptionally tight throughout the early 1990s in successive Junes, with identity checks enforced and outsiders barred. Grief cut deeply for those who had lost siblings, relatives, or friends, and who could not mourn openly. Almost overnight, the event created a new generation of dissidents and political untouchables. Student leaders such as Wang Dan or Chai Ling, who were given political asylum

---

4. Scott Simmie and Bob Nixon, *Tiananmen Square*, 194.

in the United States, were joined by a cohort of urban residents placed under house arrest for their part in demonstrations across China's cities, and by a wider body of those removed from their posts, or transferred to menial jobs, or whose promotions were consistently blocked.

Two full-length transcripts of conversations and meetings from the center of decision-making have appeared in the decades since 1989, the first in 2001 and the second in 2009. Both appeared initially in English, with publication of the "original" Chinese following soon after, distributed from Hong Kong and abroad. The second, *Gaige licheng* (改革历程 The Road to Reform, edited by Bao Pu; published English title *Prisoner of the State: The Secret Diary of Zhao Ziyang*) seems more secure in its provenance, if it is proven to be based on audio transcripts made by Zhao Ziyang and spirited out of China. According to the diary, Zhao, who was general secretary of the Communist Party in 1989 and a prominent reformist, set down his memories of the events three years later as he remained under house arrest. The volume tells of events from Zhao's perspective, sympathetic to the students and to their demands, and displays his continued questioning of the Party's narrative.

The text chosen for this chapter is similarly controversial, and employs a less reflective, personal stance than Zhao's *June Fourth—The True Story* (中国六四真相 Zhongguo liusi zhenxiang) appeared under the pseudonym Zhang Liang. The papers present a selection of accounts of open and secret meetings from the political center, including the informal committee of Eight Elders who oversaw decisions from within the Party stronghold at Zhongnanhai during the crisis. The historian Andrew Nathan, who was selected to be the recipient of the documents and went on to edit them, describes the papers as an "intimate account of top-level politics," which "possess an internal coherence, richness and human believability that would be almost impossible to fake."[5] Transcripts of debates among Chinese leaders give—if accurate—a poignant angle to events, showing, for example, that the Standing Committee of the Politburo would have voted 3-2 to continue dialogue, had it not been overruled by the extra-constitutional Elders, a group of influential former leaders. According to Nathan, the documents challenge the CCP's own line that Tiananmen was a legitimate suppression of anti-government activity.[6] Nathan's essay suggests that Jiang Zemin and Li Peng had the most to lose from publication of the documents, and it is noteworthy that those he cites as standing to gain, such as Zhu Rongji and Wen Jiabao, have enjoyed more powerful roles since. "Zhang Liang," meanwhile, notes in his preface some of the crucial lessons to be learned from the episode: that democracy in China will depend on people within China; that a reversal of the state verdict on June Fourth is inevitable; and that pro-democracy factions

5. Andrew Nathan, "Introduction," *The Tiananmen Papers*, xxiii.
6. Ibid., xx.

within the Party itself are the key to political change.[7] The first extract below is the preface by "Zhang Liang," who compiled the extracts; the second and third are entries from the chronicle.

Excerpted from Zhang Liang (pseud.), *Zhongguo liusi zhenxiang* (Hong Kong: Mingjing, 2001).

Further Reading

Bao Pu, Zhao Ziyang, Adi Ignatius, Renee Chang, and Roderick Macfarquhar. *Prisoner of the State: The Secret Journal of Premier Zhao Ziyang.* London: Simon and Schuster, 2009.
Béja, Jean-Philippe, "The Massacre's Long Shadow." *Journal of Democracy* 20/3 (2009), 5-16.
Cheng, Chu-yuan. *Behind the Tiananmen Massacre: Social and Economic Ferment in China.* Boulder: Westview Press, 1990.
Ding, Yijiang. *Chinese Democracy after Tiananmen.* Vancouver: University of British Columbia Press, 2001.
Han Minzhu, ed. *Cries for Democracy: Writings and Speeches from the 1989 Chinese Democracy Movement.* Princeton: Princeton University Press, 1990.
Han, Theodore and John Li. *Tiananmen Square, Spring 1989: A Chronology of the Chinese Democracy Movement.* Berkeley: Institute of East Asian Studies, University of California, 1992.
Lee, Feigon. *China Rising: The Meaning of Tiananmen.* Chicago: Ivan R. Dee, 1990.
Nathan, Andrew J., and Perry Link, eds. *The Tiananmen Papers.* London: Little, Brown, 2001.
Oksenberg, Michel, Lawrence R. Sullivan, and Marc Lambert, eds. *Beijing Spring, 1989: Confrontation and Conflict: The Basic Documents.* (Armonk: M. E. Sharpe, 1990.
Richelson, Jeffrey T., and Michael L. Evans, eds. *Tiananmen Square, 1989, The Declassified History.* National Security Archive Electronic Briefing Book No. 16. *http://www.gwu.edu/~nsarchiv/NSAEBB/NSAEBB16/index.html*
Salisbury, Harrison E. *Tiananmen Diary: Thirteen Days in June.* London: Unwin, 1989.
Simmie, Scott, and Bob Nixon. *Tiananmen Square.* Vancouver: Douglas and McIntyre, 1989.
Wu Hung. "Tiananmen Square: A Political History of Monuments." *Representations* 35 (1991), 84-117.

---

7. Ibid., xiii.

中国六四真相

自序

「六四」感怀

「六四」过去已经十二年。十二年，历史长河中<u>一闪即逝</u>的浪花，但对于一个人的生命来说，它又是那么的悠长。作为「六四」事件的<u>身历者</u>，遥想当年，总有一种历史的沉重感、<u>沧桑</u>感，仿佛历史就凝固在那一刻，压得人喘不过气来。「长歌当哭，是必须在痛定之后的」，当我们提笔追忆「六四」的时候，仿佛又感受到几千名青年人的血，奔洒在长安街的周围。时间是难以洗涤掉血迹的。历史和人民终将<u>抒写</u>：「六四」是二十世纪世界民主运动史上最伟大的事件之一，是二十世纪中国最伟大的民主运动。

　　「六四」不仅仅是中国青年学生追求民主的运动，也不仅仅是发生在北京的爱国民主运动「六四」参与人数之众，波及范围之广，持续时间之长，影响之空前，堪称二十世纪世界民主运动之最。然而，「六四」却以其空前的悲壮和惨烈载入了史册。「六四」失败了，它以专制的胜利和民主的失败而告终。然而，「六四」的失败又是必然的。当我们<u>痛定思痛</u>，我们必须清醒地承认这一点。「六四」几乎遍及中国的每一个大中城市、全国所有的高等院校、将近一半的中等专科学校；一部份大中城市的工矿企业、机关事业单位；极少部份的农村地区。上千万人直接或间接地参与了运动。然而，就「六四」总体而言，它又是一场自主的、自发的、无序的运动，在很大程度上，它成了人民对政府宣泄不满与愤慨的「<u>出气筒</u>」。

一闪即逝	yìshǎn jí shì	pass in an instant
身历者	shēnlìzhě	those who have been through an Experience; witness
沧桑	cāngsāng	vicissitude; great change
痛定思痛	tòngdìng sītòng	recall; draw lessons from painful experiences
抒写	shūxiě	describe; express
出气筒	chūqìtǒng	(slang) punch-bag; pressure vent

中共高层<u>开明派</u>的软弱，<u>学运</u>组织内部的不一致，知识分子与工
人、农民的脱离，没有严密的组织和纲领是「六四」失败的根本原因。

「六四」的失败，从一个侧面证明了它决不是一场有组织、有<u>预谋</u>的反
革命动乱和暴乱。以北京为中心的「六四」民主运动尽管以悲剧而告终，
但它留下的遗产却是极其宝贵的。随之而来的东欧共产主义制度的崩溃以
及苏联的解体，无疑在一定程度上是总结并吸取了中国「六四」失败教训
的结果。

纪念「六四」，不由得无限感慨。「六四」过去已经十二年，中国国
内也已发生了很大的变化。面对历史与人民，每一位热爱中国的有识之
士，是否经过了深刻的反思与省悟呢？判断中国社会经济政治的发展趋
势，绝不能感情用事，更不能脱离中国的国情来主观<u>臆测</u>。一定要冷静、
理性、客观。这里，有这样几点启示：

一、中国民主政治春天的到来靠中国人民自己。在中国国内，尽管共
产党政权已经<u>腐败透顶</u>，道德<u>沦丧</u>，但由于中国经济实力的增强，人民生
活一定程度的改善，更由于中国共产党组织自上而下加强对整个社会的控
制，几乎渗透到中国社会的每一个<u>角落</u>，目前，没有第二种力量能与中国
共产党相<u>抗衡</u>。因此，尽管民怨<u>沸腾</u>，但老百姓无奈地说：共产党不能靠
了，就谁也不靠，只靠我们自己。我们认为，共产主义在中国的终结是历
史之必然。但<u>搞垮</u>共产党的只能是共产党人自己，决不可能有第二种力
量。

中(国)共(产党)	Zhōng-gòng	Chinese Communist Party
开明派	kāimíng pài	the reformers
学(生)运(动)	xuéyùn	student movement
预谋	yùmóu	premeditate; pre-arrange
臆测	yìcè	conjecture; speculate
腐败透顶	fǔbài tòudǐng	thoroughly corrupt; rotten to core
沦丧	lúnsàng	lost; ruined
角落	jiǎoluò	corner; nook
抗衡	kànghéng	*v* rival; contend with
沸腾	fèiténg	boil; seethe over
搞垮	gǎokuǎ	undermine; cause to collapse

二、平反「六四」，是历史之必然、人民之心声。「六四」情结几乎
压得每一位中国有识之士喘不过气来，几乎所有的中国人都认为平反「六
四」是大势所趋，只是个时机问题。从「六四」发生的那天起，中共高层
领导人中就有不同意见，随着时间的流逝，特别是邓小平等中共元老与绝
大多数当事者的死去，从中共党内到中共党外，要求平反的呼声不断高
涨，并且最终将形成时代的洪流。中国共产党高层中的开明力量终将顺应
时势，把握这一历史性机会，平反「六四」，进而最终抛弃共产主义制
度。

三、中共党内开明派将是推动中国民主政治的关键力量。中国共产党
已经不是传统意义上的共产党，而是一个派系庞杂、目标各异、意识形态
混乱的大杂烩。中共内部的激进派与保守派的对立甚至比共产党与国民党
的对立还尖锐。这一点，中共与苏共很相似。因而，今天形式上的铁板一
块很有可能在一夜之间龟裂。取代共产党的将是共产党内部的新生力量，
他们对共产主义制度的痛切将甚于任何党派，他们要求建立民主政体的愿
望格外强烈，他们必将团结海内外一切民主力量，在联合的基础上，构建
中国的民主政治体制。

四、中国的民主政治建设必须靠植根于国内的民主力量才能发展。在
海外为中国的民主、自由、法治而呼吁，争取国际社会的理解和支持，很
有必要。但是，解决中国的根本问题还得立足国内。因此，立志为中国的
民主与自由献身的人们，一定要具备赵紫阳「我不入地狱，谁入地狱」

平反	píngfǎn	reverse a verdict on
有识之士	yǒushí zhī shì	person of vision or insight
元老	yuánlǎo	senior statesman; founders
杂烩	záhuì	mixed dish; medley
激进派	jījìn pài	radicals; pro-democracy faction
保守派	bǎoshǒu pài	conservatives
苏(联)共(产党)	Sū-Gòng	Communist Party of the USSR
龟裂	jūnliè	be full of cracks; break up into clods
赵紫阳	Zhào Zǐyáng	CCP gen. secretary (1919-2005) stripped of posts after June 4

的<u>无所畏惧</u>的气派。社会的进步与发展总是要以一批人的献身为代价。在中国走向民主自由的进程中，肯定会有人作出牺牲。留学海外，真正立志于为祖国献身的人们，应该<u>挺起胸膛</u>，回到祖国，与共产党中的开明人士相结合，深入城镇和广大农村，走与工农大众紧密结合的道路。在中国的广大农村，尚有四分之一老百姓的意识仍停留在二十世纪三十年代的水平。亟需大批有识之士的启蒙，中国民主政治真可谓任重而道远。

十二年过去了，「六四」并没有因为时间的推移而被人们所忘却。关于「六四」的众多疑问，至今仍<u>众说纷纭</u>，<u>莫衷一是</u>。无疑，准确、全面、客观地评价「六四」的最基础工作，就是公布「六四」真相，还历史以本来面目。作为「六四」的身历者、见证人，

我们有道义、有责任把忠实记录的关于「六四」决策的全过程公诸于世，以告慰于人民和历史。现在，这里，我们唯一能够对大家说的是：这部书的全部资料来源都是有根据的，全书以客观事实说话。为了忠实于历史，我们采用编年史实录形式，从一九八九年四月十五日<u>胡耀邦</u>去世到六月二十四日中共<u>十三届四中</u>全会闭幕，基本上每一日都按：一，中央高层决策；二，全国各地动态；三，国外反应及媒体报导进行展示，尽可能避免加上我们的主观评论，唯恐自己的观点影响读者自己的评判。本书公布的是「六四」的全部真相，尤其是中共高层关于「六四」决策的全过程，有的甚至连当今中共最高层成员都不了解。我们只期望：此书经得起历史检验。它的出版，能从根本上推进中国民主政治建设的进程。

无所畏惧	wúsuǒ wèi jù	fearless; intrepid
挺起胸膛	tǐng qi xiōngtáng	straighten up one's head and chest
众说纷纭	zhòngshuō fēnyún	opinions differ
莫衷一是	mòzhōngyíshì	unable to agree; no unanimity
胡耀邦	Hú Yàobāng	chief reformer under Deng Xiaoping, whose death in April 1989 was the immediate cause of the demonstrations at Tiananmen (1915-1989)
十三届四中	shísānjièsìzhōng	the Fourth Plenum of the Thirteenth Central Committee, which took place in June 1989

鲁迅先生说过，「真的猛士，敢于直面惨淡的人生，敢于正视淋漓的鲜血」。纪念「六四」的今天，我们只能作出这样的历史选择。是为序。

张良

二〇〇一年一月八日

(2) 政治局常委紧急会议

学生绝食后社会各界的强烈呼吁以及中共高层尤其是中共元老的强大压力下，十六日晚，也就是在杨尚昆、邓小平、李鹏、赵紫阳先后分别与戈尔巴乔夫会谈，完成中苏高级会晤最主要的议程后，赵紫阳、李鹏、乔石、胡启立、姚依林和中共元老杨尚昆、薄一波召开了中央政治局常委紧急会议。会议的气氛一开始就显得紧张。现根据会议纪录予以综述。

惨淡	cǎndàn	bleak; desolate
杨尚昆	Yáng Shàngkūn	president of PRC (1907-1998)
李鹏	Lǐ Péng	premier; member of Politburo Standing Committee (1928-)
戈尔巴乔夫	Gēěrbāqiáofū	Mikhail Gorbachev
乔石	Qiáo Shí	member of Politburo Standing Committee; in charge of security and Party discipline (1924-)
胡启立	Hú Qǐlì	member of Politburo Standing Committee; subsequently demoted (1929-)
姚依林	Yáo Yīlín	vice premier, and representative of conservative old guard (1917-1994)
薄一波	Bó Yībō	one of Eight Elders; former vice premier (1908-2007)
中央政治局常委	Zhōngyāng zhèngzhìjú chángwěi	Standing Committee of the Politburo of the CCP

赵紫阳：「现在，天安门广场学生的<u>绝食</u>请愿活动已经第四天了。学生们的健康已经受到极大的损害，有的学生的生命已处于危险之中。我们已经采取了一切可能采取的措施，对绝食学生进行治疗和抢救，保证学生的生命安全，另一方面，多次与绝食学生代表的对话进行对话，并郑重表示今后将继续听取他们的意见，希望立即停上绝食，但都未能取得预期效果。在天安门广场人群拥挤，口号标语不断和人群极度激动的情况下，绝食学生代表也表示，他们已不能控制局势。薄一波插话：「实际上这是少数人拿绝食学生当<u>人质</u>，要挟、强迫党和政府答应他们的政治条件，连一点起码的人道主义<u>都不讲了</u>。」

赵紫阳继续：「现在，如果我们再不迅速结束这种状况，听任其发展下去，很难预料不出现大家都意想不到的情况。」否定反对资产阶级自由化的口号，目的就是要取得<u>肆无忌惮</u>地反对<u>四项基本原则</u>的绝对自由。他们散布了大量谣言，攻击、<u>污蔑</u>、<u>谩骂</u>党和国家领导人，尤其是攻击为我们改革开放作出了巨大贡献的邓小平同志，其目的就是要从组织<u>颠覆</u>中国共产党的领导，推翻经过人民代表大会依法选举产生的人民政府，彻底否定<u>人民民主专政</u>。他们四出煽风点火，秘密串连，成立各种非法组织，强迫党和政府承认，就是要为他们在中国建立反对派，反对党打下基础。

杨尚昆：从这两天北京实际上处于一个无政府状态。所有的学校罢课，一些机关工作人员也上街了，还有交通等等基本上都混乱了，这种混

绝食	juéshí	hunger strike
人质	rénzhì	hostage
都不讲了	dōu bù jiǎng le	with no regard for; let alone…
肆无忌惮	sìwújìdàn	recklessly; wantonly
四项基本原则	Sìxiàng Jīběn Yuánzé	Four Cardinal Principles (i.e socialist road, people's democratic dictatorship, leadership of the CCP, Marxism-Leninism and Mao Zedong thought
污蔑	wūmiè	vilify; slander
谩骂	mànmà	hurl abuse at; vilify
颠覆	diānfù	subvert; overturn
人民民主专政	rénmín mínzhǔ zhuànzhèng	people's democratic dictatorship

乱实际上是个无政府状态。象中苏会谈这样历史性的事情，使得我们没有办法在天安门举行欢迎仪式，而临时改在飞机场，其中今天两次应该在人民大会堂会谈的，被迫改到<u>钓鱼台</u>，还取消了一些预订的节目，这样一种状态原来是规定了要向<u>烈士纪念碑</u>献花圈也没有办法进行。这个在我们对外关系」来讲是非常之坏的影响。这种状况如果继续下去，我们这个首都呵，不能称其为首都，所以形势是非常严重的。

(3) 十七日上午，中共中央政治局常委会议在邓小平家召开，邓小平、杨尚昆、薄一波和赵紫阳、李鹏、乔石、胡启立、姚依林参加。现根据会议纪录予以综述。

会议一开始，赵紫阳先简单地介绍了学潮的情况，赵紫阳说，「现在绝食的学生被推到台前去了，想下来也下不来，事情很<u>棘手</u>。当前最重要的是要说服学生把绝食和他们的要求分开来，让绝食的学生先从广场上撤下来，回到学校去。否则，广场上<u>瞬息万变</u>，什么意想不到的事情都可能发生。局势很紧张。」

杨尚昆：「学潮发展到今天，已经一个多月了。这一个多月来，首都是不是发生了动乱？是。现在已经闹得连国事都不能正常进行，连欢迎戈尔巴乔夫的仪式和接待活动都不能正常进行，闹得连走路、上下班都成了问题，首都还有什么秩序？还能说没有损害国家利益、社会利益？还不是动乱？我们谁要承认这种行动不是动乱，那还怎么进行改革、开放，进行社会主义现代化建设！但是，我们必须把煽动、制造动乱的极少数人，和动机纯洁的学生及其他善良的人们严格区分开。」

钓鱼台	Diàoyútái	State Guest House (lit. Fishing Terrace, formerly used by emperors)
烈士纪念碑	lièshì jìniànbēi	Monument to the Revolutionary Martyrs
棘手	jíshǒu	troublesome; problematic
瞬息万变	shùnxī wànbiàn	undergo great changes very rapidly

　　李鹏：「我认为，学潮的<u>升级</u>，事态发展到现在这样难以控制的局面，紫阳同志应该负最主要的责任。本来，在他出访朝鲜期间，政治局常委徵求他的意见时，他就打回电报明确表示『完全同意小平同志就对付当前动乱问题作出的决策。四月三十日回国之后，他在政治局常委会议上还再次表示，同意小平同志的讲话和四月二十六日<u>社论</u>对动乱的定性，认为前段对学潮的处理是好的。但是，没过几天，他却在五月四日下午接见<u>亚银</u>年会代表时，发表了一通同政治局常委决定、小平同志讲话和社论精神完全对立的意见，这篇讲话未徵求过常委们的任何意见。第一，在已经出现明显动乱的情况下，他却说、中国不会出现大的动乱。；第二，在大量事实已经证明动乱的实质是否定共产党领导、否定社会主义制度的情况下，他还坚持说。他们绝不是要反对我们的根本制度，而是要求我们把工作中的<u>弊病</u>改掉。；第三，在已经有种种事实说明极少数人利用学潮策动动乱的情况下，他还只是说、难免有人企图利用。从根本上否定了中央关于极少数人已经在制造动乱的正确判断。赵紫阳同志的这番讲话，是<u>鲍彤</u>事先为他起草好的。鲍彤还要求中央人民广播电台和中央电视台当天下午就立即播出。赵紫阳同志的这番讲话，经过人民日报等报纸的报导，在广大干部、群众中造成了严重的思想混乱，给动乱的组织者和策划者撑了腰、壮了胆、打了气。<u>李锡铭</u>、<u>陈希同</u>同志就反映，在紫阳同志的讲话以后，北京市承受了相当大的压力，有的说、中央出了两个声音，谁对谁错，以谁为主。有的说。要我们同中央保持一致，同哪个中央保持一致？有的高校做学生思想工作的干部感到被出卖了伤心得流下了眼泪。

升级	shēngjí	escalation
社论	shèlùn	editorial
亚(洲开发)银(行)	Yàzhōu Kāifā Yínháng	Asian Development Bank
弊病	bìbìng	malpractice
鲍彤	Bào Tóng	Zhao Ziyang's secretary, expelled from the Party and imprisoned after June 4 (1932-)
李锡铭	Lǐ Xímíng	Beijing Party secretary (1926-)
陈希同	Chén Xītóng	mayor of Beijing (1930-)

所以，出现了高校政治思想工作几乎完全<u>瘫痪</u>的局面，致使现在的局势越来越严重。」

姚依林：「紫阳同志接见亚行理事会的讲话，不讲金融问题，只讲国内学潮，要是不看标题，谁都不相信这是一篇对外国人的讲话。我认为紫阳同志的这篇讲话是有明确意图的。这篇讲话讲学生的行动是爱国的，这可以理解。然后就提出我们确实有很多腐败现象，是和学生想到一块了，我们将通过民主、法制解决这些问题。这篇讲话根本没有说<u>四二六</u>社论是否正确，绕开这个问题。这是一篇相当重要的讲话，这篇讲话等于把小平同志的意见、中央政治局常委内部的不同看法统统暴露在学生和别有用心者面前，致使学潮越闹越大，几乎达到失控的局面。还有一条，我不明白的是，为什么紫阳同志昨天在与戈尔巴乔夫会谈的时候，要把小平同志推出来，在现在这样的局势下，讲这番话，无异是要把这次事件的全部责任推到小平同志头上，把学潮的矛头对准小平同志，这等于是给已经混乱的局势火上加油。」

赵紫阳：二位先允许我对这两件事作出说明。关于我五月四日会见亚洲银行理事年会代表的讲话，一开始是想促进学潮的平息，同时也想使外资增强对中国稳定的信心，讲话发表后，开始听到的是一坏一好的反映。我当时并没有意识到有什么问题。尚昆、乔石、启立等同志都认为反映不错，李鹏同志当时还对我说，话讲得很好，他在会见亚行年会代表时，也要呼应一下。这次讲话的调子比较温和。我的这次讲话，从当时各方固的反映看，效果还可以。李鹏同志说我的讲话未经常委讨论，这是事实。不过，中央各位领导同志接待外宾时的谈话（除正式会谈方案外），历年都不提交常委讨论，一般都是根据中央的方针自己去准备。关于昨天我同戈尔巴乔夫的谈话。十三大以来，我在接待国外党的主要领导人时，曾多次向他们通报，我党十三届一中全会有个决定，小平同志作为我党主要决策

| 瘫痪 | tānhuàn | paralysis |
| 四二六 | sìèrliù | April 26 |

者的地位没有改变。我的目的是让世界上更明确知道小平同志在我们党内的地位不因退出常委而发生变化，在组织上是合法的。这次访朝，我也向金日成主席谈了这个问题。我跟戈讲这个问题实际上是惯例了。问题在于这次作了公开报导。为什么昨天讲了这个事呢？我从朝鲜回来后，听说小平同志四月二十五日关于学潮问题的讲话传达后，在社会上引起很多议论，说常委向小平同志汇报不符合组织原则。还有一大堆难听的话。我觉得我有必要加以澄清和说明。

在戈尔巴乔夫来访的前两天，我与工人和工会干部座谈对话时，会上也有人提出这类问题。当时我根据十三届一中全会的决定，作了说明，效果良好。他们说，我们过去不了解，现在知道了就好了。在此之前，陈希同同志就针对人们有关垂帘听政的错误议论向大专院校负责人做过解释，说明了党的十三届一中全会有关决定的情况，效果也是好的。陈希同同志在四月二十八日的常委会上还汇报过这个情况。因此，我就考虑，如果通过公开报导，把这一情况让群众知道，对减少议论可能有所帮助。我当时向戈尔巴乔夫同志通报的内容是，十三届一中全会郑重作出一个决定，在最重要的问题上仍然需要向邓小平同志通报并向他他请教（我有意识的没有讲，可以召集会议和由他拍板的话）。邓小平同志也总是全力支持我们的工作，支持我们集体作出的决策。照理说，这些内容的话，是不会给人以一切事情都由小平同志决定的印象的。我实在没有想到，这样做，会伤害小平同志，我愿对此承担一切责任。」

赵紫阳说这话后，邓小平说了一句份量极重的话：紫阳同志，你五月四日在亚行的那篇讲话是一个转折，从那以后学生就闹得更凶了。」邓小平接着说：是没有错，我们是要发展社会主义民主，但匆匆忙忙地搞绝对

金日成	Jīn Rìchéng	Kim Il Sung (1912-1994)
澄清	chéngqīng	clarify
垂帘听政	chuílián tīngzhèng	hold court from behind a screen; attend to affairs
拍板	pāibǎn	have the final say
照理	zhàolǐ	normally; in the course of events

不行，搞西方那一套更不行。如果我们现在十亿人搞<u>多党竞选</u>，一定会出现文化大革命中那样全面内战的混乱局面。不一定都要用枪炮，用拳头、木棍也可以打得很凶。民主是我们追求的目标，但前提必须是国家保持稳定。这次事情不一样。事情一爆发出来，就很明确。一些同志到现在还不明白问题的性质，认为这只是单纯的对待学生的问题，实际上，对方不只是那些学生，更有一些别有用心的人。他们的根本口号就是两个，一是要打倒共产党，一是要推翻社会主义制度。他们的目的就是要建立一个完全依附于西方的资产阶级共和国。不懂得这个根本问题，就是性质不清楚。我知道你们中间有争论，但现在不是来判断争论的问题，今天不讨论这个问题，只讨论究竟应该退不退？」

....

邓小平：「大家都看到了，现在，北京乃至全国的形势都相当严峻。特别是北京，无政府状态越来越严重，法制和纪律遭到破坏，许多高校陷于瘫痪，公共交通到处堵塞，<u>党政</u>领导机关受到冲击，社会治安恶化，游行的人数越来越多，已经严重干扰和破坏了生产、工作、学习和生活的正常秩序。如果再不结束这种状况，任其发展下去，我们已经取得的一切成果，都将变为泡影，中国将出现一次历史性的倒退。退，就是承认他们那<u>些</u>；不退，就是坚定不移地贯彻我们四月二十六日的社论方针。<u>陈云</u>、<u>先念</u>、<u>彭真</u>等老同志，当然包括我，看着北京的局势都忧心如焚。北京已经不能维持了，必须首先解决北京的安定问题，不然全国其它省、区、市的问题解决不了。<u>卧轨</u>、<u>打砸抢</u>，不是动乱是什么？再这样下去，

多党竞选	duōdǎng jìngxuǎn	multi-party elections
党政	dǎng-zhèng	Party and government
陈云	Chén Yún	one of Eight Elders and a founder of the PRC (1905-1995)
(李)先念	Lǐ Xiānniàn	one of Eight Elders, former state president (1909-1992)
彭真	Péng Zhēn	one of Eight Elders, former Beijing mayor (1902-1997)
卧轨	wòguǐ	lie on the rails: to protest, or commit suicide
打砸抢	dǎ-zá-qiǎng	beating, smashing, and looting

我们都要被管制了。考虑来考虑去，要请解放军出来，要在北京戒严，具体一点就是在北京市区实施戒严。戒严的目的就是为了坚决制止动乱，迅速恢复秩序，这是党和政府义不容辞的责任。我今天郑重地向中央政治局常委会提出来，希望你们考虑。」

对于邓小平的建议，赵紫阳回答，「有决断总比没有决断好。不过，小平同志，这个方针我很难执行，我有困难。」

邓小平：「少数服从多数嘛。」

赵紫阳：「我服从党的组织纪律，少数服从多数。」

会议决定：一。晚上继续召开中共中央政治局常委会议，具体部署如何实施戒严，二，中央政治局常委于十八日早晨去医院看望绝食学生；三，李鹏于十八日与学生代表进行对话，要求绝食学生全部从天安门广场撤出来。四、十八日上午，政治局常委向邓小平等中共元老报告部署戒严情况。会后，邓小平亲自打电话给陈云、李先念、彭真，并由秘书通知邓颖超、王震和洪学智、刘华清、秦基伟，于第二天上午开会，通报实际由邓小平决定而以中央政治局常委名义作出的戒严部署。

戒严	jièyán	impose martial law
部署	bùshǔ	deploy
邓颖超	Dèng Yǐngchāo	one of Eight Elders, former Politburo member, widow of Zhou Enlai (1904-1992)
王震	Wáng Zhèn	one of Eight Elders, vice president of the PRC (1908-1993)
洪学智	Hóng Xuézhì	People's Liberation Army general (1913-2006)
刘华清	Liú Huáqīng	general, former commander of the navy (1916-)
秦基伟	Qín Jīwěi	Politburo member; minister of defense (1912-1997)

9. THE 1980s ENLIGHTENMENT

River Elegy
Su Xiaokang et al.

1988 was a Dragon Year, the temporal home of disaster in Chinese superstition. True to form, tensions ran high throughout the year, as bad portents proliferated and apprehension grew that the reform process was beginning to stall. Inflation, corruption, nepotism, and a volatile economy were spreading panic across China's cities, and a mood of crisis had begun to take hold. Indeed, although much had been achieved during the wonder decade of the 1980s—economic growth, relaxation in ideological control, the rehabilitation of education, religious freedom, cultural flowering—each step forward had been checked by the conservative rearguard, and by 1988 many reformers began to fear that their luck was running out.

River Elegy was a response to this eschatological mood. A documentary series in six parts which meditates on China's past and future, it was directed by Xia Jun 夏骏, and written by Su Xiaokang 苏晓康, Xie Xuanjun 谢选俊, Wang Luxiang 王鲁湘, Zhang Gang 张钢, and Yuan Zhiming 远志明. It received its first airing on the Chinese Central Television Station in June 1988—but provoked such an extraordinary response from the viewing public that it was promptly screened again in August. In essence, *River Elegy* sounds the death knell for Chinese civilization, and reactions to it were commensurately dramatic. For some, the series was a rallying cry for the faltering reforms, a last stand for the future; while for others, it was a recklessly immoral act, responsible in part for fomenting the national self-hatred which would turn to radicalism at Tiananmen Square the following year. Political opinion reflected this schism: Vice President Wang Zhen called the series "cultural nihilism," while General Secretary Zhao Ziyang lent energetic support behind the scenes. Everyone had an opinion—"liberalists, hard-liners, Neo-Confucianists, cultural elites, ordinary citizens, and global Chinese communities"[1]—and the series was the cultural event of the year.

Much of the appeal of *River Elegy* lies in the fact that it is far more than "just" a documentary. The series blends narrated history, theory, and philosophy, and splices the ideas of Western thinkers such as Marx, Hegel, Plekhanov, Arnold Toynbee, Adam Smith, and Francis Bacon together with studio interviews with Chinese scholars and writers such as Li Yining, Wang Juntao, Zheng Yi, and Zhang Wei. Each episode is a collage of

---

1. Jaiyan Mi, "The Visual Imagined Communities: Media State, Virtual Citizenship and Television in *Heshang* (*River Elegy*)," 331.

newsreel, studio interviews with experts, images of the modern West, archival footage of Chinese leaders either dead or disgraced, excerpts from films, travel brochures, and gazetteers, and previously unaired sequences depicting the Great Leap Forward, Red Guard veneration of Mao, and study sessions from the Cultural Revolution. Literary and cultural sources are densely interwoven, intensifying this sense of a multi-media, interdisciplinary text. Above all, *River Elegy*'s fusion of the verbal and the visual sets it apart: the written text of the voiceovers, a piece of imaginative prose in its own right, is twinned with endless visual vistas of China as a place—its rivers, plateaus, and mountains—and the result is a potent sense of epic. *River Elegy* is an attempt to articulate the past creatively: an exercise in hybridity which renders history at a high emotional pitch, and is happily cavalier in its approach to documented fact. Described as everything from an "ideological discourse"[2] to a "showpiece of . . . cultural criticism,"[3] the point of the series lies precisely in its refusal to be named by genre or discipline.

Part 1, "Searching for a Dream" (寻梦 Xunmeng), describes how the Yellow River has shaped China's destiny, both cradling its civilization and slowly suffocating it. Indeed, although it matured early, China has changed little since: it simply turns on its cruel, familiar axis, and instead of learning from history, its people cleave to despots whose autocracy obviates the need for individual action. A true reorientation toward the future can come only when China turns its back on the fateful river and looks out toward the sea. Part 2, "Destiny" (命运 Mingyun), focuses on China as a geographical entity, and tells how the loess plateau and a land-locked agrarian culture have hemmed in the Chinese spirit. This insularity finds its archetypal emblem in the Great Wall, a signifier of cowardice and conservatism rather than of any transdynastic might. Part 3, "The Light of the Spirit" (灵光 Lingguang), explores the depressing paradox of China's early inventiveness and its later slump into technological stagnation. Paper, printing, gunpowder, and the compass are the offspring of China's genius, but its people stood by and watched as Europeans stole their discoveries and made them the basis of a civilization. China, once again, has only itself to blame. Ethical precepts have always fettered the pursuit of knowledge, and a desire for orthodoxy has suppressed the intellectual inventiveness needed to push science forward.

Part 4, "The New Era" (新纪元 Xin jiyuan), examines why pre-modern China failed to foment industrial revolution or nurture a market economy. A society of small landholders, engaged in small scale production, has

2. Jing Wang, *High Culture Fever: Politics, Aesthetics, and Ideology in Deng's China*, 121.
3. Edward Gunn, "The Rhetoric of *River Elegy*: From Cultural Criticism to Social Act," 14.

consistently lacked the cohesiveness to transform its macroeconomics, while China's huge population has always encouraged a wasteful attitude toward labor. Now, at long last, China is on the cusp of a new era of dynamism. Part 5, "Sorrow and Worry" (忧患 Youhuan) argues that the Yellow River is the final emblem of China's sorrows: analogies exist between the nation's natural and man-made disasters—between flooding and peasant rebellion—and catastrophe in China adheres to a grim pattern. Indeed, if the Yellow River represents disaster, then the dikes which contain it are China's social structure, presided over by a bureaucracy whose inner corruption causes the whole edifice periodically to collapse. Underlying the entire cycle is totalitarianism, the "sedimented mud" which stymies change. Part 6, "Azure" (蔚蓝色 Weilanse) offers a fitting coda to these themes, and is the focus of this chapter.

As should be clear by now, symbol is the real language of *River Elegy*. The dragon, the Great Wall, the loess plateau, and the Yellow River all "become" China—land-locked, isolationist, vulnerable to the elements, and in thrall to charismatic power. The Middle Kingdom's symbolic other, meanwhile, is the ocean, epitomized by maritime culture and the bold democratic enterprise of the Western sea-faring nations. Together, these symbols communicate the baseline message that Chinese history is a repetitive continuum, punctuated by tyranny and disaster, and beholden to what lies beyond its shores for salvation. *River Elegy* uses its palette of yellow and blue to beseech China to break through history, live by the rule of law, and join the world—not just economically but emotionally too. These symbols, both resonant and accessible, allow the series to reach the public in ways which far transcend the typical documentary mode. As Chen Xiaomei puts it, "*Heshang* struck a chord in the national sensibility by glossing over the jump from the factual to the symbolic."[4]

In many ways, *River Elegy*'s critique of China seems unremitting: an exercise in self-hatred which borders on excess. Yet commentators have been quick to note the sometimes disingenuous nature of its anguish over China, past and present. Rather than self-hatred, *River Elegy* displays a passionate cultural narcissism which fetishizes the Yellow River, the Great Wall, the dragon—through lingering pans and highly-charged language—even as it professes to despair of them. What the makers of the series lament is not so much China, as China's lost greatness, and their critique is really a paean to nationalism: if China can change, then China can be glorious again. By the same token, what some CCP cultural commissars derided as an infatuation with the West is at base a much more cynical need to "know thine enemy." Imitation is less flattery than a desire to beat the West at its own game.

---

4. Chen Xiaomei, "Occidentalism as Counter-Discourse: 'He Shang' in Post-Mao China," 701.

Just as relevant a subtext is the question of who should usher China into its new age of enlightenment. Here, the series is keen to maintain a niche for China's special people: the intellectuals. Indeed, although the authors can be swingeing in their criticism of this group, dubbing them spineless "appendages" (附庸 *fuyong)* in Part 6, they retain a conviction that China's intellectuals hold the key to the future. Only they can undertake direct dialogue with the West, learning and implementing its secrets. More to the point, the series itself, and of course its makers, are intimately implicated in this project. Like so many literati before them—from Qu Yuan (who is referenced in the pages which follow) to the May Fourth iconoclasts and beyond—Su Xiaokang et al. are engaged in the ancient intellectual practice of *youmin youguo* 忧民忧国: worrying about the welfare of the nation and its people. And to a degree, of course, this anxiety is tinged with self-interest. Despite the prominent role assigned to intellectuals within Dengist China, their position remained precarious, and it is surely this sense of insecurity which underlies *River Elegy*'s focus on the nation's "special people." Yet in the end, their suggested kinship with Qu Yuan proved all too prescient. In the aftermath of Tiananmen, Su Xiaokang, Yuan Zhiming, and Zhang Gang went into exile, Wang Luxiang was imprisoned, and Xie Xuanjun was prohibited from distributing his work.

The passage which follows is taken from the script of the final episode, "Weilanse," and it marks a bravura climax to the themes of land versus sea, democracy versus despotism, and China versus the world which *River Elegy* explores as a whole. It traverses the broad historical sweep, from the Qin emperor to Columbus and Magellan to the Sino-Japanese War. It is, moreover, deliberately cosmopolitan in its cultural references, with Qu Yuan, Liang Qichao, and the vibrant folklore of the loess plateau taking their place alongside Galileo, Adam Smith, and John Locke. The stated theme is China's stasis, its ossified society, and cramped horizons. Yet, as ever, the self-flagellation hides a greater pride, and the passage is redolent with hints of China's timeless glory.

Su Xiaokang, Wang Luxiang, et al. *Heshang*. Beijing: Xiandai chubanshe, 1988, 95-105.

Further Reading

Chen Fong-ching and Jin Guantao. *From Youthful Manuscripts to River Elegy: The Chinese Popular Cultural Movement and Political Transformation, 1979-1989*. Hong Kong: Chinese University of Hong Kong Press, 1997.

Chen Xiaomei. "Occidentalism as Counterdiscourse: 'He Shang' in Post-

Mao China." *Critical Inquiry* 18/4 (1992), 686-712.

Chen Zuyan. "'River Elegy' as Reportage Literature: Generic Experimentation and Boundaries." *China Information* 7/4 (1993), 20-32.

Chong, W. L. "Present Worries of Chinese Democrats: Notes on Fang Lizhi, Liu Binyan and the Film 'River Elegy'." *China Information* 1/3 (1989), 1-20.

———. "Su Xiaokang on His Film 'River Elegy.'" *China Information*, 4/1(1989), 44-55.

De Jong, Alice. "The Demise of the Dragon: Backgrounds to the Chinese Film 'River Elegy.'" *China Information* 4/3 (1988-89), 28-43.

Field, Stephen. "*He Shang* and the Plateau of Ultrastability." *Bulletin of Concerned Asian Scholars* 23/3 (1991), 4-13.

Gunn, Edward. "The Rhetoric of *River Elegy*: From Cultural Criticism to Social Act." *Bulletin of Concerned Asian Scholars* 23/3 (1991), 14-22.

Lin, Min, and Maria Galikowski. "From 'River Elegy' to *China Can Say No*: China's Neo-Nationalism and the Search for Collective National Identity." In Min Lin and Maria Galikowski, eds. *The Search for Modernity: Chinese Intellectuals and Cultural Discourse in the Post-Mao Era*. New York: St. Martin's Press, 1999, 89-102.

Liu, Toming Jun. "Uses and Abuses of Sentimental Nationalism: Mnemonic Disquiet in *Heshang* and *Shuobu*." *Modern Chinese Literature and Culture* 13/1 (2001), 169-209.

Ma, Shu-Yun. "The Role of Power Struggle and Economic Changes in the '*Heshang* Phenomenon' in China." *Modern Asian Studies* 30/1 (1996), 29-50.

Mi, Jaiyan. "The Visual Imagined Communities: Media State, Virtual Citizenship and Television in *Heshang* (*River Elegy*)." *Quarterly Journal of Film and Video* 22/4 (2005), 327-340.

Su Xiaokang et al. *Deathsong of the River: A Reader's Guide to the Chinese TV Series Heshang*. Ithaca: East Asian Program, Cornell University, 1991.

Wang, Jing. "*He Shang* and the Paradoxes of Chinese Enlightenment." *Bulletin of Concerned Asian Scholars* 23/3 (1991), 27-32. Reprinted in *High Culture Fever: Politics, Aesthetics, and Ideology in Deng's China*. Berkeley: University of California Press, 1997, 118-36.

Zhao, Suisheng. "Chinese Intellectuals' Quest for National Greatness and Nationalistic Writing in the 1990s." *China Quarterly* 152 (1997), 725-45.

河殇：第六集 蔚蓝色

人的血液是红色的。

几乎所有动物的血液都是红色的。

原始宗教把生命的原色规定为红。原始人在死者的遗体上用<u>铁矿石</u>涂上红色，以此<u>召唤</u>那失去的生命力。

蔚蓝色的天空，深邃而神秘。人类曾经坚信，这神秘的蔚蓝色描绘着整个宇宙，它是宇宙的颜色。

仅仅在二十多年前，当人类第一次离开地球，在太空中遥望自己的家乡时，他们才惊讶地发现，在目前已知的<u>宇宙</u>星体中，唯有我们人类的家园—— 地球，才是一颗蔚蓝色的星球。

（推出<u>片名</u>： 第六集 蔚蓝色）

生命的星球是蔚蓝色的星球。地球上的一切生命得以生存的大气和水，使地球成为蔚蓝色的星体。

覆盖地球表面十分之七的大海，也是蔚蓝色的。

大海本来就是生命的故乡。在地球的突变中，大海曾经<u>庇护</u>了人类祖先的生命。后来，当人类重新回到陆地时，他反而不适应了。在强迫自己适应大陆环境的过程中，人类创造了文明。

<u>复活节岛</u>上的这些<u>谜</u>一样的石像，告诉我们一万年以前，在太平洋上就活跃着一个古老而有活力的航海文明。这些今天看起来残破不堪的航海工具，把人类从陆地上又重新载回海中。是什么信念支持着这些原始人

铁矿石	tiěkuàngshí	iron ore; red ochre; here: a deep red iron oxide commonly used by ancient peoples as decorative body paint and for writing pictographs
召唤	zhàohuàn	summon
宇宙	yǔzhòu	the universe; the cosmos
片名	piānmíng	title of a movie (here: episode)
庇护	bìhù	shield; shelter
复活节岛	Fùhuójiédǎo	Easter Island
谜	mí	enigma; mystery

去横渡至今使人视为畏途的大海呢？这些原始人的航海活动，同<u>哥伦布</u>和<u>麦哲伦</u>那创立人类新纪元的伟大航行之间，我们能不能听见人类命运的宏伟<u>旋律</u>呢？

正是由于这种持续不衰的航海生活的存在，人类的文明才分成了内陆文明与航海文明两大单元。

这是一个濒临西太平洋的国家，同时，它又<u>雄踞</u>在欧亚大陆的东部。它的躯体是黄色的，它那像脊柱一样拱起的大河，也是黄色的。

我们看到这条<u>河姆渡遗址</u>出土的木船，就仿佛看到了遥远的中华文明的源头荡漾着蔚蓝色的波光。

但是，早在神话时，来自黄河<u>中游</u>黄土区的内陆文明，已经在不断征服下游和沿海地区了。今天，我们还能从<u>黄帝</u>大战<u>炎帝</u>和<u>蚩尤</u>的故事里，听到这历史深处的朦胧声音。

后来，周朝对殷商的征服，证明这股来自内陆<u>腹地</u>的力量，是不可抗拒的。到了战国晚期发生的楚败于秦的<u>史诗</u>般的战争，可以说是以小麦作食粮、用战车作战、并且是受到了<u>游牧</u>民族和<u>波斯</u>文化影响的黄色文明，最终战胜了以大米作食粮、懂得利用大船和水上作战、并且是受到东南亚和太平洋文化影响的蔚蓝色文明。

哥伦布	Gēlúnbù	Christopher Columbus (1451-1506)
麦哲伦	Màizhélún	Ferdinand Magellan (1480-1521)
旋律	xuánlǜ	melody
雄踞	xióngjù	grandly situated
河姆渡	Hémǔdù	a Neolithic culture (c. 5000 BCE) which flourished in modern-day Zhejiang Province
遗址	yízhǐ	ruins; relics
中游	zhōngyóu	middle reaches of a river
黄帝，炎帝，蚩尤	Huáng Dì, Yán Dì, Chī Yóu	three mythical chieftains of prehistoric China
腹地	fùdì	hinterland
史诗	shǐshī	epic
游牧	yóumù	nomadic
波斯	Bōsī	Persia

这个内陆文明的历史性胜利，是无论<u>屈原</u>那种抢天哭地的悲歌，还是<u>西楚霸王</u>那种地动山摇的反抗，都无法遏制的。

蔚蓝色的隐退，埋伏下一个民族和一种文明日后衰败的命运。太平洋那千古不息的蓝色<u>波涛</u>，一直在默默地召唤这个躺在大陆上的古老民族，偶而也引起过它的激动，把它的航船一直牵到波斯湾和阿拉伯半岛。然而，蔚蓝色海洋的吸引力，比起那黄色的土地来，毕竟要微弱多。

使那黄色文明具有巨大凝聚力的奥秘，就在于儒家文化在这片土地上逐渐取得了<u>独尊的地位</u>。

儒家的一整套思想，表达了内陆文明的生活规范和理想，它在东方封建社会的盛期，显然是比较合理的。但是，单一的思想统一削弱了多元的发展，古代生活中丰富的海洋文明的因素，就像几缕细细的清泉，<u>淌</u>到内陆文明的黄土<u>板块</u>上，立刻就无影无踪了……。

当内陆文明在华夏大地<u>蒸蒸日上</u>的时候，蔚蓝色的海洋文明，正在<u>地中海</u>悄悄崛起了。

屈原	Qū Yuán	a poet (c. 340-278 BCE) of the state of Chu during the Warring States period who was unjustly banished by the Chu king
西楚霸王	Xī-Chǔ bàwáng	the overlord of Western Chu: a name for Xiang Yu, a warrior king (232-202 BCE) of Chu who committed suicide after suffering defeat at the hands of Liu Bang, founder (c. 256-195 BCE) of the Han dynasty
波涛	bōtāo	great waves; billows
独尊的地位	dúzūn de dìwèi	pre-eminent position
淌	tǎng	drip; trickle
板块	bǎnkuài	tectonic plate
蒸蒸日上	zhēngzhēngrìshàng	thrive; flourish
地中海	Dìzhōng Hǎi	Mediterranean Sea

早在古希腊时代，雅典的民主思想，正是随着雅典的海上权力一同兴起的，海权导致了民主革命。

近代西方资产阶级革命的社会前提，也正是欧洲海外航线的开辟。从十五世纪开始航行于海天之间的那些帆船，既揭开了世界贸易和殖民活动的帷幕，同时也运载着科学和民族的希望。蔚蓝色就靠着这小帆船，获得了现代世界命运的象征意义。

于是，广大的东方市场和美洲新大陆，使小小的欧洲几乎一夜之间成为暴发户。

横渡大洋需要又坚固、又庞大、又精巧的船舶，造出这些船舶需要数学和物理学，需要技术与科学。于是，1636 年，伽利略发表了《新科学对话》。这场"对话"，就是在造船厂举行的。

英国首先由海外贸易获得巨大的利益，促进了资本的原始累积，也促进了自由思想的普及。于是，首先在英国发生了克伦威尔领导的资产阶级革命。1651 年，克伦威尔颁布航海条例。1690 年，洛克发表《政府论》。自由贸易论成为资产阶级的口号和原则。

资产主义转动着工业革命和自由贸易这两个轮子，开始了伟大的飞跃，开始了科学与民族的双重历史大合唱。

这一切，都与海洋息息相关。

中国这时候在干什么呢？

当麦哲伦正航行在他的环球航线上时，明朝嘉靖皇帝因为日本贡使打架，开始正式"闭关"。

公元 1776 年，亚当·斯密发表了著名的《国富论》。就在这本书

雅典	Yǎdiǎn	Athens
暴发户	bàofāhù	*nouveau riche*; upstart
伽利略	Jiālìlüè	Galileo
克伦威尔	Kèlúnwēi'ěr	Oliver Cromwell
颁布	bānbù	promulgate
洛克	Luòkè	John Locke
亚当·斯密	Yàdāng Sīmì	Adam Smith
《国富论》	*Guófù lùn*	*An Inquiry into the Nature and Causes of the Wealth of Nations*

中，他宣布中国的历史和文化停滞了。他说：停滞是由于不重视海外贸易，闭 关必趋于自杀。

可惜，这些话没有一个中国人能够及时听到。

终于，当虎门码头烧起那把著名的大火，揭开了耻辱的中国近代史的时候，中国同西方之间，已经隔着一条巨大的精神文化鸿沟了。一个扩张的、进行国际贸易和战争的蔚蓝色文明，同一个坚持农业经济和官僚政治的黄色文明之间的文化对抗，无疑是冰炭不相容的。

然而只要一交手，西方的坚船利炮马上就让中国的官员和士大夫们领教了蔚蓝色的强大。于是有了"洋务运动"，有了"中体西用"。

洋务派大臣们买回来了威力强大的铁甲军舰，办起了一座座兵工厂。位于上海市郊的江南兵工厂，在掌握西方技能方面远远超出日本。1870 年左右， 俄国人参观远在中国西北的兰州兵工厂时，为那里制造的枪枝质量之精良感到震惊。甲午战争开战时，中国的军舰数量比日本要多。

然而，这一切并没有阻止清王朝先败于法国，再败于日本。甲午海战失败的最直接原因，竟是由于一个腐败的承包商在许多炮弹里灌了泥沙。呈半月型展开的中国舰队，临战了还不知到底应该听从谁的指挥。

虎门	Hǔmén	Humen Bay, Guangdong province—site of the burning of opium by the imperial envoy Lin Zexu in 1839, an act of defiance against the British which triggered the Opium Wars
冰炭不相容的	bīng-tàn bù xiāngróng de	as incompatible as ice and hot coals
洋务运动	Yángwù yùndòng	the Foreign Affairs/Westernization movement of the late nineteenth century
中体西用	Zhōngtǐ Xīyòng	the principle of "Chinese learning for the essence, Western learning for the practical"
甲午战争	Jiǎwǔ Zhànzhēng	the Sino-Japanese War of 1894-95
承包商	chéngbāoshāng	contractor
半月型	bànyuèxíng	half-moon shape
指挥	zhǐhuī	command; commander

这一事 实清楚地说明了，腐败的制度所导致的必然失败，并不能靠技术来挽救。

清朝政府最早派送到英国学习海军的留学生<u>严复</u>，日后并没有去当一名战舰指挥官，而是成了思想启蒙家。

严复从对西方的大量观察中发现，欧洲文化的伟大成绩就在于发挥个人的潜力，提供了一种社会契约。这种契约能使竞争以及资本主义的其它一切功能，都有利于促进社会变革。同样，通过利用个人的"意志力"一种人类的"<u>浮士德</u>"和"<u>普罗米修斯</u>"式的能力，就能创造出一种生机勃勃的文化。

然而，当严复参与其事的<u>百日维新</u>惨败之时，日本的<u>明治维新</u>却成功了。当这位中国近代的伟大启蒙者在封建势力的打击下，一步步放弃改良思想，最终倒退到<u>孔孟</u>之道的怀抱里去的时候，他在英国海军大学的同学<u>伊藤博文</u>，却连任日本首相，率领这个岛国迅速跨进世界强国之林。

严复乃至近代许多伟大思想先驱如<u>康有为</u>、<u>梁启超</u>、<u>章太炎</u>等等的

严复	Yán Fù	scholar and translator (1854-1921), famous for introducing aspects of Western thought to China during the late Qing period
浮士德	Fúshìdé	Faust
普罗米修斯	Pǔluómǐxiūsī	Prometheus
百日维新	Bǎirì Wéixīn	Hundred Days Reform of 1898
明治维新	Míngzhì Wéixīn	Meiji Restoration of 1868
孔孟	Kǒng-Mèng	Confucius and Mencius
伊藤博文	Itô Hirubumi	Japanese statesman (1841-1909) who served as Prime Minister four times, and orchestrated Japan's rise to world power status
康有为	Kāng Yǒuwéi	classical scholar (1858-1927) and a leading light of the Hundred Days Reform
梁启超	Liáng Qǐchāo	scholar (1873-1929) who played a seminal role in the late-Qing reform movement
章太炎	Zhāng Tàiyán	late-Qing scholar and advocate of reform (1868-1936)

悲剧命运，似乎都证明了，即使最优秀的中国人在革命和激进了一阵子以后，到头来都摆脱不了退回<u>儒家</u>的归宿。

直到八十年代的今天，在"中国文化热"的大讨论中，人们依然在继续着中西文化优劣的百年未决的争辩。无论是"<u>全盘西化</u>"的一派幻想，还是"儒家文明第三繁荣期"的<u>一厢情愿</u>，一切仿佛还在原地踏步。难怪有的青年学者这样感叹道：巨大的文化财产变成了巨大的文化包袱，巨大的文化优越感变成了巨大的文化负罪感，这不能不说是中国现代化过程中的一个巨大心理障碍。

变法之艰难，或许就难在我们总在担心"中国人还是中国人吗？"我们似乎并不知道，在以往西方的二三百年里，不论是<u>文艺复兴</u>、宗教改革，还是启蒙运动，西欧人至少从未担心过，在改革之后是否会成为不是意大利人了、不是德意志人了、不是法兰西人了。唯独在中国，这是最大的<u>忌讳</u>。

这或许正是那黄色文明的沉重之处和浅薄之处！

两千多年前的哲学家庄子，给我们讲过一个寓言：

黄河之神<u>河伯</u>，在秋天涨大水的时候发现自己很伟大，居然在两岸之间分辨不清牛马。他尽情往下游漂去，突然看见了大海，<u>竟茫然若失</u>。海的主宰<u>北海若</u>告诉他，不能和<u>井蛙</u>谈论大海，因为它只知道自己那点小小的地盘，无法想象大海的博大。而现在，我的河伯，你终于走出了<u>壅塞</u>的河道，看见了大海的恢宏。你知道了局限，也就进入了一个更高的境界。

儒家	Rújiā	Confucian school
全盘西化	quánpán Xīhuà	wholesale Westernization
一厢情愿	yìxiāngqíngyuàn	one's own wishful thinking
文艺复兴	Wényì Fùxīng	the Renaissance
忌讳	jìhuì	taboo
河伯	Hé Bó	Spirit of the Yellow River
茫然若失	mángrán ruòshī	lost in thought; at a loss
北海若	Běi Hǎi Ruò	Spirit of the North Sea, a character in the "Autumn Floods" chapter of *Zhuangzi*
井蛙	jǐngwā	a person with a limited outlook
壅塞	yōngsè	clogged up; jammed

这是一个象征。它说的并不是古代中国，它好象是在预言今天。

古老的黄河之神，真正看清大海的面貌，认识大海的博大与力量，不过一个世纪。它面向大海发出的那一声长长的叹息，穿过一百多年的历史，一直回响到今天。

（再一次推出片名：蔚蓝色）

这片土黄色的大地不能教给我们，什么是真正的科学精神。

<u>肆虐</u>的黄河不能教给我们，什么是真正的民主意识。

单靠这片黄土和这条黄河，已经养育不起日益膨胀的人口，已经孕育不了文化，它不再有过去的营养和精力。

儒家文化或许有种种古老完善的"<u>法宝</u>"，但它几千年来偏偏造就不出一个民族的<u>进取</u>精神、一个国家的<u>法治</u>秩序、一种文化的更新机制；相反，它在走向衰落之中，形成了一种可怕的自杀机制，不断摧残自己的精华，杀死自己内部有生命力的因素，窒息这个民族的一代又一代精英。纵使它有千年珍奇，今天也是难免<u>玉石俱焚</u>了。

历史证明：按照一种内陆文化的统治模式来进行现代化建设，虽然也能容纳现代科技的某些新成果，甚至<u>卫星</u>可以上天，原子弹可以爆炸，但却不能根本性地<u>赋予</u>整个民族以一种强大的文明活力。

只有当蔚蓝色的海风终于化为雨水，重新滋润这片干旱的黄土地时，这些只在春节喜庆日子里才迸发出来的令人惊异的活力，才有可能使巨大的黄土高原重新获得生机。

在黄土高原的腹地延安，到处都可以看到来自上海、浙江等沿海省市的小姑娘、小伙子们开设的服装店、理发店。沿海地区涌来的商品散布

肆虐	sìnüè	ravage; devastate; rampant
法宝	fǎbǎo	talisman; magic formula; charms
进取	jìnqǔ	keep forging ahead; enterprising
法治	fǎzhì	rule of law
玉石俱焚	yùshíjùfén	destroy wantonly
卫星	wèixīng	satellite
赋予	fùyǔ	endow

在大街小巷。神圣的、土灰色的<u>宝塔山</u>，在这红红绿绿、<u>熙熙攘攘</u>的市场后面，渐渐淡化为一个朦胧的背景。

（陕北<u>安塞</u>千人打<u>腰鼓</u>。）

这些老汉和小伙子，他们的祖先曾经从这内陆腹地出发，征服了全中国，如今却随着这片萎缩了的土地，一起萎缩了他们曾经那么旺盛的精力。令人难以置信的是，这几个小伙子，竟然是这支气势<u>磅礴</u>的千人腰鼓队的成员。难道他们的生命力，永远只能消耗在打腰鼓的渲泄中吗？

(Cont.)

宝塔山	Bǎotǎ shān	Baota hill in Yan'an
熙熙攘攘	xīxīrǎngrǎng	bustling with activity
安塞腰鼓	Ānsàiyāogǔ	an energetic folk dance, expressive of peasant life on the loess plateau, which is performed in northern Shaanxi Province
磅礴	pángbó	majestic; all-embracing

10. CHINESE NEO-NATIONALISM

China Can Say No
Song Qiang et al.

China Can Say No is the seminal text of popular Chinese nationalism in the 1990s. Published in 1996, during the immediate aftermath of the military confrontation between China and the United States in the Taiwan Strait, the 130,000 copies of its first print run sold out in weeks. The book had clearly touched a nerve, and its authors—Song Qiang 松强, Zhang Zangzang 张藏藏, Qiao Bian 乔边, Gu Qingsheng 古清生, and Tang Zhengyu 汤正宇—drew hundreds of letters of support from all over China. Other writers jumped swiftly on the bandwagon, and 1996 saw a slew of texts in a similar naysaying style, including *How China Can Say No* (中国何以说不 Zhongguo heyi shuo bu), *China Can Still Say No* (中国还是可以说不 Zhongguo haishi keyi shuo bu), *Behind the Demonization of China* (妖魔化中国的背后 Yaomohua Zhongguo de beihou), and *The True Story of the Sino-American Contest* (中美较量大写真 Zhong-Mei jiaoliang daxiezhen). The 1999 bombing by the United States of the Chinese embassy in Belgrade unleashed a further torrent of "no" literature, and by the turn of the century, xenophobic nationalism had become a competitive niche market. As John W. Garver puts it, "almost every bookshop and street-vendor's stall in any large Chinese city offered dozens of such titles, often displayed together on special tables in well-trafficked areas of the store."[1]

The genesis of *China Can Say No*, and its legion spin-offs, is complex. In some senses, the text belongs to the broader "Say No" genre (inaugurated in 1989 by Morita Akio and Ishihara Shintarō's *The Japan That Can Say No*) which has sprung up across parts of East Asia in recent years. In other ways, the rampant patriotism it promotes can be seen as a response to the collapse of Cold War power relations, one which finds parallels far beyond the region. Yet ultimately the text's origins lie at home, and can be traced back to the trauma of Tiananmen. The violent crackdown of 1989 caused a crisis of legitimacy for the Chinese government, and in the years which followed the Party sought to reclaim the justness of its mandate by raising a brand of crowd-pleasing nationalism to the status of official ideology. At the core of this policy was the Campaign of Patriotic Education, a raft of China-loving measures which required secondary school students to learn patriotic songs, university freshmen students to take courses in Chinese history, and workers to visit patriotic bases. Moreover, as the nationalist turn became more pronounced, it found ready sponsors amongs writers and

---

1. John W. Garver, "Review: More from the 'Say No Club,'" 152.

intellectuals. Both the national studies (国学 *guoxue*) and so-called "post-ism" (后 学 *houxue*—the attempt to indigenize aspects of Western postmodernism) movements which came to prominence in the mid-1990s were assertions of Chineseness in a Western-dominated world. In this context of state and scholarly patriotism, it was perhaps inevitable that a popular, populist nationalism would also have its day. Spurning an academic approach to international relations, *China Can Say No* marketed itself as precisely this: a mirror of how real Chinese felt about their nation and its place in the world during the post-Cold War era.[2] In many ways, therefore, its insights are indispensable.

The premise of the polemic is that many Chinese of the Tiananmen generation were too rash in their embrace of Euro-American ideas and ideologies during the 1980s; indeed, the worldview of *River Elegy*, the subject of the previous chapter, is implicitly critiqued. Instead of unreasoning idolatry of the West, what China needs is a new discourse of patriotism, a robust reiteration of what Chineseness is and does. In *China Can Say No*, this neo-nationalism operates across two axes: China as victim and the United States as foe. The notion of China as the target of ceaseless foreign aggression is, of course, an entrenched one, and as Geremie Barmé puts it, "Questions of racial and political impotence have been central to Chinese thoughts and debates" since the nineteenth century.[3] But recent years have seen both the Chinese authorities and the populace itself grow ever more irate about China's injured past, as year-on-year economic growth has caused national pride to swell. *China Can Say No* sets out to fan these flames: the world "owes" China for 150 years of suffering, and the time has come to pay. Like the Campaign of Patriotic Education which preceded it (which turned the commemoration of the May Fourth Movement and the 150th anniversary of the Opium War in 1990 into an exercise in foreigner-bashing), the book is as much about xenophobia as it is an entreaty to love China. Its rhetoric re-visits the indignities of the nation's past in order to stoke a sense of grievance, and anti-imperialism is its major fuel.

The flipside of victimology, meanwhile, is the search for someone to blame—and by the mid- to late-1990s it had become clear that the chief nemesis of China's post-Mao renaissance was the United States. In April 1991, *People's Daily* openly named the United States as the major foreign force hostile to China, and since then the point has become established fact in many circles. America blocked Beijing's bid to join the World Trade Organization; its human rights diplomacy and interventions in China's

---

2. As Ben Xu puts it, these writings "are accepted as mass-consumption goods rather than as academic works." See Xu, "Chinese Populist Nationalism: Its Intellectual Politics and Moral Dilemma," 14.

3. Geremie Barmé, "To Screw Foreigners Is Patriotic: China's Avant-Garde Nationalists," 210.

internal affairs were an exercise in hypocrisy; and its arms sales to Taiwan, its naval intervention in the Taiwan Strait, and its hospitality to Taiwanese President Lee Teng-hui added up, in Chinese eyes, to an agenda of support for Taiwanese independence. Vitriol against the United States drives the narrative of *China Can Say No*, inflaming writers and readers alike, and in some ways, this fury is understandable. As Suisheng Zhao puts it, America struggles with the reality of a rising China, "fearing China's strength, but also fearing its weakness; fearing China's wealth, but also fearing its poverty; fearing China's stability, but also fearing its chaos."[4]

Justified or otherwise, there can be no doubting either the passion contained within *China Can Say No* or the passion which it generated among readers. And this latter reaction, in particular, begs the question: Why has the public been so ready and willing to turn an ear to voices which "say no"? The most likely answer is that patriotism fills the void left by the disavowal of Maoism: it is a precious grand narrative in a society whose value system has been upended, and whose insecurities have grown quite acute in the free-for-all of the reform era. Certainly, the CCP—living as it may be on borrowed time—has capitalized on this mood, and conservative officials were quick to lend their support to *China Can Say No* and its team of authors. In this sense, the writers of the book, with their zeal for prosecuting the nation's enemies and reluctance to raise the problems of "socialism with Chinese characteristics," are intellectuals in the service of the state, spurning the radicalism of 1980s for a more revisionist stance. Especially striking in this regard is the ambivalence of the text toward the Maoist past. As Chris Hughes has put it, "The idea that mainland China can achieve economic miracles if the population just gives up its lunch-time nap"[5] is ominously reminiscent of the backyard steel foundries of the Great Leap Forward, and the oft-repeated mantra to "overtake Britain and catch up with America." What is more, all the writers perform numerous self-criticisms about the right-wing view of world politics they held in the past, with minimal awareness that the ultranationalism they currently espouse is every bit as reactionary.

This combination of reticence about the problems of China's present and odd nostalgia for those of its past has caused many other commentators to come down hard on what they perceive as the true causes of ultranationalism. According to these critics, it is repressed shame at China's inhospitality to democratic ideas—and the silence which many of its intellectuals have maintained on the subject since Tiananmen—which drives the discourse of xenophobia. Shame, unspoken, turns into defensive rage, which then lashes out at easier targets. Thus John Fitzgerald claims that "the 'say no' authors appear to resent the twist of

---

4. Suisheng Zhao, "Chinese Intellectuals' Quest for National Greatness and Nationalistic Writing in the 1990s," 741.
5. Chris Hughes, "A Western Scholar Looks at *The China That Can Say No*," 92.

fate which delivered them into the world as citizens of a state that cannot afford the liberties that citizens of other states take for granted,"[6] while John W. Garver goes further and argues that the polemics of the naysayers are nothing more than "cathartic projections of responsibility for China's problems onto putatively hostile foreign powers."[7]

Many of these points appear in sharp relief in the passages excerpted below. All three extracts—whether their subject is the containment of China, the Taiwan problem, or US hegemony in the round—adopt a tone which alternates from indignant to sarcastic to self-justificatory. As the essayists swing from demonology (of the United States) to victimology (of China), they play just as fast and loose with historical truth as do the American politicians who are the target of their collective polemic. In so doing, these passages reveal the demagogic nature of Chinese neo-nationalism: sleights of hand and rhetorical flourishes are par for the course, and the writers routinely appeal to the size of China's population and the longevity of its civilization as if they were natural signifiers of the nation's justness. Yet above all, perhaps, the message of the extracts is menacing. China may be the victim of history, but now the "sleeping dragon" of cliché has woken, and *China Can Say No* relishes the opportunity to warn America of what awaits if this dragon is unwisely roused.

1. He Beilin. "Qianyan." In Song Qiang, Zhang Zangzang, and Qiao Bian, *Zhongguo keyi shuo bu. Lengzhanhou shidai de zhengzhi yu qinggan jueze.* Beijing: Zhonghua gongshang lianhe chubanshe, 1996, 1-3.

2. Zhang Zangzang. "Ezhi, fan'ezhi, fanguolai ezhi." In Song Qiang, Zhang Zangzang, and Qiao Bian, *Zhongguo keyi shuo bu. Lengzhanhou shidai de zhengzhi yu qinggan jueze.* Beijing: Zhonghua gongshang lianhe chubanshe, 1996, 61-63.

3. Zhang Zangzang. "Zai Taiwan wentishang Meiguo bu yao zouhuo." In Song Qiang, Zhang Zangzang, and Qiao Bian, *Zhongguo keyi shuo bu. Lengzhanhou shidai de zhengzhi yu qinggan jueze.* Beijing: Zhonghua gongshang lianhe chubanshe, 1996, 71-64.

Further Reading

Barmé, Geremie. "To Screw Foreigners Is Patriotic: China's Avant-Garde Nationalists." *China Journal* 34 (1995), 209-34.
Des Forges, Roger, and Luo Xu. "China as a Non-Hegemonic Superpower?

6. John Fitzgerald, "China and the Quest for Dignity," 55.
7. Garver, "Review: More from the 'Say No Club,'" 158.

The Uses of History among the *China Can Say No* Writers and
Their Critics." *Critical Asian Studies* 33/4 (2001), 483-507.

Fitzgerald, John. "China and the Quest for Dignity." *National Interest*
55 (1999), 47-59.

Gao Mobo. "Sino-US Love and Hate Relations." *Journal of Contemporary
Asia* 30/4 (2000), 547-61.

Garver, John W. "Review: More from the 'Say No Club.'" *China
Journal* 45 (2001), 151-58.

Gries, Peter H. *China's New Nationalism: Pride, Politics, and Diplomacy.*
Berkeley and Los Angeles: University of California Press, 2004.

Hughes, Chris. "A Western Scholar Looks at *The China That Can Say
No.*" *Sinorama* 21/11 (1996), 89-95.

Li Hongshan. "China Talks Back: Anti-Americanism or Nationalism? A
Review of Recent 'Anti-American' Books in China." *Journal of
Contemporary China* 6/14 (1997), 153-60.

Lin, Min, and Maria Galikowski. "From 'River Elegy' to *China Can Say
No*: China's Neo-Nationalism and the Search for Collective
National Identity." In Min Lin and Maria Galikowski, eds. *The
Search for Modernity: Chinese Intellectuals and Cultural
Discourse in the Post-Mao Era*, 89-102. New York: St. Martin's
Press, 1999.

Liu, Toming Jun. "Uses and Abuses of Sentimental Nationalism:
Mnemonic Disquiet in *Heshang* and *Shuobu*." *Modern Chinese
Literature and Culture* 13/1 (2001), 169-209.

Wang, Fei-Ling. "Ignorance, Arrogance, and Radical Nationalism: A
Review of *China Can Say No*." *Journal of Contemporary China*
6/14 (1997),161-65.

Xu, Ben. "Chinese Populist Nationalism: Its Intellectual Politics and Moral
Dilemma." *Representations* 76/4 (2001), 120-40.

Zhao, Suisheng. *A Nation-State by Construction. Dynamics of Modern
Chinese Nationalism.* Stanford: Stanford University Press, 2004.

———. "A State-led Nationalism: The Patriotic Education
Campaign in Post-Tiananmen China." *Communist and Post-
Communist Studies* 31/3 (1998), 287-302.

———. "Chinese Intellectuals' Quest for National Greatness and
Nationalistic Writing in the 1990s." *China Quarterly* 152 (1997),
725-45.

中国可以说不

前言

这不是一份民族主义宣言，也不是确立中国在国际政治中的位置的战略<u>大纲</u>。

把它看成是广泛的民意的映射或许更确切一些。

很多事实和<u>迹象</u>表明，冷战之后，作为一个独存的社会主义大国，中国的走向尤为使人关注；出于<u>根深蒂固</u>的意识形态<u>歧见</u>，出于力图单独<u>主宰</u>世界的超霸心态，美国对于中国崛起这一现象更多地显示出痛苦和不安。在他们看来，不久的将来也许只有中国才能<u>制衡</u>其文化霸权、经济霸权和军事霸权。于是，一个来自"自由世界"的针对中国的大阴谋开始<u>酝酿</u>发酵……

之所以说是阴谋，是因为美国说的是一套，做的又是一套。

当他们重申台湾是中国的领土时，他们的第七舰队却<u>游弋</u>在台海附近，并<u>趾高气扬</u>地告诉世界："谁也别忘了，美国海军是世界第一。"

当他们<u>悦耳动听</u>地唱着要帮助中国尽早加入世界贸易组织时，欧盟一位高级人士私底下却表明：我们这方面没有什么大问题，主要是美国在阻挠。

当中国多次阐明自己在人权问题上的立场，并希望就这一领域进行对话而不要对抗时，美国的<u>费拉罗</u>女士却<u>贼喊捉贼</u>地说，中国在联合

大纲	dàgāng	outline; synopsis; summary
迹象	jìxiàng	sign; indication
根深蒂固	gēnshēndìgù	deep-rooted; inveterate
歧见	qíjiàn	conflicting ideas; opinions
主宰	zhǔzǎi	dictate; dominate; sovereign
制衡	zhìhéng	checks and balances
酝酿	yùnniàng	ferment
游弋	yóuyì	cruise
趾高气扬	zhǐgāoqìyáng	arrogant; strutting
悦耳动听	yuè'ěr dòngtīng	pleasing to the ear
费拉罗	Fèilāluó	Geraldine Ferraro (1935-), former US ambassador to the UN Human Rights Commission
贼喊捉贼	zéihǎnzhuōzéi	a thief who cries, "Stop thief!": hypocrite

国人权委员会年会针对西方国家的举动所提出的"不予审议"的动议就是对抗。

当美国到处叫嚷中国搞武器扩散加深了世界敏感地区的危机时，他们自己却爆出了"伊朗门"事件……

言而总之，在所有领域对中国予以"遏制"，这已经成为美国的一项基本国策。一场针对中国的新冷战正由美国发动起来。

本书的一位作者说：我原本是一位国际主义者，但自从看到美英等国在中国申办奥运会问题上的种种举止，深受刺激，打从以后我就慢慢地变成一个民族主义者了。

我相信，中国有很多人都具有相同或相似的心路历程。

顺便说一句。本书的五位作者都是三十岁上下的年轻人，有报社记者、大学教师、诗人及自由撰稿人。他们跟《日本能够说不》、《可以说不的亚洲》的作者盛田昭夫、石原慎太郎、马哈蒂尔无论在 资历、身分和地位上都不可同日而语。写作此书，更多的出自一种情感选择—因为他们也不是国际问题专家。但唯其如此，该书才具有了更广泛坚实的民意基础。

中国说不，并不是寻求对抗，而是要在更平等的氛围下寻求对话。这也是本书一以贯之的主题。而以美国为首的西方国家里那些怀念冷战时代、热衷于制定"对抗"和"遏制"政策的政客们应该明白，他们已经使中国人特别是中国青年厌烦、反感到了极点。

遏制	èzhì	containment; to contain
举止	jǔzhǐ	bearing; manner
撰稿人	zhuàn'gǎorén	author; drafter of a manuscript
盛田昭夫	Morita Akio	co-author (1921–99) of *The Japan That Can Say No*
石原慎太郎	Ishihara Shintarô	co-author (1932-) of *The Japan That Can Say No* and *The Asia that Can Say No*
马哈蒂尔	Mǎhādìěr	Mahathir Mohammed (1925-), co-author of *The Asia That Can Say No*
同日而语	tóngrì'éryǔ	mention in the same breath
唯其如此	wéiqí rúcǐ	precisely because of this
一以贯之	yìyǐguànzhī	consistent; pervasive

有必要给出如下结论：

美国谁也领导不了，它只能领导它自己；

日本谁也领导不了，它有时连自己都无法领导；

中国谁也不想领导，中国只想领导自己。

请阅读正文。

1996 年 4 月 26 日

第二篇： 第二章
遏制，反遏制，反过来遏制

1．"遏制中国"己成为美国的一项长期战略

尽管美国本土的一些<u>有识之士</u>也在告诫自己的政府"不要同中国打冷战"，比如<u>基辛格</u>，他就认为同中国对抗对于美国来说代价太高了。但在事实上，美国近几年来对中国实施的完全是一种遏制政策，用他们自己的话讲，叫"<u>软硬兼施</u>"，尽管形式上各不相同，其目的是一致的。这也就是中美关系何以走到目前这样的危险边缘的主要根源。

深刻的意识形态歧见，西方文明对东方的<u>倾覆</u>姿势，霸道的国家主义和<u>领袖欲</u>是美国人之所以"遏制"的基本出发点。另外，我认为，整个美国对中国所形成的知识有相当大一部分是错误的；从这个角度讲，中国人对美国的了解要深刻、明晰和全面得多。一九九二年上半年，我曾与一个在北京某高校就读的美国留学生韩盖德同桌共餐。<u>席间</u>，我们因为西藏问题争论得差点<u>不欢而散</u>。韩盖德的观点是：自从中国"侵占"西藏后，每年都要从那里<u>攫取</u>上百亿元的财富，并由此造成了整个西藏的贫困落后，人民<u>生灵涂炭</u>——这简直就无从讨论了，他可能以为达赖喇嘛时期的西藏是多么丰衣足食、歌舞升平、<u>繁华似锦</u>呢。"我们美国人就是这么认为的。"——韩盖德反复这样强调。想一下吧，在一个传媒高度"自由"、"发达"、"公正"的国度里，竟然对中国生发出那么多"稚童"的观念，对东方的历史与现实的认识有如此大的偏差，这是多么可怕又可悲的一件事！

有识之士	yǒushízhīshì	a person with breadth of vision
基辛格	Jīxīngé	Henry Kissinger (1923-)
软硬兼施	ruǎnyìngjiānshī	use both hard and soft tactics; use both carrot and stick
倾覆	qīngfù	overturn; topple
领袖欲	lǐngxiùyù	the drive to lead
席间	xíjiān	in the course of a banquet or meal
不欢而散	bùhuān'érsàn	part on bad terms
攫取	juéqǔ	seize; grab
生灵涂炭	shēnglíngtútàn	abject misery
繁华似锦	fánhuásìjǐn	intellectually and artistically vibrant

　　认为中国是一个苏联式的<u>扩张主义者</u>，是一个邪恶的帝国，有必要"让它呆在窝里，别出来<u>惹事生非</u>"（美国一<u>参议员</u>语），这是美国对中国进行遏制的另一个主要依据。最近，中国军队在台海进行的一系列军事演习，以及此前的中国政府在<u>南沙群岛</u>、<u>钓鱼岛</u>等的一贯立场，都被美国视为中国搞军事扩张的一个征兆。但是，请问美国的政府和国会，一个国家有没有对包括本国在内的几个国家有争议的领土提出主权的权利？难道中国只有很大度地<u>拱手相让</u>才能证明中国没有野心？至于台湾问题，之所以发展到这一步，一与台湾岛的台独<u>猖獗</u>有关，第二显然与美国的不可告人的用心有关。美国的那些政治家内心绝对不会愿意大陆与台湾顺顺利利地实行统一的。如果统一，他们手里对付中国的<u>筹码</u>不是又少了份量很大的一块吗？

　　其实，在这个问题上，我认为中国人的态度既理智又明确。第一，我们希望能和平统一台湾；第二，如果台湾宣布独立或被外国势力所干预，我们不承诺放弃使用武力。这两个观点，我觉得每一个富有智识和公义的人都应该能够理解。不管李登辉如何辩解，我们只要读一读他与日本作家<u>司马辽太郎</u>的谈话就可以对其用心予以洞察。所以，如果把中美关系的今日格局仅仅理解成为两个国家相互之间的误解和<u>意气用事</u>就有点<u>牵强</u>了。

扩张主义者	kuòzhāngzhǔyìzhě	expansionist
惹事生非	rěshìshēngfēi	stir up trouble
参议员	cānyìyuán	senator
南沙群岛	Nánshā Qúndǎo	the Nansha (Spratly) Islands, variously claimed by China, Taiwan, Vietnam, Malaysia, and the Philippines
钓鱼岛	Diàoyú Dǎo	the Diaoyu/Senkaku Islands, claimed by China, Japan, and Taiwan
拱手相让	gǒngshǒu-xiāngràng	surrender something submissively
猖獗	chāngjué	rampant
筹码	chóumǎ	chip; counter
司马辽太郎	Shiba Ryōtarō	Japan's foremost historical novelist (1923-1996)
意气用事	yìqìyòngshì	act on impulse
牵强	qiānqiǎng	forced; farfetched

为什么偏偏要中国承诺放弃使用武力？你们美国的南北战争为什么不能放弃武力好好地坐下来谈呢？谈一百年也没有什么嘛，应该<u>风物长宜放眼量</u>嘛。所以说，<u>己所不欲，勿施于人</u>。

在这个问题上，美国人不要总以为"<u>老子天下第一</u>"，以领导世界为己任。在台海演习时，美国的<u>决策</u>是愚蠢的和不<u>慎重</u>的，第七舰队进入台湾海峡才是一种公然的<u>挑衅</u>。美国防部长<u>佩里</u>居然以这样的口吻威胁中国："谁也不要忘了，美国的海军是世界第一。"我也以这样的口吻来<u>奉劝</u>美国："谁也不要忘了，中国的人口是世界第一。"如果有谁认为和中国在台湾问题上有<u>讨价还价</u>的余地那就大错特错了。

为了维持自己的长久的霸权地位和冷战后格局，<u>不择手段</u>地使用阴谋、谣言及武力威胁与贸易<u>制裁</u>，它除了能短时间地延缓中国的 现代化进程外，其后果对美国和整个西方世界来讲也是灾难性的。请看看《中国青年报》在1995年所作的一项民意测验的结果吧，美国已经成了中国青年最为讨厌的国家了——与一个有十数亿人口、有几千年文明史、正在重新崛起的东方大国蓄意为敌，其政策也太不明智了。

(Cont.)

风物长宜放眼量	fēngwù chángyí fàng yǎnliàng	take the long view on things
己所不欲，勿施于人	jǐ suǒ bú yù wù shī yú rén	do as you would be done by others
老子天下第一	lǎozi tiānxià dìyī	think of oneself as the most important person in the world
挑衅	tiǎoxìn	provocation
佩里	Pèilǐ	William Perry (1927-), former US secretary of defense
奉劝	fèngquàn	offer a piece of advice
讨价还价	tǎojiàhuánjià	haggle
不择手段	bùzéshǒuduàn	by hook or by crook; by any means
制裁	zhìcái	sanctions

第二篇： 第四章
在台湾问题上美国不要走火

针对台岛内的<u>分裂主义</u>倾向<u>甚嚣尘上</u>，中国力求通过各种方式予以阻遏，虽然现在的局势从表面上看趋于平静，但是，<u>树欲动而风不止</u>，转机并未真正出现。

其根本原因在于，美国及少数西方国家并不真正愿意看到大陆与台湾实行统一——即使如美国所宣称的那样，以和平的方式统一，恐怕美国人在内心深处也是极不痛快的。

一个正在逐渐显露其重要性的、在意识形态上迥异的国家处于分裂状态对于美国的全球战略是大有好处的。这种分裂分治的现实可以逼迫中国的现代化进程不断受到<u>羁绊</u>和干扰，而美国又可以随时随地<u>打楔子</u>。含混不清的态度，此一时彼一时的表述，<u>国会</u>与政府之间的看似对立又能迅速协调的政治把戏——以此手腕来操纵两岸关系的<u>风云</u>，并且还能巧妙地深藏私心，实在有点<u>自欺欺人</u>。

比如说："签订了<u>中美三项联合公报</u>，然后再通过国会整出一部《<u>与台湾关系法</u>》，一旦台独主义者<u>马蹄声急</u>，而中国政府、不得不严肃

分裂主义	fēnlièzhǔyì	splittism; separatism
甚嚣尘上	shènxiāochénshàng	noise and dust; to cause a furor
树欲动而风不止	shù yù dòng ér fēng bùzhǐ	here: the situation is escalating
羁绊	jībàn	fetter; yoke
打楔子	dǎ xiēzi	drive a wedge between
国会	Guóhuì	Congress
风云	fēngyún	volatile situation
自欺欺人	zìqīqīrén	deceive oneself as much as others
中美三项联合公报	Zhōng-Měi sān Xiàng Liánhé Gōngbào	the three Joint US-PRC Communiqués of 1972, 1979, and 1982
与台湾关系法	Yǔ Táiwān Guānxìfǎ	the Taiwan Relations Act of 1979
马蹄声急	mǎtíshēngjí	lit. "the sound of horses hooves"; here, to step up the pace of one's activities

地表明态度时，华 盛顿的国会山便<u>扑腾</u>起来，一边叫嚷要重新定义《与台湾关系法》，使其能临驾于中美联合公报之上，一边找出词条，因为在那个"关系法"中，美国人只是"支持两岸和平统一"，所以，武力是非法的，是会带来严重后果的。如果中国不承诺不使用武力，美国就有"保卫台湾"的权利和义务。

可以这么说，<u>台独</u>势力的发展壮大其实与美国不无干系；<u>中央情报局</u>的帐号上为台湾的分裂主义分子拔出多少<u>款项</u>以便其羽翼渐丰可能在不久的将来也会<u>大白于天下</u>。然后，美国人再要求你和平统一。此时，台湾似乎成了美国利益的一个符号，而不是中国隔海相望的领土。

进而言之，美国的战略是，第一，使和平统一成为不可能；第二，剥夺中国在任何情况下有使用和平线以外的手段的权利：第三，使台湾问题国际化，让中国不能<u>妄动</u>，否则，就是对亚太乃至整个世界的安全构成威胁，因而必须遭致惩罚和<u>唾弃</u>。

但是，美国不要忘了，中国人在台湾问题上并不会按照它的思路走。进一步说，中国的原则的确定并不是哪个领导人甚至哪一届政府<u>心血来潮</u>时一笔挥就的。有关台湾问题的原则，既体现了国民的意志，又考虑到两岸的各类变数及外国势力干预的各种可能性。正如江泽民所言，在台湾问题上，（中国）没有哪个领导人敢于无原则的妥协，因为那将会使其成为历史的罪人。

美国将两艘<u>航空母舰</u>派往台湾海域，以"尽可能地发出强硬而明确的信息"。

这个信息是明确的：如果两岸开战——谁都不希望出现这种场面——美国将毫不犹豫地进行军事干预。

扑腾	pūteng	get the jitters
台独	Táidú	Taiwan independence movement
中央情报局	Zhōngyāng Qíngbàojú	CIA
款项	kuǎnxiàng	funds
大白于天下	dàbái yú tiānxià	come out into the open
妄动	wàngdòng	act rashly
唾弃	tuòqì	spurn
心血来潮	xīnxuèláicháo	seized by a whim
航空母舰	hángkōng mǔjiàn	aircraft carrier

这个信息同时也是含糊的：因为它仅仅是信息；如果美国要<u>付诸实施</u>，我相信它也会计算到底将会付出多大的代价。

首先，它能够像对付伊拉克那样，让许多西方国家集合在它的周围，以联合国的名义"合法"地与中国对抗吗？"

其二，它能在亚洲国家找到<u>一呼百应</u>的盟友吗？

其三，中国不是伊拉克：中国没有去侵犯另一个国家，中国是在为主权、领土完整而战（这一点，联合国的决议已经昭明）；中国也不可能像伊拉克那样在<u>狂轰滥炸</u>之下顷刻便<u>俯首称臣</u>。并且，美国在亚洲的几次战争并未能全身而退，如果<u>悍然</u>与中国对阵，那意味着它所进行的是本世纪最大而且最胜负莫测的赌博。

这并非说，中国的军事实力已经可以与美国抗衡，更不能表明中国<u>穷兵黩武</u>。如果中国甘愿付出高昂的代价，也只是因为如前所述，谁坐视台湾的独立，谁就会成为千古罪人。

我们也应该向美国传递以上这样一个明确的、强硬的信息。

所以，美国目前应该做的，是尽量少让台湾问题复杂化，很清楚，整个事情的转折点正是因为美国<u>自食其言</u>，使李登辉获得了赴美签证——它的象征意义及微妙性并非美国不能了解的。如果以此来探实中国的忍耐限度——试试水温——那么中国无疑会被<u>激怒</u>，因为美国选择的是一个最为敏感最有禁忌的部位。说得不客气一点，台湾问题就是中国的"<u>私处</u>"。基辛格博士说："如果敌视中国成了我们外交政策中的一种经常现象，我们就将找不到同盟者。对中国而言，台湾不是一个外国，而是一个1895年被日本占领，从而开始了对中国领土蚕食的岛屿。中国对这种被认为是分割行动的反应，犹如当年美国北方各州对南方各州企图脱离美国的反应。"

付诸实施	fùzhū shíshī	put into effect; to carry out
一呼百应	yìhūbǎiyìng	hundreds respond to a single call
狂轰滥炸	kuánghōnglànzhà	indiscriminate bombing
俯首称臣	fǔshǒuchēngchén	surrender
悍然	hànrán	brazenly
穷兵黩武	qióngbīngdúwǔ	aggressively militaristic
自食其言	zìshíqíyán	break one's promise
激怒	jīnù	infuriate
私处	sīchù	private parts

不能据此说，基辛格就是一个<u>亲华</u>人士，只不过这位美国的前政府高级官员更具有正直开明的气度、尊重历史和自己心灵的勇气及个人智识与战略目光。我们也不能说，美国国内的其他人士（如<u>金里奇</u>、<u>杰西·赫尔姆斯</u>等）对待台湾问题的态度与基辛格相比仅仅是认识上的差距。唯一的结论就是，中国统一被视为一种危害美国的长久利益的行为，必须尽其所能，使台湾海峡成为一道不可逾越的界限。

但是，很显然，一旦问题变得严峻和必须选择时，美国将"很难找到同盟者"。

(Cont.)

亲华	qīn-Huá	pro-Chinese
金里奇	Jīnlǐqí	Newt Gingrich (1943-),
		Republican politician
杰西·赫尔姆斯	Jiéxī	Jesse Helms (1921-2008),
	Hè'ěrmǔsī	Republican politician

11. THE EMERGENCE OF CIVIL SOCIETY

Building a Civil Society in China
Deng Zhenglai and Jing Yuejin

The origins of the term "civil society" are famously complex, just as definitions of it remain elusive. Thinkers as diverse as Adam Ferguson, Hegel, Alexis de Tocqueville, and Jürgen Habermas have contributed to its evolution in philosophy from the eighteenth century onward, and the concept comes with a heavy freight of hope, idealism, and moral expectation. Indeed, as Heath Chamberlain puts it, "civil society" has come to signify the "reign of virtue,"[1] an ideal of political checks and balances to which all societies should aspire. In its simplest formulation, civil society refers to the set of institutions, organizations, and engagements which exist between state, family, and market; and it both overlaps with these entities and remains distinct from them. Examples of civil society in action include charities and philanthropic institutions, social and political movements, professional associations, business coalitions, voluntary groups, NGOs, quangos, faith-based organizations, and advocacy groups. All are fundamentally alike in the balance they strive to maintain between collective enterprise and independent character.

Applying the term to China, in whatever guise, has proved to be a fraught exercise for Western scholars. Timothy Brook and B. Michael Frolic observe that "the relationship between state and society in China has been a perennial topic in Western intellectual circles since Hegel theorized China as a state without a society,"[2] and the reform years have only seen this clamor about civil society grow louder, with the work of the German philosopher and sociologist Habermas acting as a particular inspiration. During the Dengist period, a slow separation of the government from the Party began to occur, feeding the theory that hard authoritarianism might yield to other modes of state-society relations. The events of 1989 put this theory to the brutal test, and although the regime stamped on the shoots of democratic change, interest in the notion that civil society might one day bring forth more egalitarian rule has not abated—either in the West or, increasingly, in China itself.

Up to a point, the desire to read contemporary China in terms of civil society is of a piece with developments elsewhere in the post-communist world. During the 1980s, democracy groups across Central and Eastern Europe seized upon the concept as an enabler of their hopes, as regimes began to crumble and new possibilities of governance emerged. Yet at the

---

1. Heath Chamberlain, "On the Search for Civil Society in China," 200.
2. Timothy Brook and B. Michael Frolic, "The Ambiguous Challenge of Civil Society," 3.

same time, the struggle for definition which attends the notion of "civil society" everywhere seems only more acute in the case of China, whose distance in both time and space from the origins of the term poses problems all of its own. The result is that, for all their enthusiasm for a Chinese "civil society," Western commentators still spend as much time defining their terms of engagement as they do analyzing actual Chinese praxis. And as Richard Madsen reminds us, these terms have "often been vaguely defined and inconsistently used, with the result that the research questions built out of them have often been unfocused and unanswerable."[3]

Certainly, the vogue for research on civil society in China has to keep an eye out for the pitfalls which plague every transfer of ideas from the West to "the rest." Thus the field must hold back from conflating civil society in China with Western patterns of socio-civic development, and at the same time attend with sufficient care to the modes of civility and society which have emerged in China's own historical experience. Studies which explore manifestations of civil society in China's pre-modern history, such as the studies by William Rowe and Mary B. Rankin of the public sphere during the late Qing period, are salutary in this regard.[4] At the same time, however, the temptation to fetishize Chinese uniqueness lingers on, with crude contrasts between Western "individualism" and the "communal" values of China proving a particular sticking point. And from here, of course, it is only a short step to tired old clichés about the Chinese preference for autocracy over self-determination. Either way, Brook and Frolic are surely right to observe that "civil society is a model, not a reality," and in this sense, China must remain at the heart of the analysis if we are to put flesh on the bones of theory. Indeed, instead of looking eastward from the West, perhaps we should take China's experience as an opportunity to rethink, and even remodel, Western-based definitions of what civil society is and does.

At the very least, incorporating the term "civil society" into the conceptual apparatus of China studies offers a new window on the relationship between state and society in a swiftly evolving polity. Here, many commentators seem to be in broad agreement that the notion of civil society as a counterpoise to the state does not speak too persuasively of China's current situation. The "state versus society" paradigm—received wisdom in the West—does not stand up to close inspection in China, where accommodation with the state, rather than resistance to it, has been the order of the day. Rather than proceeding from the premise that "the existence and viability of civil society vary directly with the distance (or absence) of state power," the Chinese case offers ample evidence that

3. Richard Madsen, "The Public Sphere, Civil Society and Moral Community: A Research Agenda for Contemporary China Studies," 184.

4. See William Rowe, "The Public Sphere in Modern China," 309-29; and Mary B. Rankin, "Some Observations on a Chinese Public Sphere," 158-182.

"civil society is as much a creature of the state as it is of society."[5] Fledgling bodies of China's post-Tiananmen civil society—NGOs, social service agencies, non-profit organizations, semi-autonomous media, religious groups, specialist associations, and all the concerned parties who run them—depend on their links with the organs of the state, and work hard to foster them. Just as relevantly, the state is also disinclined to view an incipient civil society as its antagonist, for reasons of both convenience and survival. For a start, extending patronage to key social organizations is a matter of plain expediency, since such partnerships assist the state as it seeks to administer a vast and complex society. Still more pragmatic is the motive of self-protection. China's government has good reason to supervise, infiltrate, and co-opt forces which it does not initiate or control, so as to safeguard its hold on power. The result of this is a relationship of symbiosis which brings benefits to both sides.

In other words, state and society are "densely interactive realms" in China—so much so, in fact, that commentators have taken this density of interaction as the starting point for theories of what might constitute a specifically Chinese civil society. Thus Chamberlain claims that civil society is an entity separate from both the state and society in China. Philip C. Huang goes further to argue that it is a "third space," located between the two and in which both participate: "something with distinct characteristics and a logic of its own over and above the influences of state and society."[6] For others, this intensive interpenetration of forces makes the term "civil society" a straight misnomer in the Chinese context.[7] The debate among Western and Western-based scholars ultimately begs a question which, as Shu-Yun Ma notes, has thus far been disappointingly overlooked:[8] What do Chinese commentators themselves make of the notion of civil society in China? The present chapter brings this question directly into the frame, and focuses on an important text from the immediate post-Tiananmen period, Deng Zhenglai 邓正来 and Jing Yuejin's 景跃进 "Building a Civil Society in China" (建构中国的市民社会 Jian'gou Zhongguo de shimin shehui).

For Deng and Jing, civil society holds out nothing less than the promise of a resolution for the cyclical failures of Chinese modernity. They argue that the quest for progress has always followed the same pattern: popular desire for political change leads to a crisis of legitimacy among power-holders,

---

5. Chamberlain, "On the Search for Civil Society in China," 204.

6. Philip C. Huang, "'Public Sphere'/'Civil Society' in China?: The Third Realm between State and Society," 225.

7. See, for example, Edward X. Gu, "Cultural Intellectuals and the Politics of the Cultural Public Space in Communist China (1979-1989): A Case Study of Three Intellectual Groups," 427.

8. Shu-Yun Ma, "The Chinese Discourse on Civil Society," 180-93.

which in its turn triggers social chaos; and as a response to this chaos, the political structure typically avails itself of military power to restore its mandate, thus causing any political transformation to be stillborn. The key problem here, according to Deng and Jing, is a cognitive one: the perennial insistence of Chinese intellectuals on political authority as the departure point for change. Civil society, as these two authors imagine it, is "a binary concept which fuses state and society," and, as such, replaces this top-to-bottom epistemology with a more dynamic, interactive process in which the two can meet in the middle. More precisely, Deng and Jing foresee a model of cooperation in which the state steadily withdraws from socio-economic domains outside its proper purview, while citizens capitalize on this concessionary mood to push for the creation of a civil society from the bottom up. And as these citizens gradually enter the public sphere and begin to shape public policy, they can forge positive relationships with the state which have the potential to break the impasse of China's modern history and create a context for peaceful, organic change.

Deng Zhenglai and Jing Yuejin. "Jian'gou Zhongguo de shemin shehui." In Deng Zhenglai, *Guojia yu shehui: Zhongguo shimin shehui yanjiu*. Chengdu: Sichuan renmin chubanshe, 1997, 1-8.

Further Reading

Brook, Timothy, and B. Michael Frolic. "The Ambiguous Challenge of Civil Society." In Timothy Brook and B. Michael Frolic, eds. *Civil Society in China*. Armonk, New York: M. E. Sharpe, 1997.

Chamberlain, Heath B. "On the Search for Civil Society in China." *Modern China* 19/2 (1993), 199-215.

Gold, Thomas. "Party-State Versus Society in China." In Joyce K. Kallgren, ed. *Building a Nation-State: China after Forty Years*, 125-151. Berkeley: University of California at Berkeley, Centre for Chinese Studies, 1990.

———. "The Resurgence of Civil Society in China." *Journal of Democracy* 1/1 (1990), 18-31.

Gu, Edward X. "Cultural Intellectuals and the Politics of the Cultural Public Space in Communist China (1979-1989): A Case Study of Three Intellectual Groups." *Journal of Asian Studies* 58/2 (1999), 389-431.

Huang, Philip C. "'Public Sphere'/'Civil Society' in China?: The Third Realm between State and Society." *Modern China* 19/2 (1993), 216-40.

Ma, Shu-Yun. "The Chinese Discourse on Civil Society." *The China Quarterly* 137 (1994), 180-93.

Madsen, Richard. "The Public Sphere, Civil Society and Moral Community: A Research Agenda for Contemporary China Studies."

Modern China 19/2 (1993), 183-98.

Pye, Lucian. "China: Erratic State, Frustrated Society." *Foreign Affairs* 69/4 (1990), 56-74.

————. "The State and the Individual: An Overview." *China Quarterly* 127 (1991), 443-66.

Rankin, Mary B. "Some Observations on a Chinese Public Sphere." *Modern China* 19/2 (1993), 158-82.

Rowe, William T. "The Public Sphere in Modern China." *Modern China*, 16/3 (1990), 309-329.

Strand, David. "Protest in Beijing: Civil Society and Public Sphere in China." *Problems of Communism* 39/3 (1990), 1-19.

Sullivan, Lawrence R. "The Emergence of Civil Society in China, Spring 1989." In Tony Saich, ed. *The Chinese People's Movement: Perspectives on Spring 1989*, 126-44. Armonk: M. E. Sharpe, 1990.

Wakeman, Frederic. "The Civil Society and Public Sphere Debate: Western Reflections on Chinese Political Culture." *Modern China* 19/2 (1993), 108-38.

建构中国的市民社会

一、引言

1.1　自鸦片战争始，中国现代化便始终面临着一个严峻的结构性挑战：作为现代化的迟发型国家，中国必须作出相当幅度的政治和社会结构调整，以容纳和推进现代化的发展。在这一结构调整过程中，需要解决的核心问题被认为是如何改造传统的政治结构和权威形态，使其在新的基础上重新<u>获致合法性</u>和社会支持力量，并转换成具有现代化<u>导向</u>的政治核心。

1.2　这一挑战构成了中国现代化的两难困境。于学理层面上讲，上述转型过程的顺利进行，必须满足两个基本条件：一方面要避免基于原有结构的政府权威在变革中过度<u>流失</u>，从而保证一定的社会秩序和政府动员社会资源的能力，避免因政治危机而引起的社会失序和动乱，为推进现代化提供必要的政治社会条件；另一方面，为了保证这种威权真正具有＂现代化导向＂，必须防止转型中的政府权威因其不具外部社会制约或因社会失序而出现的向传统＂回归＂。

回顾历史，我们不无遗憾地发现，这两个必须满足的基本条件却构成了中国现代化过程中<u>相倚</u>的两极：政治变革导致权威的合法性危机，进而引起社会结构的解体、普遍的失范、甚或国家的分裂；作为对这种失序状态的响应和补救，政治结构往往向传统回归，借助军事力量并利用原有的或改造过的象征性符号系统来解决合法性危机的问题，这又使政治结构转型<u>胎死腹中</u>。

1949 年以后，在高度政治<u>集权</u>和计划经济的框架中，历史上出现的 两极徘徊衍变为＂<u>一放就乱，一乱就统，一统就死</u>＂（中央与地方关系方

获致	huòzhì	achieve
合法性	héfǎxìng	legitimacy
导向	dǎoxiàng	orientation
流失	liúshī	be eroded
相倚	xiāngyǐ	mutually dependent
胎死腹中	tāisǐfùzhōng	be aborted
集权	jíquán	centralization of state power
一放就乱，一乱就统 一统就死	yí fàng jiù luàn, yí luàn jiù tǒng, yì tǒng jiù sǐ	relax control and chaos follows but crack down and everything stagnates

152

面），以及 " 精简－膨胀－再精简－再膨胀 "（政府机构改革方面）的恶性循环。

1.3 1978 年改革开放以来，围绕中国现代化道路的诸种争论和理论主张，尤其是关于政治体制改革和经济体制改革关系的讨论，可以说是国人在新的历史条件下，试图对这一历史性挑战寻求一个时下的解决方式的尝试。

新权威主义对改革中出现的社会失序现象充满忧虑，故其强调权威的重要性，主张在旧体制向现代商品经济和民主政治发展的过程中，需要强有力的具有现代化导向的政治权威，以此做为社会整合和保证秩序的工具，为商品经济的发展提供良好的社会政治环境和条件。在此基础上发展起来的新保守主义（从某种程度上讲，其性质与新权威主义有所区别）则更为明确地主张从传统文化中去寻找支撑这种权威的社会和文化资源。

作为对立面的民主先导论则强调原有政治集权体制对中国现代化过程的障碍作用，它主张中国的改革必须以政治体制改革为先导，认定没有民主政治的推进和实现，就不可能有中国经济的现代化。

1.4 我们的兴趣和关注的焦点毋宁是：二十世纪九十年代的今天，我们究竟应当以怎样的认知方式来看待中国现代化的这一两难症结？ 作为对中国现代化问题持严肃且理性态度的知识分子，我们认为，要摆脱中国现代化过程中的两难境地，首先必须从认识上实现一种思维的转向，不能像以往的论者那样，把目光的聚焦点只放在政治权威的转型上，因为中国现代化两难症结真正的和根本的要害，在于国家与社会两者之间没有形成适宜于现代化发展的良性解构，确切地说，在于社会一直没有形成独立的、自治的结构性领域。无论是国家权力的过度集中，还是政治权威急剧流

精简	jīngjiǎn	retrench
主张	zhǔzhāng	position; proposition; stand
新权威主义	xīnquánwēizhǔyì	neo-authoritarianism
新保守主义	xīnbǎoshǒuzhǔyì	neo-conservatism
民主先导论	mínzhǔ xiāndǎolùn	the theory of democracy first
症结	zhèngjié	the crux (of the problem)
境地	jìngdì	plight; condition
聚焦点	jùjiāodiǎn	focal point; central issue
要害	yàohài	crucial point
急剧	jíjù	suddenly; sharply

失，除了本身（内部结构）的原因外，无不与国家和社会的关系（外部结构）密切相关，因此，在现代化基本问题的认定上，必须用＂国家与社会的二元观＂替代＂权威本位（转型）观＂。

中国现代化若要摆脱历史的恶性循环，走出两难困境，就必须在理论上和实践上回答国家与社会的关系问题。这是一个摆在我们面前的、无可回避的艰巨课题。

1.5　为了引起理论界对这一重大问题的思考，为了有利于实践中解决好国家与社会的关系问题，根据中国改革开放的现实和历史的经验教训，我们在认真的思考和反思后，认为有必要建立中国市民社会的理论。我们认为：

作为中国现代化过程的一种战略性思考，这一理论的根本目标在于：从自下而上的角度，致力于营建健康的中国市民社会。透过中国市民社会的建构，逐渐确立国家与市民社会的二元结构，并在此基础上形成一种良性的互动关系，惟其如此，才能避免历史上多次出现的两极摆动，推进中国的经济体制和政治体制改革，最终实现中国的现代化。

建构中国市民社会的主要作用表现在以下几个方面：

在计划经济体制解体亦即国家放弃用行政手段组织经济活动的过程中，市民社会能积极主动地承担起培育市场和发展商品经济的历史任务，并在这一过程中造就一大批独立自主的从事商品经济活动的市场主体。换言之，在国家部分退出社会经济领域以后，市民社会一方面能防止＂空位＂的发生，在另一方面则为自身的营造打下经济基础。

在中国从传统社会向现代社会转型期间需要集中权威的同时，作为一种独立自主的力量，市民社会能够成为遏制这种权威向专制退回的＂最后堡垒＂；另外，市民社会在日常生活中具有抑制国家权力过分胀的作用。

在中国改革开放必然向政治领域纵深发展的过程中，市民社会通过发

二元观	èryuánguān	binary concept
艰巨	jiānjù	formidable; arduous
遏制	èzhì	contain; restrain
专制	zhuānzhì	autocracy
堡垒	bǎolěi	fortress; rampart of defense
纵深	zòngshēn	in depth and in breadth

展市场经济和培育多元自治的结社组织，能够为实现民主政治创设社会条件。

市民社会内部发展起来的契约性规则、自治能力和利益格局是社会稳定的保险机制和控制机制。由于社会生活和经济生活的非政治化，政治上的变动对社会其它部分生的连带反应大大减弱。同时，社会内部利益格局的多元化，也会使社会整体不稳定的可能性大大降低。

建构中国市民社会的具体策略是：采取理性的渐进的分两步走的办法，亦即我们所主张的＂两个阶段发展论＂。第一阶段为形成阶段，其间由国家和市民社会成员共举：国家在从上至下策动进一步改革的同时，加速变更政府职能，主动地、逐 渐地撤出不应干涉的社会经济领域；社会成员则充分利用改革的有利条件和契机，有意识地、理性地由下至上推动市民社会的营建。这一阶段的活动主要集中和反映在经济领域。第二阶段为成熟阶段，其间社会成员在继续发展和完善自身的同时，逐渐进入＂公域＂，参与和影响国家的决策,并与国家形成良性的互动系。

1.6　迄今，知识界和理论界对中国现代化的认知和研究主要着眼于自上而下的过程。新权威主义与民主先导论对中国现代化道路的选择虽各不相同，但是它们对这一问题的思考方向却是相同的，即在改革的思路上都沿循自上而下的理论走向。考虑到中国社会的历史特点及现代化激活的特殊方式，这种自上而下的路向是可以理解的。但是必须指出，如果说以往对中国现代化的研究始终局限于自上而下的路径乃是一种遗憾的话，那么在改革开放生机勃勃的今天，我们依旧囿于这一思维定式，对自下而上

结社	jiéshè	(to form an) association
契约性规则	qìyuēxìng guīzé	contractual rules
两个阶段发展论	liǎnggè jiēduàn fāzhǎnlùn	theory of two stages of development
策动	cèdòng	instigate
职能	zhínéng	function
撤出	chèchū	withdraw from
契机	qìjī	juncture; turning point
激活	jīhuó	activate
生机勃勃	shēngjībóbó	full of vitality
囿于	yòuyú	be constrained by

地推动现代化过程的社会劳动者行动的意义和作用缺乏关照，就不仅只是一种遗憾，而是还有一种大失误。

建构中国的市民社会还应当消除几种观念上的误识，一种是认为市民社会在性质上是资产阶级的，因此倡导市民社会就是主张和维护资产阶级的利益，甚至是鼓吹资本主义；这种认识的失误之处在于把市民社会简单地等同于资产阶级。事实上，资产阶级的兴起只是西方市民社会的一种类型。从历史发展角度看，市民社会作为近现代国家的对应物，具有普遍的特性，中国亦不例外。另一种误识认为，强调市民社会的独立性和自治性，就是不要国家，主张无政府主义。这种认识混淆了国家干预的必要性和它的合理界限。提出市民社会的独立性和自治性并不是否定国家干预的必要性，而是力图对国家的干预划出一定的界限。最后，还有一种错误观念，认为市民社会是对抗甚或反抗国家的；这种观念源于中国传统文化中的民反官思维模式。然而如上所述，市民社会具有抑制国家权力过度膨胀的作用，但这种作用的目的并不是反抗国家，而是在国家与市民社会的二元结构中保持必要的平衡。上述种种认识上的误导，都会从不同的方面危及和影响市民社会的健康发展，故应予以必要的警戒。

二、何谓中国的市民社会

2.1 近代西方市民社会的形成乃是与西方 " 近代国家 " 或所谓 " 民族国家 " 的出现密切相关联的；从人类社会发展的复杂性和多样性角度看，市民社会在不同的历史阶段以及不同的文化背景和国别，其涵义、构成、作用和性质也会有所不同。市民社会绝对不是一种自然的和不变的东西，

倡导	chàngdǎo	propose; initiate
对应物	duìyìngwù	a homologous entity
无政府主义	wúzhèngfǔzhǔyì	anarchism
界限	jièxiàn	boundary; limits; demarcation line
民反官	mín fǎn guān	the people against the government
误导	wùdǎo	misconception
危及	wēijí	endanger
涵义	hányì	meaning; connotation

而是一种历史现象；不是一致的共同模式，而是具有特质的社会现象。因此，我们应将市民社会放到特定的历史环境中加以考察。另一方面，市民社会又具有众多的共同特性，如以市场经济为基础，以契约性关系为<u>中轴</u>，以尊重和保护社会成员的基本权利为前提等等。因此，全面把握市民社会的本质，必须将它的普遍性质和特殊型态，<u>有机</u>地结合起来。

2.2 根据中国历史的背景和当下的现实，我们认为，中国的市民社会乃是指社会成员按照契约性规则，以<u>自愿</u>为前提和以自治为基础进行经济活动、社会活动的私域，以及进行<u>议政参政</u>活动的非官方公域。它的具体内涵是：

中国市民社会是由独立自主的个人、群体、社团和<u>利益集团</u>构成的，其间不包括<u>履行</u>政府职能、具有＂国家政治人＂身份公职人员、<u>执政党</u>组织、军人和警察，也不包括<u>自给自足</u>、完全依附于土地的纯粹农民。在中国市民社会中,企业家阶层与知识分子是<u>中坚</u>力量,其原因是：企业家是营建、发展和完善市场经济的主要力量；企业家在市场交易活动中依契约规则本能地维护自利的同时能平等地对待他利，从而是平等契约精神的<u>发扬光大</u>者；企业家在市场经济活动中深刻地<u>体认</u>到负面自由（免受外部力量侵犯和免遭陷入社会混乱和失序的<u>侵扰</u>）的重要意义，从而是稳定秩序和维护市民社会的主导力量；企业家握有相当的财力和物力，是国家税收的主要承担者，从而是能影响国家有关决策的一方利益者；企业家所拥有的经济 实力和地位，使他们在组织和资助各种群体、社团和利益集团的活动

中轴	zhōngzhóu	axis
有机	yǒujī	organic
自愿	zìyuàn	act voluntarily
议政参政	yìzhèng cānzhèng	discuss and take part in affairs of government
利益集团	lìyì jítuán	interest groups
履行	lǚxíng	perform; carry out
执政党	zhízhèngdǎng	ruling party
自给自足	zìjǐzìzú	self-sufficient
中坚	zhōngjiān	nucleus; hard core; backbone
发扬光大	fāyángguāngdà	carry forward; enhance
体认	tǐrèn	perceive intuitively
侵扰	qīnrǎo	invade and harass

中，起着主导者的作用，从而是组织市民社会的领导力量。中国的知识分子，一般都具有现代意识和现代化知识；由于社会结构的分化，一部分知识分子转换角色，积极投身于企业家行列，成为引导经济健康发展的中坚力量；而未投入经济活动领域的知识分子，在教育、<u>启蒙</u>、文化建设、研究、理论指导等方面起着不可替代的作用，他们是推进和指导市民社会健康发展的知识源泉和<u>动力源泉</u>。

应当指出的是，虽然中国农民从整体上说还没有完全脱离土地，但是中国改革开放带来的<u>乡镇</u>企业繁荣，培育出了一大批虽具农民身份乡镇企业家和乡镇企业工人。随着农村商品经济的发展，他们将成为中国市民社会中一支不可或缺的力量。

中国市民社会的内在联系既不是传统的血缘亲情关系，也不是<u>垂直指令性</u>的行政关系，而是内生于市场交易活动的契约性关系。这就是说，市民社会内部每一方在为获取他方所有而自己又需要的一部分<u>权益</u>的同时，必须让渡自己的部分权益；换言之，在获致这一部分权益的同时，也就承诺了对这部分权益所必须履行的义务。这种契约性关系的确立，首先是对市民社会中各个成员的基本人权和产权的肯定。因为人们在<u>缔结</u>契约或与他人发生契约性关系之前，都必须被假定已具有某些事前已拥有的权利和资源，否则从道德上讲，他们不具有理由也不可能把一些权益让渡给他人。再者，这种契约性规则一旦得以确立，它便对市民社会中每个成员的行为选择构成了外在的约束空间；每一个受制于这种契约性关系的成员，可以在<u>遵奉</u>这种规则的范围内理性地竞取自己的利益，并在自己的生活范围内充分自主和独立。

(Cont.)

启蒙	qǐméng	enlightenment; instruct the young or ignorant
动力	dònglì	motive force; dynamic power
源泉	yuánquán	source; fountainhead
乡镇	xiāng-zhèn	villages and towns
垂直	chuízhí	vertical
指令性	zhǐlìngxìng	directive; commanding
权益	quányì	rights and interests
缔结	dìjié	establish
遵奉	zūnfèng	obey; revere

12. THE NEW LEFT AND THE CRITIQUE OF CONSUMERISM

The Invisible Politics of Mass Culture
Dai Jinhua

Dai Jinhua 戴锦华 (1959-) is a professor at Peking University, and one of China's leading cultural theorists. Her scholarship traverses film studies, feminist Marxism, and the workings of mass culture, and her writings have won her audiences both at home and in the international academic community. In many ways, Dai is an old-school public intellectual, a figure who—in Richard Posner's words—draws on his or her scholarly resources to address "a broad though educated public on issues with a political or ideological dimension."[1] In particular, Dai frequently makes the "New Left" (新左派 Xin Zuopai) and its politics her platform for incisive critiques of China's swelling middle classes and their steadily deflating social conscience.

The "New Left" or the "New Left Wing" (新左翼 Xin Zuoyi) is a loose coalition of Neo-Marxist thought which emerged in the mid-1990s as the idealism of Tiananmen died a death, and a backlash against the democracy movement and its "excesses" began to gather force. In addition to Dai Jinhua, key figures in this coalition include Wang Hui 汪晖, Cui Zhiyuan 崔之元, Gan Yang 甘阳, and Liu Kang 刘康. As a broad group, these intellectuals pit themselves against the "telos of progress" Western-style, and they try instead to recover the lost purity of the socialist impulse. As Kalpana Misra puts it, they are profoundly troubled by such problems as "the increasing gap between socialist norms and official policies, the emergence of class stratification, erosion of Communist values, [and] the integration of China into the global capitalist system."[2] Already suspicious of both Western ideologies and the capitalist machine, the New Leftists hardened their stance in the late 1990s as NATO bombed the Chinese embassy in Belgrade and the Asian financial crisis took hold.

The natural antagonists of the New Left on the Chinese politico-intellectual scene throughout this period have been the liberals, prominent among whom are Zhu Xueqin 朱学勤, He Qinglian 何清涟, and Qin Hui 秦晖. They are also very fretful about the problems which developmentalism has brought in its train, but are more inclined to view these as the inevitable

---

1. Richard Posner, *Public Intellectuals. A Study of Decline* (Cambridge: Harvard University Press, 2002), 170.
2. Kalpana Misra, "Neo-Left and Neo-Right in Post-Tiananmen China," 718, n1.

teething troubles of a nation reborn after years of revolution than as signs that China should turn away from the free market. If anything, in fact, they claim that China has not changed enough, and that only when a more liberal ethos is embraced across the board will wealth multiply more equitably, socio-economic tensions ease, and the nation live up to its promise. For the New Leftists, however, this liberal trust in the market is utopian—and glibly so—in its hope that prosperity for all will issue forth from full-blown liberalization. A further bugbear is what New Leftists see as the reluctance of many liberals to face up to the intimate ways in which politics and the economy are yoked together. This reluctance, according to the New Left, also makes the liberals complicit in the general depoliticization of culture and its steady surrender to the demands of the market. The liberals, for their part, have retaliated by claiming that the New Left's concern with class as a category of analysis makes it the handmaiden of hardline Party ideology. The two groups have debated fiercely with each other in recent years, producing polemics and counter-polemics which suggest a rigid polarization of opinion.

It would, however, be a mistake to view the New Leftist manifesto as either consistent or free of contradiction. Even the term "New Left" has failed to muster a consensus around it, with Wang Hui arguing that the Western connotations of this title are ill-suited to a movement which roots itself so adamantly in Chinese reality.[3] Yet at the same time, this desire for distance from the West coexists with the simple fact that some of the movement's major spokespeople are themselves Western-educated intellectuals, several of whom continue to work in Western academic institutions and to publish in English as much as they do in Chinese. More importantly, the sheer diversity of their work reveals that New Leftism is a fluid position which shares space with many other zones in the Chinese ideological field. In this sense, to define New Leftism in prescriptive terms is to impose cohesiveness of ideology and intent over a body of opinion which is far from unified. That said, most commentators associated with the New Leftist project do share a nexus of core concerns. All interrogate the validity of Western theory for China, all are dedicated to probing the legacy of Chinese communism, and all pursue justice for those left behind by breakneck economic growth.

First of all, the attentions of New Leftists are focused in large part "on a quest for Chinese solutions to the problems encountered in the reform process."[4] At base, this quest centers on a kind of "hermeneutics of suspicion," in which the origins and motives of Western attempts to theorize China and the world are subjected to sustained postmodern skepticism. This is not to say that Occidental ideas are eschewed altogether.

---

3. Wang Hui, "The New Criticism," in Wang Chaohua, ed., *One China, Many Paths*, 62.
4. Kalpana Misra, "Neo-Left and Neo-Right," 731.

On the contrary, their wide reading in Western thought has led many New Leftists to approach China theoretically, and they are well versed in the writings of Michel Foucault, Louis Althusser, Antonio Gramsci, and Fredric Jameson. In particular, many were "exposed to a neo-Marxist line of contemporary Western theory which had been profoundly influenced by Maoism and Mao's Cultural Revolution theory."[5] Several New Leftists have gone on to harness this Marxist deconstructionist thought to question the relevance of Enlightenment modernity for China, and to reclaim Chinese reality for Chinese thinkers and their homegrown solutions.

New Leftists are equally committed to revisiting history, and no period preoccupies them more than China's revolutionary past. For many of these thinkers, the revolution has been too hastily besmirched in the years since Mao's death, and it now deserves rehabilitation as a unique time of meaning, faith, and rebirth. In particular, some New Leftist thinkers feel a certain nostalgia for mass movements, and the transformative effects they can have on society. Inevitably, the period most ripe for their revisionist eye is the Cultural Revolution. Cui Zhiyuan, for one, has argued for the "reasonable elements" within radical Maoism, one of which might well be to "repeat the Cultural Revolution every seven to eight years."[6] Less controversially, Cui also claims that the Cultural Revolution brought not just mob rule and kangaroo courts, but also the beginnings of reform—indeed, much of the economic success of the 1980s and beyond is arguably attributable to policies implemented during those ten turbulent years. Dai Jinhua also inclines towards this view. As Jing Wang and Tani Barlow have observed, she "stresses critical self-reflection and warns against the all-out negation of the immediate historical past, hinting at the huge price that the modern Chinese have paid for the radical breaks advocated by first the May Fourth intellectuals, later, Maoists and now, anti-Maoists."[7]

Just as crucial is the New Leftist call for social justice and its critique of the disparities which lie all too visibly beneath the self-congratulatory rhetoric of the reform period. Many New Leftists fear that China is in the grip of "closet rightists" whose aim is to convert political power into personal wealth by fostering crony capitalism between Party leaders and business executives. The result is desperate inequity, with the eastern seaboard growing fat on globalization while millions of Chinese elsewhere are bled dry as they struggle to compete in this hard new market reality. Here again, New Leftists have recourse to the revolutionary past, arguing that a core facet of Maoism was its desire for a modernity which rejected the dog-eat-dog competitiveness of Western capitalism. More pragmatically, they make the case that regional disparity poses huge risks

5. Guo Jian, "Resisting Modernity in Contemporary China," 368.
6. Quoted in Guo Jian, "Resisting Modernity in Contemporary China," 368.
7. Jing Wang and Tani E. Barlow, "Introduction," in Dai Jinhua, *Cinema and Desire: Feminist Marxism and Cultural Politics in the Work of Dai Jinhua*, 5.

for the preservation of order, as wage gaps and unemployment squeeze governmental resources. Their solution is for the state to rein the market in more closely, armed with what Ban Wang calls "a public policy for the common good and protectionist measures to shore up the national economy."[8]

The piece by Dai Jinhua excerpted here, "The Invisible Politics of Mass Culture" (大众文化的隐形政治学 Dazhong wenhua de yinxing zhengzhixue) slots New Leftist thinking into an intriguingly culturalist frame. The square or plaza (广场 guangchang) is Dai's central metaphor, and she analyzes how public space in China has switched its identity from religiously political to ruthlessly commercial in recent years. Tiananmen Square, once the holiest of Chinese squares, is at the core of her argument, and its 1989 watershed marks the beginning of this semantic shift. The fact that China's reforms have resulted in the term *guangchang* being emptied of its revolutionary content betrays, according to Dai, a steady loss of social welfare, social equality, and social conscience. As even Mao and the revolution have become subject to gross commodification, it is time for intellectuals to speak up and bring politics back into national life. The onus falls on them to impugn the devastating fall-out of change, and to petition the state to ensure that women, the unemployed, the young, the old, and the sick find proper provision in a society where guaranteed employment, social services, and health care are now a thing of the past.

Dai Jinhua. "Dazhong wenhua de yinxing zhengzhi xue." *Tianya* 2 (1999), 32-37.

Further Reading

Dai Jinhua. *Cinema and Desire: Feminist Marxism and Cultural Politics in the Work of Dai Jinhua*, ed. Jing Wang and Tani E. Barlow. London: Verso, 2002.

Davies, Gloria, ed. *Voicing Concern: Contemporary Chinese Critical Inquiry*. Lanham: Rowman and Littlefield, 2001.

Dirlik, Arif. "China's Critical Intelligentsia." *New Left Review* 28 (July-August 2004), 130-38.

Guo Jian. "Resisting Modernity in Contemporary China: The Cultural Revolution and Postmodernism." *Modern China* 25/3 (1999), 343-76.

Misra, Kalpana. "Neo-Left and Neo-Right in Post-Tiananmen China." *Asian Survey* 43/5 (2003), 717-44.

Wang, Ban. Review of *One China, Many Paths* by Chaohua Wang,

---

8. Ban Wang, review of *One China, Many Paths* by Chaohua Wang, *Modern Chinese Literature and Culture* Resource Center Publications.

Modern Chinese Literature and Culture Resource Center Publications, stable url: http://mclc.osu.edu/rc/pubs/reviews/wang2.htm.

Wang, Chaohua, ed. *One China, Many Paths*. London and New York: Verso, 2003.

Wang Hui. "The Historical Origin of Chinese 'Neoliberalism.' Another Discussion on the Ideological Situation in Contemporary Mainland China and the Issue of Modernity." *Chinese Economy* 36/4 (July-August 2003), 3-42.

———. "Fire at the Castle Gate." *New Left Review* 6 (November–December 2000), 69-99.

Xu Youyu. "The Debates between Liberalism and the New Left in China since the 1990s." *Contemporary Chinese Thought* 34/3 (2003), 6-17.

Ye Xiaoqing. "In Search of a 'Third Way': a Conversation Regarding 'Liberalism' and the 'New Left Wing'." In Gloria Davies, ed. *Voicing Concern: Contemporary Chinese Critical Inquiry*, 185-98. Lanham: Rowman and Littlefield, 2001.

大众文化的隐形政治学

广场-市场

在九十年代中国的文化风景线上，一个有趣的<u>译名</u>，或许可以成为解读这一时代的<u>索引</u>之一。随着诸多现代、后现代风格的摩天大楼于中国都市<u>拔地而起</u>，不断突破和改写着城市的天际线；诸多的大型商城、购物中心、专卖店、连锁店、<u>仓储</u>式商场，以及这些新的建筑群所终日吞吐的人流，无疑成了这一风景线上最引人注目的段落。此间，Plaza--这类集商城、超级市场、餐厅、连锁快餐店、健身馆、办公楼（今日之所谓"<u>写字楼</u>"）、宾馆、商务中心于一体的巨型建筑，或许提供了中国大都市国际化、或曰全球化的最佳例证。如何以自己民族的语言命名这类新的空间，或许是每一个<u>后发现代化国家</u>诸多问题背后的<u>细枝末节</u>之一。于是，在1995-1996年前后，这类空间在借用人们熟悉的称谓"大厦"、"中心"之后，获得了一个"新"的译名：Plaza（广场）。一时间，烟尘四起的建筑工地围墙上，"广场"的字样随处可见。作为一种中国特色，一如你会在一个偏远的县城中遇到一个被称为"中国大饭店"的小餐馆；继Plaza之为"广场"之后，形形色色的大型或中型专卖店，亦开始称"广场"：诸如"电器广场"或"时装广场"。而在1993年前后，爆炸式地出现的数量浩繁的报纸周末版和消闲、娱乐型报刊，则同样以"广场"来命名种种时尚<u>栏目</u>。

来自西班牙语的Plaza，意为被重要建筑所环绕的圆形广场。在资本主义文明兴起的欧洲现代都市中，Plaza从一开始，便不仅有着政治、文化中心的功能，而且<u>充当</u>着城市的商业中心。而将巨型商城称为Plaza（广场），却有着欧洲-美国-亚洲发达国家、地区(对我们说来，最重要的是香港)的语词旅行脉络。将类似建筑直译为广场，就所谓规范汉语而言，并非

译名	yìmíng	translated term; transliteration
索引	suǒyǐn	index
拔地而起	bádì'érqǐ	rise suddenly from the ground
仓储	cāngchǔ	keep in storage
写字楼	xiězìlóu	office building
后发现代化国家	hòufā xiàndàihuà guójiā	later modernizing state
细枝末节	xìzhīmòjié	minor details; non-essentials
栏目	lánmù	title of a column
充当	chōngdāng	serve as; act as

一个恰当的意译。但一如当代中国、乃至整个现代中国的文化史上的诸多例证，一个新的名称总是携带着新的希望，新的兴奋甚或狂喜。于是"丰联广场"便成了一个远比"燕莎购物中心"更诱人的称谓。

"广场"在现代中国史上，始终不是一个普通的名词。我们或许可以说，作为中国知识分子记忆清单的必然组成部分，"广场"不仅指涉着一个现代空间。爆发于天安门广场的五四运动成了中国现代史（当然更是中国现代文化史）的开端。伴随着社会主义中国的建立，天安门广场成了开国大典、阅兵式之所在，因而成了新中国及社会主义政权的象征，亦指称着人民：消融了阶级和个体差异的巨大的群体。而1966-1967年间，毛泽东八次接见红卫兵，则在广场--天安门广场这一特定的空间上，添加了集权与革命、膜拜与狂欢、极端权力与秩序的坍塌、青年学生的激情与对过剩权力的分享的冲突意义。爆发于1976年的天安门广场上的"四·五运动"—事实上成了结束"文革"及"四人帮"政权的先导，但仍在搬演社会主义的经典样式：群众运动（以及不无荒诞的"诗歌运动"）恢复了现代社会的广场和平示威的形式。

如果说，法国大革命为现代法国提供了自己的革命模式：城市起义、街垒战、人民临时政权；那么，五四运动则提供了现代中国的革命方式：以青年学生为先导，以广场运动为高潮，并以最终引发全社会、尤其是上海工人的参与而改写并载入历史。因此，广场，作为中国文化语境中特定的能指，联系着不同历史阶段中的"革命"与政治的记忆；其自身便是"中国版"的现代性话语的重要组成部分，并且记录着中国现代化进程的特

丰联广场	Fēnglián Guǎngchǎng	Beijing's Fenglian Plaza
燕莎购物中心	Yānshā Gòuwù Zhōngxīn	Beijing's Yansha Mall
清单	qīngdān	detailed list; inventory
开国大典	kāiguó dàdiǎn	inauguration; foundation ceremony for a state
阅兵式	yuèbīngshì	parade; military review
集权	jíquán	dictatorship; totalitarianism
膜拜	móbài	prostrate oneself in worship
坍塌	tāntā	collapse
荒诞	huāngdàn	absurd; ridiculous
街垒战	jiēlěizhàn	street fighting
能指	néngzhǐ	signifier

殊实践。广场，在中国几乎是一个专有名词，特指着具有神圣感的天安门广场，当代中国的政治中心；于是，当Plaza被称之为"广场"的时候，便不仅是某种时髦的称谓，而且在有意无意间显现了九十年代中国一种特定的意识形态症候与其实践内容。

挪用与遮蔽

或许可以说，在当代中国文化，尤其是新时期文化中，存在着某种"广场情结"。因此针对着这一多重编码的形象，类似的僭越与亵渎在八十年代后期已悄然开始。在1987-1988年间，广场与社会主义革命时代神圣的禁忌便开始成为游戏和调侃的对象。1987年著名的第五代导演田壮壮成功的商业电影《摇滚青年》中，出现了天安门红墙下的摇滚场景。在1988年（所谓"电影王朔年"）四部改编自王朔小说的影片便有两部出现了主人公在天安门广场上恶作剧的插曲。1989年中央电视台的元旦联欢晚会上，相声演员姜昆用一个关于"天安门广场改成农贸市场"的"谣言"，令观众大为开心；在一段时间之内这一说法几乎被视为有趣的社会和政治预言。

如果说，八、九十年代之交的毛泽东热、"文革"热、政治怀旧潮，在对昔日禁忌、神圣、意识形态的消费中，构成了复杂的政治情绪的发露；那么，在九十年代前半期，它在消费和消解昔日意识形态的同时，成功地充当着一架特殊的文化浮桥，将政治禁忌与创伤记忆转换为一种新的

挪用	nuóyòng	appropriation
编码	biānmǎ	code
僭越	jiànyuè	transgression
亵渎	xièdú	profanity; blasphemy
调侃	tiáokǎn	ridicule; mock
田壮壮	Tián Zhuàngzhuàng	(1952-) fifth generation filmmaker
王朔	Wáng Shuò	(1958-) controversial contemporary novelist
插曲	chāqǔ	episode; theatrical interlude; songs in a film or play
联欢晚会	liánhuānwǎnhuì	a television gala show
相声	xiàngsheng	comic dialogue; cross-talk
姜昆	Jiāng Kūn	(1950-) leading performer of *xiangsheng*
浮桥	fúqiáo	floating bridge

文化时尚。因此，Plaza--商城被名之为"广场"，便不仅是一种政治性的僭越，而且更接近于一次<u>置换</u>与挪用。我们知道，一次不"恰当"的挪用，固然包含着对被挪用者的<u>冒犯</u>与僭越；但它同时可能成为对挪用对象的<u>借重</u>与仿同。如果说，在社会主义中国的历史上，天安门广场曾在新的"中国中心"想象里，被指认为"世界革命的中心"，"红色的心脏"；那么，高速公路、连锁店、摩天大楼、大型商城、<u>奢华</u>消费的人流则以一幅典型的世界无名大都市的图画，成就着全球一体化的景观，成就着所谓"后工业社会"特有的"高速公路两侧的快餐店风景"。七、八十年代之交，中国经历着再一次的"遭遇世界"。这一<u>悲喜剧式</u>的遭遇，一度有力地碎裂了很多人心目中中国作为世界革命中心的想象。于是，作为一次新的合法化论证，在对毛泽东"第三世界/发展中国家"的论述的有效挪用中，中国似乎开始接受自己在（西方中心的）世界历史中"滞后的现实"，开始承认置身于（西方中心的）世界边缘位置。整个八十年代，最为有效而有力的主流意识形态表述，是官方与精英知识分子达成的深刻共识，即"改革开放"，"走向世界"，"历史进步战胜历史循环"，"现代文明战胜东方<u>愚昧</u>"，"朝向蔚蓝色文明"，"地球村与中国的<u>球籍</u>问题"。类似的主流意识形态话语，无疑将中国对自身边缘位置的接受，定义为朝向世界中心、突破中心并终有一天<u>取而代之</u>的伟大进军。尽管此间经历了八十年代终结处的风波，但以1992年邓小平<u>南巡</u>讲话为转折，社会主义市场经济或曰全球化、商业化的过程，陡然由<u>潜流</u>奔涌而出。中国社会一夜间再度由沉寂而<u>市声鼎沸</u>，似乎成为"历史规律"不可抗拒的明证。于是，以Plaza作为昔日之广场的替代物，于是似 乎成了一个

置换	zhìhuàn	displacement
冒犯	màofàn	offense; affront
借重	jièzhòng	enlist the help of
奢华	shēhuá	extravagant
悲喜剧式	bēixǐjùshì	tragicomic
愚昧	yúmèi	ignorance
球籍	qiújí	membership in the community of nations
取而代之	qǔ'érdàizhī	replace; supersede
南巡	nánxún	Deng Xiaoping's tour of the South in 1992
潜流	qiánliú	undercurrent
市声鼎沸	shìshēng dǐngfèi	haggling voices of the market

"恰如其分"的逻辑结果。

　　从某种意义上说，对"广场"这一特定能指的挪用，是一次遮蔽中的暴露；它似乎在明确地告知一个革命时代的过去，一个消费时代的降临。这里有两个颇为趣的例证。1996年，作为一次经典的政治教育活动，举办了大型图片和实物展览：《红岩》。展览所呈现的本是现代中国史上黑暗而酷烈的一幕：它揭露了在"中美合作所"--美国CIA与国民党当局的情报机构辖下的两所监禁政治犯的秘密监狱—"白公馆"和"渣滓洞"中的暴行，即共产党人及形形色色政治异见者，当年被施以酷刑，最终在1949年前被集体灭绝。六十年代，亲历者的回忆录《在烈火中永生》、借此创作的著名长篇小说《红岩》以及根据小说改编的电影《烈火中永生》，不仅成为六十年代中国文化的代表，而且无疑是革命文化的经典之作。它指称着伟大而圣洁的共产主义精神，指称着共产党人不可摧毁、永难毁灭的信仰与意志。对于中年以上的中国人说来，它赫然端居于人们的记忆清单之中，至少在二十年乃至更长的岁月中成为最感人且迷人的英雄范式。然而，这同一主题的展览，到了1996年却成了出资承办这一展览的企业"富贵花开公司"的商业广告行为。比"红岩"更为响亮的，是"富贵花开公司"的广告词："让烈士的鲜血浇灌富贵花开"。在此，笔者毋需赘言"富贵花开"作为典型

恰如其分	qiàrúqífèn	apt; appropriate
红岩	Hóngyán	"Red Crag," an exhibition in memory of revolutionary martyrs; also the title of a novel about the period by Luo Guangbin 罗广斌 and Yang Yiyan 杨益言
辖	xiá	have jurisdiction over
监禁	jiānjìn	take into custody
白公馆, 渣滓洞	Báigōngguǎn, Zhāzǐdòng	two GMD jails in Chongqing
酷刑	kùxíng	torture
亲历者	qīnlìzhě	someone with first-hand experience e.g., of an event
《烈火中永生》	*Lièhuǒzhōng yǒngshēng*	*Eternity in Flames* (1965), a film directed by Shui Hua 水华
赫然	hèrán	impressively
端居	duānjū	here: at the top of the list
毋需赘言	wúxū zhuìyán	no need to add superfluous words

的"旧中国"阶级社会与市民文化的向往，与革命烈士为之献身的共产主义图景间存在着怎样巨大的裂痕；但与政治波普的有意识戏仿不同，它与其说是对立的意识形态话语之不谐的展示，不如说是一次（尽管不一定成功的）置换与缝合。共产主义前景、社会主义实践被全球化景观、小康社会的未来、更为富有且舒适的"现世"（不如说是消费主义的）生活所取代。一如可口可乐公司的驻中国机构，以中国五六十年代劳动模范奖状为范本，设计了对自己公司职员的奖励标志。

另一个例子或许更为直观而清晰。那是1996-1997年间矗立在北京老城的主干道长安街中心地段的巨幅广告，三棱柱形的活动翻板不间断地依次变换、展示着三幅画面。其中之一是一幅政治性的公益广告：红色衬底上白色的等线体字样书写着："深化改革，建设有中国特色的社会主义"；继而出现的则是连续两幅画面华丽、色调迷人的"轩尼诗 (Hennessy) X.O"的广告。我们间或可以将其视为一处呈现九十年代文化冲突的空间：公益广告所采取的经典社会主义宣传品的形式，及其内容所昭示的当代中国作为最后一个社会主义堡垒的意义；与之共处的是轩尼诗广告所负载的跨国资本形象、消费主义所感召的奢靡、豪华的西方"现代"生活范本。这里无疑存在着某种"冷战"时代形同水火的意识形态对立，存在着F.杰姆逊所谓第三世界的民族国家文化与帝国主义文化的"生死搏斗"。但事实上，这正是一处颇为典型的九十年代文化的共用空间：它所展现的与其说是一种冲突，不如说是一次合谋。其1:2的时空比，则暗示着一次中心偏移与中心再置的过程。

波普	bōpǔ	pop (art etc.)
戏仿	xìfǎng	parody
不谐	bùxié	disharmony
缝合	fénghé	suture
奖状	jiǎngzhuàng	certificate of merit
三棱柱形	sānléngzhùxíng	an upright prism
不间断地	bùjiānduànde	continuous
公益	gōngyì	public welfare
奢靡	shēmí	extravagant
F.杰姆逊	F.Jiémǔxùn	Fredric Jameson (1934-)
生死搏斗	shēngsǐ bódòu	life-and-death struggle
时空比	shíkōngbǐ	ratio of time and space

经济拯救取代（经典社会主义的或政治民主的）政治拯救，成为别无选择的中国未来之路；作为全球化过程必然的<u>伴生物</u>，消费主义便成了九十年代中国很多地方社会、文化景观最强有力的构造者。然而，这里发生着的并非一个<u>线性</u>过程。如果说，在上海--中国第一工业都市，昔日的东方第一港、"<u>十里洋场</u>"、西方"冒险家的乐园"--人民广场确已<u>连缀</u>在消费风景之中；那么，在北京--中国的政治文化中心，"广场"仍<u>并置</u>在两种乃至多种意识形态的社会运作之中。当众多的商城、商厦、购物中心、连锁店、专卖店吞吐并分割着都市的人流，天安门广场仍是国庆盛典及1997年6月30日为庆祝"对香港恢复<u>行使主权</u>"而组织彻夜联欢的场所。而在南中国的第一都市广州，一种更为"和谐"的组合是"青年文化广场"：大商城间的空间成了"社会主义精神文明建设"项目--青年联欢及组织"文艺演出"的场所。因此，"广场"称谓的挪用，是一份繁复而深刻的暴露与遮蔽，它暴露并遮蔽着转型期中国极度复杂的意识形态现实，暴露并遮蔽着经济起飞的繁荣背后跨国资本的大规模渗透。但对于九十年代很多中国人来说，远为重要的，是迷人的消费主义风景线，遮蔽了急剧的市场化过程中中国社会所经历的社会再度分化的沉重现实。

"无名"的阶级现实

九十年代，围绕着Plaza，在中国都市铺展开去的全球化风景，不仅是商城、商厦，也不仅是<u>星罗棋布</u>于中国主要都市的<u>麦当劳</u>、<u>必胜客</u>；而且还有充满"<u>欧陆</u>风情"的"布艺商店"（家居、室内装饰店）、"花艺教室"（花店）、"饼屋"（面包房，这一次是台湾译名）、咖啡馆、酒吧和迪厅

伴生物	bànshēngwù	corollary; by-product
线性	xiànxìng	linear
十里洋场	shílǐyángchǎng	a metropolis infested with foreign adventurers; the old name for Shanghai's Nanjing Road, also called 上海滩
连缀	liánzhuì	join together; to cluster
并置	bìngzhì	collocate; to place side by side
盛典	shèngdiǎn	grand ceremony
行使主权	xíngshǐzhǔquán	exercise sovereignty
星罗棋布	xīngluóqíbù	spread all over
麦当劳	Màidāngláo	Macdonalds
必胜客	Bìshèngkè	Pizza Hut
欧陆	Ōulù	European

（舞厅），还有拔地而起的"高尚住宅"区，以及以"一方<u>世外桃源</u>，欧式私家别墅"、"时代经典，现代传奇"或"艺术大地"为广告或为名称的别墅群。曾作为八十年代精英知识分子话语核心的"走向世界"、"球籍"、"落后挨打"、"撞击世纪之门"，在这新的都市风景间也成为可望并可及的"景点"：商业国际电脑网络的<u>节点</u>站的广告云："中国人离信息高速公路到底有多远？--向北1500米"；长安街上的咖啡馆取名为<u>"五月花"</u>，<u>地质</u>科学院办的对外营业餐厅名曰"地球村"。命名为"世纪"、"新世纪"、"现代"或"当代"的商城、饭店，名目各异的公司<u>多如牛毛</u>，<u>不胜枚举</u>。一时间，中国人作为"快乐的消费者"取代了"幸福的人民"或"愤怒的公民"的形象。似乎是一次"逻辑"的延伸，"在消费上消灭阶级"的"后现代"社会图景，取代了无阶级、无差异、<u>各取所需</u>、物质产品极大丰富的共产主义远景，成了人们所向往、追逐的现世天堂。

与此同时，于1994年以后再度急剧膨胀和爆炸的大众传媒系统（电视台、有线电视台、报纸周末版及周报、大型豪华型休闲刊物），以及成功市场化的出版业，不仅丰满并<u>装点</u>着全球化进程中的中国生活，而且也常常屏壁式地遮挡社会现实。比如新富（New Rich）群体的<u>崭露头角</u>引人注目；与此相关的文化呈现是呼唤、构造中国的中产阶级社群。作为八十年代知识分子话语构造成功的一例，九十年代的社会文化"常识"之一，是精英文化与流行文化<u>共享</u>的对"中产阶级"的<u>情有独钟</u>。因为在八十年代的文化讨论中，尤其是在对战后实现经济起飞的亚洲国家之例证的<u>援引</u>中，一

世外	shìwài	beyond the mundane world
桃源	táoyuán	utopia
节点	jiédiǎn	node
五月花	wǔyuèhuā	the "Mayflower" ship
地质	dìzhì	geology
多如牛毛	duōrúniúmáo	countless
不胜枚举	bùshèngméijǔ	too many to innumerate
各取所需	gèqǔsuǒxū	each take what they need
装点	zhuāngdiǎn	decorate
崭露头角	zhǎnlù tóujiǎo	burst onto the scene
共享	gòngxiǎng	enjoy together; to share
情有独钟	qíngyǒudúzhōng	have a passion for something
援引	yuányǐn	cite examples

个庞大的、成为社会主体的中产阶级群体的形成，标识着经济起飞的实现，指称着对第三世界国家地位的逃离，意味着社会民主将伴随不可抗拒的"自然"进程（以非革命的方式）来临。此间，为八十年代有关讨论所忽略、为九十年代的类似表述有意遗忘的，是无人问及十三亿人口之众的中国，面对着瓜分完毕、极度成熟的全球化市场，背负着难于记数的历史重负，有没有可能成为一个以中产阶级为主体的国度；更没有关心那些无法<u>跻身</u>于中产阶级的人群（"大众"或"小众"）将面临着怎样的生存。

(Cont.)

| 跻身 | jīshēn | ascend, to be ranked among, rise to a higher position |

13. CHINESE INTELLECTUALS AND CHRISTIANITY

A Sociological Commentary on the Phenomenon of "Cultural" Christians
Liu Xiaofeng

When the academic and journalist Ian Buruma went to investigate the fate, ten years on, of the four writers of the documentary *River Elegy* (河觞 Heshang) who had escaped from China, he was curious to find out why three had turned to Christianity.[1] The link between political crises and religious zeal interested Buruma, who noted the fervor of attachment to the mainland among Chinese Christians in the United States, pointing out that Christianity could be a vehicle for Chinese nationalism now just as it had been for the revolutionary leader Sun Yat-sen earlier in the century. Christianity has continued to grow in China since Buruma's article was published in the late 1990s. Although the figures released by the official church are around 25 million for Protestants and Catholics combined, there are few who would dispute the greater accuracy of unofficial figures, which push the numbers of unregistered church believers up toward 80 or 100 million or beyond. While Christianity has been predominantly the domain of the rural and the female throughout the twentieth century, new growth is increasingly urban, male, and intellectual.

Christianity came to China through the Church of the East (the Nestorians) around the seventh century, but it was not until the Ming and Qing eras that it became a notable force, largely through the impact of the Roman Catholic Jesuits and others at the imperial court. Swathes of Protestant missionaries in the nineteenth century brought a new aspect: translated Bibles, together with vernacular education and widespread literacy drives. The legacy of nineteenth-century Western-imported Christianity is currently being reassessed in China. For decades it was vilified in communist writings as imperialist or colonialist, a dangerous import that had been shipped in on the back of the opium vessels. But now the more positive aspects of the Christian heritage are being openly studied: the hospital building programs, the establishment of schools and universities, the impact of Christian literature on the modern vernacular language (白话 *baihua*), and the influence of faith on the lives of individual Chinese people.

Many Chinese Christians have come to their faith through the perceived moral force of Christianity. Countless late-Qing and twentieth-century intellectuals were drawn to the Christian faith because of what they saw as

---

1. Ian Buruma, "The Pilgrimage from Tiananmen Square." *New York Times* April 11, 1999.

the compelling moral goodness of Jesus as described in the Bible. This concurred with the thrust of Confucian doctrine, which aimed at becoming a sage, or at the very least a *junzi* 君子, the gentleman of noble character who occupied the next step down the aspirational rung and who embodied the highest values. In both Christianity and Confucianism, the moral self was to be continually refined and fulfilled through a process of increasing self-awareness. The core of much writing by early twentieth-century Christians, particularly those still schooled in the classical canon, was Jesus himself: Jesus as sage, Jesus as revolutionary hero. The theme of a socially relevant Christianity has reappeared under different guises as circumstances have changed. For Bishop Ding Guangxun 丁光训 (K. H. Ting) and a generation of church leaders from the 1950s onward, Marxist charges against religion posed a grave threat, and in response, Christianity geared itself toward the building of a socialist society, contributing to the common good by exhorting believers to love each other and by encouraging the personal development of the "new human" (新人 *xinren*) in China. In the late 1980s and 1990s, a number of newer scholars—often "cultural Christians" or academics sympathetic to Christianity—have continued these calls for religion to benefit society. Many, from government ministers downward, have acknowledged that Christianity can have a positive influence on society by encouraging a dutiful workforce and by promoting harmonious relationships and good deeds. The so-called "spiritual vacuum" that worries commentators on contemporary China is a factor in encouraging even ardent communists to consider the social gain from organized religion. Academics such as Yang Huilin 杨慧林 at Renmin University in Beijing have advocated a "non-religious" interpretation of Christianity, which makes it suitable to the Chinese cultural situation.[2]

The political movements and campaigns which have dominated Chinese social life throughout the PRC era form the backdrop to the institutional church. Throughout the height of the Communist period, Christianity was anathema to the state, and professing Christians suffered much, sometimes enduring more than other "non-red" categories of people. As churches and seminaries were disbanded throughout the late 1960s and 1970s, survival was a priority for the church, and serious theological or biblical studies were an inconceivable luxury. In the Protestant church, a fault line runs between the China Christian Council (CCC) and house church leaders. The division between registered and unregistered churches is painful for many, and is predicated on a sense of betrayal among those who chose not to register their churches with the government on ideological grounds during the 1950s and 1960s. Many of this latter group have served long prison sentences, suffering greatly in comparison with those who registered and

2. See Yang Huilin, "Inculturation or Contextualization: Interpretation of Christianity in the Context of Chinese Culture," 7-32.

thus acceded to the Party line on religious matters. The sense of betrayal on the part of the underground or family churches means that many are deeply suspicious of sanctioned theologians, who are often much more liberal in their theology. Just as with many contemporary debates in the West, the authority of scripture is at the heart of much of the tension.

Many academic theologians without a church affiliation cultivate a neutral, scholarly perspective, and some leading names among them have become public figures with a growing voice on moral and philosophical issues. Even Bishop Ding conceded that theology being done outside the church in China is superior to that within it. Academic departments in universities are frequently better equipped than seminaries, and often have brighter students. Even after the reform period brought significant development to universities, theology faculties were still regarded as suspect. So it is not surprising that many of the forty or so university master's programs in Christian theology which were instituted across Chinese universities in the late 1990s and early 2000s come under the rubric of philosophy departments, or fall within programs like sociology of religion. Because of the emphasis on state needs and priorities, the study of the Christian faith at Chinese universities has concentrated on the sociology of religion, on comparative philosophies, and on safely-distant church history.

Two developments of note have recently taken place: the phenomenon of "cultural Christians" (文化基督徒 *wenhua jidutu*),[3] which refers to academics and intellectuals from all disciplines who are in sympathy with Christian moral or ethical teaching, but are not necessarily believers; and the growing field of Sino-Christian theology. Fredrik Fällman has analyzed the use of the term "cultural Christians," and differentiates four groups: (1) scholars studying Christianity from an academic viewpoint, and who try to keep a neutral position towards the church; (2) scholars sympathetic to Christianity, but who do not openly confess faith and do not associate with churches; (3) scholars who profess faith, but do not attend church and are not baptized; (4) scholars who are baptized and regularly attend church, a group that is relatively small. Fällman holds that the third group is closest to the original idea of "cultural Christians."[4]

Liu Xiaofeng 刘小枫 (1956-), whose article below examines both social aspects of Christianity and the phenomenon of "cultural Christians," has at times been regarded as one of their most vocal representatives. A leading proponent of Sino-Christian theology, Liu was for many years professor at Sun Yat-Sen University in Guangdong, and since 2008 has held a post at Renmin University in Beijing. Investigating the Christian faith first

---

3. For discussion and analysis of the term, see Fredrik Fällman, *Salvation and Modernity*, 38-43.
4. Fällman, *Salvation and Modernity*, 43-48.

through literature and Western philosophy, Liu's academic focus ultimately remains within Christian philosophy, as it discusses questions of God's love and beauty, and the impact of the Christian message. In the 1980s, when a number of "cultural Christians" started to speak and write openly about their faith, several dissociated themselves from churches, ritual, and baptism—although many have changed their stance since.[5] In his most well-known works, *Salvation and Easy Wandering* and *Toward the Truth on the Cross*, Liu introduced a selection of Christian theology to Chinese readers, comparing Western and Christian culture and philosophy with Chinese cultural and philosophical traditions. He advocates a pluralistic modern China where Christianity plays a role in public discourse, and where Christian ethics can serve as the foundation of values in society.[6]

Proponents of Sino-Christian studies have aimed to construct a branch of Chinese theology that emphasizes the humanistic and academic character of the discipline. Sino-Christian theology does not insist on the precondition of belief, and does not proselytize, but aims to bring Christian theology into mainstream Chinese culture.[7] Adherents of Sino-Christian studies argue that theology in the West is of and for the church, while in China it is of and for Chinese academia. Two facets capture the zeitgeist: the upsurge of interest in religion, and the adamantly Chinese nature of its scholarship, which is conducted on Chinese terms, rather than following a Western lead or Western interests. As the number of Christians in China continues to shoot upward, it will be intriguing to observe how this strident new Chinese theology might influence society.

Liu Xiaofeng, "'Wenhua' jidutu xianxiang de shehuixue pingzhu."

Further Reading

Aikman, David. *Jesus in Beijing*. London: Monarch, 2005.
Bays, Daniel H., ed. *Christianity in China: The Eighteenth Century to the Present*. Stanford: Stanford University Press, 1996.
Gernet, Jacques. *China and the Christian Impact: A Conflict of Cultures*. Cambridge: Cambridge University Press, 1985.
Fällman, Fredrik. *Salvation and Modernity: Intellectuals and Faith in Contemporary China*. Stockholm: Stockholm University, 2004.

5. Liu Xiaofeng, *Zhengjiu yu xiaoyao* (拯救与逍遥 Salvation and Easy Wandering; Shanghai: Shanghai Sanlian, 2001); and *Zouxiang shizijia shang de zhen* (走向十字架上的真 Toward the Truth on the Cross, Shanghai: Shanghai Sanlian, 1995), 124-27.
6. Fällman, *Salvation and Modernity*, 55-61.
7. See Li Qiuling, "Historical Reflections on 'Sino-Christian Theology,'" 56. The Beijing academic He Guanghu has advocated, in contrast, a "mother-tongue" theology which draws on the riches of Chinese culture as expressed through its language.

Lai, Pan-chiu, and Jason Lam, eds. *Sino-Christian Theology: a Theological Qua Cultural Movement in Contemporary China.* Frankfurt: Peter Lang, 2010.

Li Qiuling. "Historical Reflections on 'Sino-Christian Theology,'" *China Study Journal* (Spring/Summer, 2007), 54-67.

Lian Xi. *Redeemed by Fire: The Rise of Popular Christianity in Modern China.* New Haven: Yale University Press, 2010.

Lambert, Tony. *China's Christian Millions.* London: Monarch, 2001.

Malek, Roman, ed. *The Chinese Face of Jesus Christ*, vol. 1. Sankt Augustin: Institut Monumenta Serica, 2002.

Standaert, Nicolas, ed. *A Handbook of Christianity in China,* vol. 1. Leiden: Brill, 2001.

Starr, Chloë, ed. *Reading Christian Scripture in China.* London: T&T Clark, 2008.

Tiedemann, R. G. ed. *A Handbook of Christianity in China,* vol. 2. Leiden: Brill, 2009.

Yang Huilin. "Inculturation or Contextualization: Interpretation of Christianity in the Context of Chinese Culture." *Contemporary Chinese Thought* 36/1 (2004), 7-32.

Liu Xiaofeng

"文化"基督徒现象的社会学评注

一

自本世纪中叶以来，基督教的合法<u>传言活动</u>在大陆实际中断，<u>无神论</u>意识形态取得了<u>实质性</u>的社会法权，以至于<u>基督教的信仰</u>和社会生活只会引起人们的政治警觉意识。然而，近十年来，社会层面对基督教的政治警觉意识至少在城市区域有明显减弱，基督教的认信在已成为社会基础意识的无神论语境中<u>自发漫生</u>。尤为引人注目的是文化知识界中出现了宗教意向和对基督信仰的兴趣。这一精神意识之趋向在文学、艺术、哲学和人文科学领域中，尽管实际上不仅<u>丝毫不具</u>普遍性，而且显得脆弱孤单，但确有增长的趋势，以至于某些<u>教会权威人士</u>声称，基督教将在教会之外得到更大的发展。

教会权威人士将这些具有基督认信趋向的文人学者称之为"文化基督徒"。按照这一命名，是否也意指大陆将会出现一种"文化的"基督教形式呢？

<u>神学家们</u>若仅用信仰意识危机来解释这一现象，或对这种实际上仍然相当微弱的"基督教热"过于乐观，就会使问题简单化。如果说已有"文化基督徒"的出现，或者将会有一种"文化基督教"形式出现，这只表明<u>汉语神学</u>已面临着一些新的神学课题。例如：所谓的"文化基督教"的含义及神学性质是什么？它在汉语基督神学发展史中的未来含义是什么？"文化基督徒"作为一种教会外的基督认信形式与教会的关系如何？以及从整个汉语文化的未来发展来看，"文化基督徒"的角色是什么？

传言活动	chuányán huódòng	evangelism; propagandizing
无神论	wúshénlùn	atheism
实质性	shízhìxìng	essential; substantive
基督教的信仰	Jīdūjiào de xìnyǎng	Christian faith
自发漫生	zìfā mànshēng	spontaneously spread
丝毫不具	sīháo bújù	doesn't have any… at all
教会权威人士	jiàohùi quánwēi rénshì	people in authority in the church
神学家们	shénxuéjiāmen	theologians
汉语神学	Hànyǔ shénxué	Chinese language theology

二

严格来讲，当代大陆并不存在一种所谓的"文化基督教"。事实上，仅可以说，在知识界中，基督信仰和神学已成为知识分子的重要关注对象之一（而非唯一）。与此相关，某些知识分子（<u>文人学者</u>）至少已采纳了某种基督教的思想立场——必得承认，在基督教中并非只有一种统一的神学思想立场。因而，那些已采纳了某种基督神学立场的知识分子将会发展出一种什么样态的神学，乃是一项有意义的神学课题；此外，这些知识分子采纳的是哪一种神学思想立场，与西方众多神学走向中的哪一种定向有<u>亲和性</u>，亦是一项引人注目的知识社会学课题。

教会权威人士称这些采纳了某种基督神学思想立场的知识分子为"文化基督徒"，其含义似乎是指，他们并非真正的基督徒，只是把基督教作为一种文化思想来接受并为之<u>辩护</u>，或从事着一种基督教文化研究而已。

这一命名之意指带有相当的含混性：首先，如果有人仅只把基督认信作为一种文化思想来采纳，尚不能具有"基督徒"之名。"基督徒"之存在必植根于信仰——对<u>那稣基督</u>和其父上帝的信仰、对基督死而复活的信仰，具有信仰的重生经验，并在行为上以那稣基督的<u>圣训</u>为个人生活的品质。实际上，在那些采纳了某种基督神学思想的中国卸识分子中，仅有极少一部分人具有这种信仰的重生经验。

另一方面，即使是那些已获得基督信仰之认信的知识分子，由于其存在形 式与大教会或小教会（小教派或<u>家庭教会</u>）都不发生关系（这既有政治处境的原因，也有大小教会本身之存在方式的处境<u>约束</u>的原因），甚至由于连最基本的<u>团契</u>生活也没有（这又有政治和地域上的原因），这些知识分子的"基督性"身分就显得极不明朗。也许我们不得不区分"基督徒"与"基督教徒"的名份，甚至也可以在早期基督教史中找到"基督徒"而非"教徒"

文人学者	wénrén xuézhě	intellectuals; scholars
亲和性	qīnhéxìng	affinity
辩护	biànhù	defend; speak in favor of
耶稣基督	Yēsū Jīdū	Jesus Christ
圣训	shèngxùn	commandments; instructions
家庭教会	jiātíng jiàohuì	"family church"; unregistered church
约束	yuēshù	restrain; dominate
团契	tuánqì	fellowship; community

的认信形式，然而，在今天来看，那些在教会组织之外，更与教会之宗派形式无关的认信基督的人，能被教会认可为基督徒吗？

这一问题不是无关紧要的。随着大陆社会文化<u>语境</u>的逐渐多元化，将会有更多的知识分子认识基督。于是，可能会有更多的教会外的"文化基督徒"，以至将出现一种"文化的"基督思想形式。对这一现象要作出神学解释，恐怕并不容易被<u>建制教会</u>接受——不妨想想朋霍费尔 (Bonhoeffer) 的一些神学主张所引致的争议。

"文化"一词的含义同样易于引起误解。如果要恰当地理解或解释所谓"文化"基督徒或"文化"基督思想，就必须注意"文化"一词在大陆的意识形态语境中所具有的<u>曲折</u>含义。只有从中国特定的意识形态话语背景中，才能充分理解"文化"一词的实际用法。

三

汉语基督教的发展，一直与西方传教活动有关，以至于基督教在中国一直被视为外来宗教，并导致至今没有了结的汉文化观念与基督教思想之争。这一历史原因使得基督性与人性之生存论关系在汉语神学思想中一直<u>蔽而不明</u>。 然而，"文化基督徒"现象之出现，与西方传教活动无关，甚至也与本土教会的宣教活动——它当然受到实质性的限制——无关。这一现象在知识社会学上的意义引人注目。至少可以提到如下一些知识社会学问题。

首先，汉文化与基督教之关系，必须从新的<u>视域</u>来考虑。民族文化论问题事实上已转换为生存本体论问题。汉文化与基督教之关系不再是一个中西文化之对话问题，而是一个生存本体论上的对话问题。汉语基督思想之发展，由外传转化为内部的自生，不仅将改变整个汉语文化与基督思想的传统关系，也将改变发展着的汉语文化本身，汉语基督神学亦应具有新的视域。

语境	yǔjìng	context
建制教会	jiànzhì jiàohuì	the established church
曲折	qūzhé	intricate; complex
蔽而不明	bì ér bùmíng	obscure; unclear
视域	shìyù	field of vision

由于"文化基督徒"现象是在中国基本上不存在宣教活动的背景上发生的，"五四"时期由中国某些教会人士提出的"<u>三自</u>"<u>纲领</u>显得失去了时代的恰切性。大陆的教会神学面临着另一方面的挑战：它将会有什么新的样态呢？与此相关，由于这一现象与西方传教活动无关，"五四"时期提出的，且至今仍在讨论的所谓<u>本色化神学</u>主张，也因此丧失了时代的恰切性，"文化基督徒"现象明显不是汉语文化的基督教现象，而是基督性的汉语文化现象。至于国家的教会、民族化的基督教之类的主张，不管从历史——<u>纳粹</u>时期的"德意志基督教"——还是从现实来看，都值得引起神学家们的警觉。

基督教的传统分裂——尤其 Hans Kung 所谓的"古典冲突"——本与中国无关。然而，传教士们（尤其是<u>新教</u>）把教会的宗派形式带到了中国，以至基督教在汉语境中的发展倍受损害。例如，在西方，无论天主教还是新教，God 之名只有一个，在中国却出现了两个 God 之名（天主和上帝）——以致三个 God 之名（外加一个"神"）。"文化基督徒"现象之出现，至少在神学定向上是普世性的，从而与本世纪的普世趋向自然<u>吻合</u>。

四

Ernst Troeltsch 指出，基督教的存在形式自始有三种：大教会 (Kirche)、小教派 (Sekte) 和神秘派 (Mystik)。大教会往往自认是此世的上帝之国和<u>救恩</u>机构，表现出主动适应此世的态度，要成为大众的教

三自	Sān Zì	"Three Self" principles, i.e., self-supporting, self-propagating, and self-governing. Elucidated early in the twentieth century, these became the hallmark of the state Protestant church in the PRC
纲领	gānglǐng	guiding principle
本色化神学	běnsèhuà shénxué	indigenized theology
纳粹	Nàcuì	Nazi
新教	Xīnjiào	Protestant
吻合	wěnhé	identical; a good fit with
救恩	jiùēn	salvation; saving grace

会，并一再表现出与国家权力相谐调的趋向；小教派是以注重"重生"经验为基础的信徒小团体，看重律法轻视恩典，有强烈的脱离此世的愿望，其信徒成员多为下层阶层，坚拒基督教的文化形态，故小教派根本没有任何神学可言，而且排外性很重；神秘派虽然也注重个人的属灵经验，却趋向于个体宗教的存在形式，有削弱建制教会形式的趋向，即使神秘派也有以个体为基础的团契，也不存在恒久和固定的建制形式，并把宗教虔敬感作为文化活动的创造性动力，注重基督宗教的文化形态和人文科学的、反省性的神学，神秘派一般属于知识分子阶层。

如果用 Troeltsch 的这一界定来分析当代大陆基督教的诸形态，也许富有激发性。我无意去为 Troeltsch 的基督教社会学作论证，而是把它作为一种宗教社会学的分析图式，有效地描述当代大陆基督教诸存在形式的特点。

"三自"组织或爱国会可视为当代大陆的"大教会"，它们对社会、国家及民族的态度，以及与国家权力谐调的趋向，都表明其身分特征；家庭教会尤其是新教的家庭教会以及历史上形成的小教派，不管在形态和实质上，都表现为小教派的形式——天主教的家庭教会也许是例外，值得做个案分析；而日渐形成的"文化基督徒"，则在形态和实质上趋向于神秘派形式，如果在 Troeltsch 的用法上来理解"神秘派"这个词，而不是将它与中古世纪欧洲神秘派或当今的所谓"灵恩派"相联的话。有三个要点值得强调：a. 明显的个体宗教形式比；b. 注重基督教之文化性和文化之基督性言述，在文化知识阶层拓展；c. 自发地趋向科学的、反思性的神学。

当代大陆的"大教会"多少有保留地承认"神秘派"，而"小教派"则对"神秘派"基本持否定态度，"神秘派"们也视"小教派"之信仰形式为"不可理解"——一位文人曾告诉我，他参加家庭教会后不久，终于不能忍受在他看来有过多中国民间宗教成分的信仰形式，便偷了一本圣经后脱离教会。

重生	chóngshēng	rebirth
恩典	ēndiǎn	grace; favor
虔敬感	qiánjìnggǎn	feeling of devotion
天主教	Tiānzhǔjiào	(Roman) Catholicism
灵恩派	líng'ēnpài	Charismatics; Pentecostals
拓展	tuòzhǎn	expand; continue

汉语基督教至今在基本神学或系统神学方面极为贫乏，百年来如此。"文化基督徒"倘若真的会形成，将在人文科学的、<u>反思</u>性神学的定向上推进基本—系统神学以及基督哲学及文化学在汉语域中的建立。这至少可以在形式上补全汉语基督教的形态。基督教中的 Troeltsch 意义上的三种存在形式之间的相互排斥，是不恰当的。无论从神学还是从社会学来讲，三种形式之间的自由和睦关系都是可以论证的，尽管相互批评亦为必要。

五

莫尔特曼 (J. Moltmann) 在谈到自己的神学构想时说，他的认信最初不是由圣经和教义问答手册唤醒的，因此，他感到自己必须在神学中发现对他自己来说是全新的一切。对于大陆的"文化基督徒"，这种经验不是陌生的。如果随着"神秘派"的形成而出现一种人文科学的、反思性神学，其样态必然会与传统的教会神学有所不同。什么叫做"在神学中发现对我们来说是全新的一切"？莫尔特曼的意思指，神学问题是从自身时代的存在处境中产生的，而不是从过去的神学思想体系和结论中产生的。同样，汉语"神秘派"神学也从自身的存在处境中得到自己的神学问题。

这种神学之形成，其神学处境至少有两个维度：一方面是与无神论意识形态之关系，另一方面是与教会神学之关系。这两方面都带有独特的处境性。在"五四"时期，基督思想与无神论的各种<u>人文</u>和科学世界观发生过激烈的争辩。这场争辩后来被中断。无神论的，但同时也是一种准宗教性和带有信仰性质的人民意识形态话语，是"文化基督徒"首要的神学处境。这绝非是有神论与无神论之间的对话问题，一个引人注目的现象充分说明了这一点：基督思想在当代文化界中<u>初露端倪</u>，最为强烈的不容忍性反应首先不是来自国家意识形态，而是来自同样受到国家意识形态限制的<u>人本主义</u>的马克思主义派。信仰论的意识形态批判和意识形态的信仰论批判是文化神学的首要课题。

反思	fǎnsī	self-examination; profound re-think
人文	rénwén	humanistic
初露端倪	chūlù duānní	initially surfaced
人本主义	rénběnzhǔyì	humanism

从教会神学方面来看，极端的<u>自由主义</u>和极端的<u>基要主义</u>过去是、迄今仍是神学的另一维度的基本处境。一方面，极端自由派（<u>吴耀宗</u>）使得基督信仰靠近历史理性主义信仰，另一方面，极端基要派（<u>王明道</u>、<u>倪柝声</u>）又从另一极端使基督信仰成了过于排斥性的律法宗教。前者的局限在于，基督信仰与无神论的<u>准宗教</u>的人民意识形态的<u>趋同</u>，后者的局限在于，丧失了基督信仰的挚爱优先性和普济性。因此，对基督教社会主义思想的神学批判和拓展神学的社会批判定向是汉语基督神学的重要课题。

汉语基督思想尚只有教会神学形态，缺乏一种人文科学性的、反思性的神学形态，这对基督文化在汉语境中的发展极为不利，尤其当考虑到无神论信仰是历史的和现实的基本处境，情形更为明朗。其结果不外是：基督信仰要不是在现实的社会处境和文化处境中被其它世界观或信仰论化解，便是以圣俗之分为界，使基督信仰处于与世隔绝的状态，被迫<u>划地为牢</u>。

当代大陆的基督"神秘主义"萌生于无神论的存在处境，植根于这一处境，并要仍然置身于这一处境，在这一处境中伸展，而非"<u>入圣超凡</u>"，进入人民意识形态为教会构筑的围墙之内。

自由主义	zìyóuzhǔyì	liberal(ism)
基要主义	jīyàozhǔyì	fundamentalism
吴耀宗	Wú Yàozōng	one of founders of Three-Self Patriotic Movement in the 1950s (1893-1979); propounded a "social gospel"
王明道	Wáng Míngdào	well-known conservative preacher and writer who taught himself theology (1900-91)
倪柝声	Ní Tuòshēng	"Watchman Nee," founder of Little Flock Church and advocate of the Restoration movement to early church principles (1903-72)
准宗教	zhǔnzōngjiào	quasi-religion
趋同	qūtóng	trend towards uniformity
划(画)地为牢	huàdì wéiláo	restrict activities to a designated sphere
入圣超凡	rùshèng chāofán	attain sainthood and transcend worldliness

　　如果它要发展一种<u>处境神学</u>，那么，其样态亦非独创独有，而是在诸多方面与欧美神学之现当代定向相关联，这是因为，从现代性语境来看，基本思想处境在生存本体论上是相同的。因而，处境神学同样应是：

　　1. 批判的神学，这种批判是双向的批判：既（向外）指向各种现代人本意识形态和信仰，也（向内）指向神学和教会本身；既是一种社会批判和意识形态批判，也是一种神学和宗教的自我批判 (Hans Kung, J.B. Metz)，批判之标准来自基督的十字架，来自圣经中的上帝之言，被钉十字架的上帝是神学的基础和批判 (J. Moltmann)。

　　2. 自由的神学，而非<u>独断论</u>的神学：神学在性质上是人与上帝、人与人的对话；神学话语是人言，不是圣言；在神学中没有人为的神圣权威或自封的<u>正统</u>，神学永远处于走向圣言的途中(Karl Barth)。

　　3. 科学的神学，这不仅指神学与社会科学和其它人文科学的对话，更是指神学自身的人文科学化 (T.F. Torrance, G. Ebeling, W. Pannenberg)。

　　4. <u>生存释义</u>论的和<u>先验论</u>的神学，神学应透入到生存论和先验论的层次，走向圣言与此在的先验存在论关系的实事本身(zur Sachen selbst)，突破汉语神学界至今还在<u>纠缠</u>的中西景观的<u>二元对立</u>，使汉语神学思想不是要立在文化民族主义景观之上，而是人与上帝的生存论关系之上 (Bultmann, Rahner).

　　5. <u>言成肉身的神学</u>，所谓"肉身"在此既是指生存的时代处境，也是指传统的发展着的民族文化本身；因而汉语基督神学既是处境化的，使基督精神在时代处境中成何的神学 (Bonhoeffer)，也是在文化中展开的神学：文化是肉身、是形式，上帝的话是灵魂、是实质，基督精神也展现为文化的形态 (R.Guardini, H.U. von Balthasar, P.Tillich)。

处境神学	chùjìng shénxué	contextual theology
独断论	dúduànlùn	dogmatism
正统	zhèngtǒng	orthodox ideas
生存释义	shēngcúnshìyì	existential hermeneutics
先验论(的)	xiānyànlùn (de)	transcendental
纠缠	jiūchán	tangle
二元对立	èryuán duìlì	binary opposition
言成肉身的神学	yánchéng ròushēn de shénxué	incarnational theology

汉语基督神学不是中国化的神学，而是在汉语的存在处境和语言中生成的神学。神学在本质上没有中西之分。

六

当把基督文化在中国的发展与历史上佛教在中国的发展加以比较，就某些方面来看，是富有意义的。

首先，基督思想经典著作之翻译与<u>佛典</u>的翻译，实不可同日而语，这是汉语基督文化发展中存在的重大问题之一。中国教会至今尚未重视系统的、全面的基督思想经典翻译工作。唯一有过的一项系统翻译计划《基督教历代名著集成》，不仅依然残缺不全、现当代部分相当薄弱，而且翻译质量（尤其中文表达）亦颇有问题。即使如此，这一翻译计划最初仍主要是由西教士推动和主持的。如果汉语神学家们仍不注意基督思想经典的系统翻译，基督文化在汉语境之发展前景不会明朗。——不妨看一看基督文化在韩国之发展及其基督教文献翻译之盛况。

佛教传入中国后发展出多维度的中国佛教，既有民间大众化的不究佛理的<u>净土宗</u>，实践与佛理并举的<u>禅宗</u>，亦有偏重思辨学理的<u>唯识宗</u>，并形成各自的传统。相形之下，基督教在中国之发展，几乎是不相称的。尤其值得注意的是，基督教在汉语境之发展类似于净土宗的定向颇为显著，这种与民间宗教相结合的定向，倘若没有注重教义及理性化神学之文化神示为补偏因素，最终难以应付现代化社会之挑战。

汉语基督神学之历史尚浅，近十年出现的"文化基督徒"现象的意义在于，基督认信由外传转变为自发寻求，这将是汉语神学发展史上的一个<u>转掠点</u>。

佛典	Fódiǎn	Buddhist scriptures
净土宗	Jìngtǔzōng	Pure Land Buddhism
禅宗	Chánzōng	Chan (Zen) Buddhism
唯识宗	Wéishízōng	Vijnaptimatrata School
转掠点	zhuǎnlièdiǎn	turning point

14. TAIWANESE IDENTITY

The Rising People
Hsu Hsin-liang

The last two decades have witnessed an extraordinary surge of interest in issues of identity across the spectrum of Taiwanese society. Animating not only political and social life, but also every aspect of culture from literature and film to art and museum studies, the vogue for identity has inspired reams of commentary, both inside and outside Taiwan. The key impetus for this fascination with what it means to be Taiwanese was provided by the gradual liberalization of public life which began in the early 1980s, and culminated in the lifting of martial law in 1987. Political opposition was legalized, restrictions on print media were lifted, and before long the public sphere became, in the words Tu Wei-ming, freely "saturated with partisan messages"[1]—each with a different notion of Taiwan and Taiwaneseness to promote.

Most strikingly, the landmark events of the 1980s have led to the ascendancy of "Taiwan consciousness," and to the entrenchment of nativization (本土化 *bentuhua*) as the ruling discourse in both politics and culture. In practice, this has meant a focus on local customs, culture, and history, and a shift away from the notion that Taiwan is a nation of displaced Chinese who owe ultimate allegiance to the vast land across the Taiwan straits. Yet issues of identity have remained fraught throughout the last two decades; and while a "return to the native" is palpable across the board, it is also clear that numerous competing interests battle for space as Taiwanese society strives to define itself. This conflict is hardly surprising when we consider Taiwan's complex ethnic composition. The island's inhabitants consist of four main groups: aborigines, known as *yuanzhumin* 原住民, who subdivide into nine tribal groups; Hakka people (客家人 Kejiaren) most of whom hail originally from Guangdong; Southern Min people from Fujian (often called 本省人 *benshengren*); and "mainlanders" (外省人 *waishengren*) who decamped to Taiwan with Chiang Kai-shek in the wake of the Communist victory of 1949. Southern Mins and Hakkas constitute over 80 percent of the population, with mainlanders making up 16 percent, and aborigines less than 2 percent.

Right across the recent debates, one theme emerges with consistent clarity: the role which history, and historical memory, plays in the evolution of identities on Taiwan. Up to a point, this focus on the past and its remembrance is well-nigh axiomatic. Scholars agree that identity is linked

---

1. Tu Wei-ming, "Cultural Identity and the Politics of Recognition in Contemporary Taiwan," 72.

to memory and history in profoundly constitutive ways; and when a nation's past is as checkered as that of Taiwan, these connections become all the more potent. Ever since the early seventeenth century, when Taiwan's aborigines and its earliest Han settlers were confronted in swift succession by Portuguese, Spanish, and Dutch adventurers, the island has found itself at the whim of opportunist powers keen to exploit its strategic location. Stability of sorts came after Taiwan was brought under the control of the Qing dynasty in 1683, although waves of immigration from the seaboard provinces over the next two centuries ensured that the island retained its frontier spirit. Taiwan's status was set on a formal footing when it was made a province of China in 1885; yet only ten years later, the bruising defeat of the Qing in the Sino-Japanese war led to the ceding of this imperial outpost to Japan.

The Japanese occupation, which lasted until 1945, marked the first time that identity became a fiercely contested issue in Taiwan. Local customs were stamped out, and colonial officials pushed Japanization via policies of acculturation, with the learning of Japanese language and lifestyle lying at the core of their project. The colonial population became imperial subjects (皇民 *huangmin*; Japanese: *kōmin*), whose loyalties lay with the Japanese emperor and whose identities were forcibly recast as Japanese. Yet effective as many of these policies were, resistance to the Japanese never really abated—despite its often savage suppression. These twin forces of assimiliation and resistance brought the question of identity to the fore with unprecedented intensity, and debate still continues today over which force proved more decisive. Some argue that resistance took the form of a sharpened sense of fellowship and affinity with the Chinese mainland. Others, however, contend that the local consciousness which emerged at this time was rooted in Taiwanese soil and reflected a nascent nativism.

Either way, Japanese defeat in World War II and Taiwan's retrocession to mainland China brought another reappraisal of local identities. When the Nationalists arrived on Taiwan in 1945, the island's new rulers made the reversal of Japanization a basic plank of policy. Mandarin replaced Japanese, mainland history was chronicled in school textbooks, monuments were built to Chinese heroes, and the story of Taiwan's past was consigned to individual memory. This enforced paradigm shift was problematic for the vast majority of Taiwanese. Almost all struggled with the new official language, and their lack of fluency barred them from joining the ruling class, which was composed largely of expatriated mainlanders. Worse still, inflation, corruption, unemployment, and food shortages were rife during the early Nationalist years, leaving some feeling oddly nostalgic for the orderliness of the Japanese interlude. This trauma reached its nadir with the February 28th Incident of 1947. The immediate spur to unrest was the arrest of a local woman selling cigarettes without a license, but events quickly took on a momentum of their own, and escalated into a spontaneous uprising which caught the provincial government unawares. The crackdown which followed remains the subject of intense debate today, with estimates of the death toll ranging from an implausibly low five hundred to an upper limit of tens of thousands of victims. Leaders of the protest movement were the professed targets, but the suppression saw countless prominent Taiwanese rounded up and executed. The intelligentsia, in particular, was ruthlessly culled. With the Communist victory on the mainland, moreover, came a new and much more immediate threat to Nationalist authority, and the hunt for Communist renegades led to the persecution of still greater numbers of local people. Thousands were incarcerated in the "White Terror" campaign which raged during the 1950s, many of whom remained in prison until the early 1980s.

The effects of February 28th and the White Terror on the evolution of Taiwanese identities are incalculable.[2] That said, the silencing of the intellectual community through violence and intimidation was perhaps the most significant factor, since with the literati dead, imprisoned, or cowed into inactivity, Taiwanese were effectively deprived of the cultural expression which is integral to the maintenance of identity. Forced underground, grief festered into resentment. In the meantime, the climate of fear which shrouded Taiwan gave the Nationalists a wide latitude for the imposition of control, and over the next twenty years, society's energies were diverted away from politics and channelled instead toward the goal of economic growth. This goal was attained in grand fashion, as Taiwan transformed itself from a rural backwater into a first-tier Asian economy. As the years passed, however, Taiwan's miracle began to force movement in the political impasse. Empowered by success, a new middle class emerged and began to search once again for a political identity—a quest which coincided crucially with the severe diminution of Taiwan's international status during the 1970s. This decade saw Taiwan lose its United Nations seat, and also the formal support of its two major allies: the United States and Japan. This loss of face impacted both on the credibility of the Nationalists as guardians of Taiwan's sovereignty, and on the evolution of local feeling across the island. As Taiwan lost its recognised "rights" over politico-cultural China, the island's people began to ask if they might represent themselves instead. As part of this process, challenges to the state were mounted by the newly-formed opposition (党外 *dangwai*) from the early 1970s onward, as the power of the Taiwan episteme grew. The Democratic Progressive Party (DPP) was established in 1986 under a powerfully nativist aegis, and its many subsequent successes culminated in the election of Chen Shui-bian as president in 2000.

---

2. For a full study, see Robert Edmondson, "The February 28th Incident and National Identity," 25-46.

Yet the establishment of Taiwanization as the dominant political, social, and cultural mode on the island has by no means led to a fusion of horizons on what it means to be Taiwanese at the *fin-de-siècle* and beyond. For Taiwanese nationalists, a unified identity rooted in Taiwan is the only way to achieve closure on the past and head off the threats posed by the PRC. For many others, however, the anti-Chinese, pro-independence stance of the Taiwanese nationalists is disturbing—if only because this stance may provoke bellicose elements within the mainland government. Others, meanwhile, view themselves as politically Taiwanese, yet at the same time retain an apolitical attachment toward traditional Han culture. And all the while, Taiwan's position as a "world island," fully assimilated into the transnational economy and fully apprised of global cultural currents, has brought implications of its own. To complicate the picture still further, the emergence of so-called Greater China—an axis of economic and cultural integration which links Taiwan, Hong Kong, mainland China, and the diaspora—has led some Taiwanese to consider afresh their identity as ethnic Chinese.

Inevitably, this brew of ethnic, cultural, and political friction sometimes bubbles over into outright conflict—and never more so than at election time, when politicians from across the spectrum play the identity card not wisely but too well. Intermittent tensions of this kind have led a number of prominent public figures to seek a way out of the identity impasse. Notable here is the call made by former president Lee Teng-hui in the late 1990s for a "new Taiwanese" identity, an inclusive definition which includes anyone willing to "strive and struggle for Taiwan."[3] Partaking of the same discursive impulse is Hsu Hsin-liang's (1941-) 1995 book *The Rising People*, the focus of the present chapter. In this text, Hsu—a former chairman of the DPP—argues for the Taiwanese as a people imbued with the migrant spirit, whose ingenuity at assimilating new influences, and exploiting them for commercial gain, gives them a distinctive national character which has the potential to transcend the divisions of the past.

Hsu Hsin-liang. *Xinxing minzu.* Taibei: Yuanliu chuban gongsi, 1995, 179-88.

Further Reading

Bosco, Joseph. "The Emergence of a Taiwanese Popular Culture." In Murray A. Rubinstein, ed. *The Other Taiwan*, 392-403. Armonk: M. E. Sharpe, 1994.

---

3. Quoted in J. Bruce Jacobs and I-Hao Ben Liu, "Lee Teng-hui and the Idea of Taiwan," 385.

Ching, Leo. *Becoming "Japanese": Colonial Taiwan and the Politics of Identity Formation.* Berkeley and Los Angeles: University of California Press, 2001.

Chu Yun-han and Jih-wen Lin. "Political Development in 20th-Century Taiwan: State-Building, Regime Transformation and the Construction of National Identity." In Richard L. Edmonds and Steven M. Goldstein, eds., *Taiwan in the Twentieth Century: A Retrospective View*, 102-29. Cambridge: Cambridge University Press, 2001.

Corcuff, Stéphane, ed. *Memories of the Future. National Identity Issues and the Search for a New Taiwan.* Armonk: M. E. Sharpe, 2002.

Edmondson, Robert. "The February 28th Incident and National Identity." In Stéphane Corcuff, ed. *Memories of the Future: National Identity Issues and the Search for a New Taiwan*, 25-46. Armonk: M. E. Sharpe, 2002.

Gold, Thomas. "Taiwan Society at the *Fin de Siècle*." In David Shambaugh, ed. *Contemporary Taiwan*, 47-70. Oxford: Clarendon Press, 1998.

Hsiau A-chin. *Contemporary Taiwanese Cultural Nationalism.* London and New York: Routledge, 2000.

Hughes, Christopher. *Taiwan and Chinese Nationalism. National Identity and Status in International Society.* London and New York: Routledge, 1997.

Jacobs, J. Bruce, and I-Hao Ben Liu. "Lee Teng-hui and the Idea of Taiwan." *China Quarterly* 190 (2007), 375-93.

Kuo Yu-fen. "Consuming Differences: 'Hello Kitty' and the Identity Crisis in Taiwan." *Postcolonial Studies* 6/2 (2003), 175-89.

Rigger, Shelley. "Competing Conceptions of Taiwan's Identity: The Irresolvable Conflict in Cross-strait Relations." *Journal of Contemporary China* 6/15 (1997), 307-17.

Tu Wei-ming. "Cultural Identity and the Politics of Recognition in Contemporary Taiwan." In David Shambaugh, ed. *Contemporary Taiwan*, 71-96. Oxford: Oxford University Press, 1998.

Wachman, Alan M. *Taiwan: National Identity and Democratization.* Armonk: M. E. Sharpe, 1994.

———. "Competing Identities in Taiwan." In Murray A. Rubinstein, ed. *The Other Taiwan*, 17-80. Armonk: M. E. Sharpe, 1994.

Wang, Edward Q. "Taiwan's Search for National History: A Trend in Historiography." *East Asian History* 24 (2002), 93-116.

Winckler, Edwin A. "Cultural Policy on Postwar Taiwan." In Stevan Harrell and Huang Chun-chieh, eds. *Cultural Change in Postwar Taiwan*, 22-46. Boulder: Westview Press, 1994.

新興民族

第八章 台灣新興的歷史過程

一個移民社會一定是個創造力飽滿的社會。移民最大的特點正在於無法把舊日生活裡所有既成的東西都隨身攜帶<u>飄洋過海</u>。移民就是最大的捨棄。捨棄原有的一切，到新的地方從頭開始。移民社會裡，<u>疆界</u>的概念不是<u>死板固定</u>的，而是隨時可以更動的，隨時都有人在想像疆界之外是不是另有一片<u>沃饒</u>的新天地。

異質<u>島嶼</u>特殊的歷史積累

台灣有什麼條件可以成為一個新興民族？面對世界局勢的全新挑戰，我們有什麼理由認定台灣能作出最好的回應？憑什麼在各個國家激烈競逐的舞台上，台灣可以因懂得比別人多、活動力比別人強，<u>脫穎而出</u>？

這一連串的問題，總歸起來只有一個答案：因為台灣有特殊的歷史積累，歷史發展給了這一代台灣人這個奮起<u>遠颺</u>的寶貴機會。

過去，在國民黨的教育底下，我們從來不曾認真地理解台灣歷史。在「中國<u>掛帥</u>」的原則下，台灣只是一個邊疆的小島，幾乎完全沒有歷史地位，沒有歷史價值。<u>扭曲</u>的歷史意識，使我們對這塊土地充滿<u>自卑</u>情

飄洋過海	piāoyángguòhǎi	travel far across the sea
疆界	jiāngjiè	boundary; border
死板固定	sǐbǎngùdìng	rigid; inflexible
沃饒	wòráo	fertile
島嶼	dǎoyǔ	island
脫穎而出	tuōyǐng'érchū	come to the fore
遠颺	yuǎnyáng	flee to a far-off place
掛帥	guàshuài	dominate; assume command
扭曲	niǔqū	distort
自卑	zìbēi	feel inferior

結，以為台灣代表的就只有逃難，只有委屈，「希望」與「發展」都要到
對岸大陸才能找到。

　　擺脫這種畸形心態，回復以台灣自身為主體的歷史眼光，我們會發
現，其實一代又一代台灣人所受的折磨苦難，正是在為我們儲積適切回應
挑戰的能力。在歷史中我們容或看見悲傷打擊，卻不應該看見悲觀絕望；
相反地，我們找到對未來可以樂觀的理由。

　　台灣的歷史經驗與其特殊的地理位置息息相關。作為一個四面環海的
島嶼，台灣有十足的理由應該依海為生，發展出海洋型的文化特質。然
而，隔著一道平均寬度不過才一百五十公里的海峽，台灣卻又與全世界內
向性大陸個性最強烈的國家——中國——緊密相鄰。隨著漢人的東渡，無
可避免地也把中國式保守的大陸型世界觀帶到台灣來，於是，海洋與大陸
的依違游移，就成為台灣歷史的一齣主要戲碼。

　　不管從海洋或大陸的角度來看，台灣都是一個很難歸類的異質島嶼。
它既不完全屬於海洋，又不完全屬於大陸，也因此，它得天獨厚地取得同
時面對海洋又學習大陸的優越條件。

　　中國大陸那種文化的一元性格，以及金觀濤所批判的「超穩定結
構」，和台灣歷史的實況格格不入。台灣短短四百年的漢人開發史，充滿
起起伏伏的戲劇性變動，最重要的，充滿了多種文明登岸逐鹿折衝的深刻
印跡。

畸形	jīxíng	lopsided; unbalanced
息息相關	xīxīxiāngguān	closely linked
海峽	hǎixiá	strait; channel
東渡	dōngdù	take a voyage eastwards
大陸型	dàlùxíng	continental type
依違游移	yīwéiyóuyí	vacillate
得天獨厚	détiāndúhòu	particularly favored by nature
金觀濤	Jīn Guāntāo	contemporary scholar and theoretician (1947-) who argues for the ultra-stability of Chinese culture
起起伏伏	qǐqǐfúfú	rise and fall; ups and downs
逐鹿折衝	zhúlùzhéchōng	bid for power and subdue one's enemies

台灣開發伊始，最具影響力的，首推代表歐洲現代資本主義力量東來的葡萄牙與荷蘭殖民者，以及明朝時與日本勾結作夥的海盜兼海商。

商業性農業的視野，海洋的魅力

西方帝國主義殖民者，率先在台灣建立以出口為導向的商業性農作墾殖。以後歷經鄭領、清治以迄日據時代，台灣經濟一直有相當重要的一部份依賴農產品出口來支撐。換句話說，台灣的農業很早以來就不是以自給自足為目標的，農業產品受到商業利益左右的情況相當普遍。

即使是處於所謂的「農業時代」，台灣社會的型態也和中國式的農村大異其趣。中國式的農村基本上自成一個生產與消費的單位，村莊裡生產所有的生活必需品，與外界溝通往來可有可無，程度減至最低。這樣的生產制度所培育出來的文化，一定是安土重遷的，死守家園的，而且對出了村莊邊界外的地方充滿恐懼與敵意。另一個特色是這種村民的物質生活條件不會超出基本生存線多少，村裡會用「安貧」或「知足」一類的哲學來勸阻其成員向外發展，不要他們向廣大的世界探頭窺視。

伊始	yīshǐ	beginning; from this time onward
勾結	gōujié	collaborate with
率先	shuàixiān	take the lead
墾殖	kěnzhí	reclaim and cultivate wasteland (and establish settlements)
鄭領	Zhèng-lǐng	the period during the 17th century when Taiwan was ruled by members of the Zheng family, a clan of pirate warlords and Ming loyalists
清治	Qīng-zhì	the period when Taiwan was under the control of the Qing dynasty (1683-1895)
自给自足	zìjǐzìzú	self-sufficient
大異其趣	dàyìqíqù	have very different tastes/styles
安土重遷	āntǔzhòngqiān	deeply attached to one's native place and reluctant to leave it
安貧	ānpín	satisfied with a simple life
知足	zhīzú	content with one's lot
勸阻	quànzǔ	dissuade somebody from doing something

　　這種類型的「農業文化」，是中國大陸發展經濟最大且最難克服的阻力。值得格外指出的是：台灣的農業社會，一直就不是這種內向閉鎖型的。用中國農村的形象來想像台灣過去的農業社會，一定會得出離譜的答案。

　　台灣農業很早就商業化，意謂著即使是鄉間農民都必須與外界隨時保持聯絡。這套制度裡一貫有很多層<u>介於</u>農人和商人間的中間角色，他們把出口市場的變動傳遞給農民，又把農產品運送到各地港口。他們就是農民們取得較為開放世界視野的一個窗口。

　　商業化的農業活動，還意謂著台灣的農民很早就具有較為先進的經濟概念。至少在生產與直接消費之外，他們必須懂得一套數字性的計算方式，才能夠掌握自己的利益<u>盈虧</u>。一個中國農民對<u>收成</u>的評估，主要參考點可能就只有「夠不夠今年全家溫飽」，台灣的農民卻要算收成可能帶來多少金錢。在這種情況下，貨幣意識很早就在台灣普遍散佈，<u>史家黃仁宇</u>批評中國社會落後是<u>肇因</u>於「數字上不能管理」的問題，台灣因商業性農業的發展經驗，而減輕了問題的嚴重性。

　　商業性的農業不是為了自己吃飽而種作，而是為了追求最大的收成收益。在這樣的前提下，<u>勢必</u>會鼓勵農民嘗試不同的作物，並且盡可能地以各種方式——如<u>施肥</u>、<u>輪作</u>等——來提高地力。總的影響就是逼迫農民不能光只是習慣地年復一年用同樣的方法種同樣的東西，而必須求變化，求突破，作實驗，冒風險。這是我們祖先們走過的一條不一樣的農業之路，他們早就不是保守的農人了。現在那麼多人深深感受到台灣人內在的

介於	jièyú	situated in between
盈虧	yíngkuī	gain and loss
收成	shōuchéng	harvest; crop
黃仁宇	Huáng Rényǔ	Ray Huang (1918-2000), historian and former Nationalist soldier, famous for his *China: A Macro History*
肇因	zhàoyīn	cause; origin
勢必	shìbì	bound to; certainly will
施肥	shīféi	apply fertilizer
輪作	lúnzuò	crop rotation

「賭徒個性」，未嘗不是這種不怕風險、只求突破的集體記憶的浮顯呢！

海盜經驗則教會台灣人海洋的開放魅力。大陸型的文明把海洋視為可怕而無法超越的障壁；海洋型文明卻認為海洋是最佳的運動路徑，不像高山窪谷的陸地那般滯礙難行，海洋可以在最短時間內讓人用最省力的方法挪移到最遠。海盜可以說是大陸型文明孕育出來的怪胎，他們因為瞭解海洋，便藉著海洋作掩護，襲擊掠奪懼怕海洋的大陸性社會。

從顏思齊到鄭芝龍再到鄭成功，以台灣為基地，出現一個龐大的海上王國。他們與明朝來往，卻不臣屬於明朝。他們的文化屬性摻雜了許多日本、琉球的成份，他們的財富更是遠超過明朝中國人的一般水準。這是海洋帶來的財富，也是海洋所開放的機會。

揭開移民墾荒新階段的序幕

清康熙二十二年（西元一六八三年），施琅攻台，消滅明鄭殘餘勢力，將台灣正式納入清朝的版圖。台灣的歷史遂由前一個「海洋時期」被拉入「大陸時期」，也揭開台灣移民墾荒新階段的序幕。

從這個時期開始，台灣表現出愈來愈強烈的移民社會特色。

我們千萬不要忽視了移民社會特色對台灣歷史走向的重大左右能力。一個由移民所組成的社會，其內在匯集了許多特殊的條件，往往彼此撞擊而迸發出其他類型社會不會有的能量。

賭徒	dǔtú	gambler
滯礙難行	zhì'àinánxíng	obstructed and difficult to cross
怪胎	guàitāi	freak
顏思齊	Yán Sīqí	17th-century pirate who led Han immigrants to Taiwan from the mainland
鄭芝龍	Zhèng Zhīlóng	merchant and pirate leader (1604-1661), father of Koxinga
琉球	Liúqiú	Ryukyu Islands
序幕	xùmù	prologue; prelude
施琅	Shī Láng	admiral (1621-1696) of the Qing fleets which defeated the Zheng family and conquered Taiwan in 1683
明鄭	Míng-Zhèng	the period during which Taiwan was ruled by the Zheng family (1662-1683)

尤其是台灣早期的移民，他們甚至不是在正常情況下離家出航的，他們必須先克服渡航禁令等重重的國家公權力恐嚇，才能夠以極其簡陋的航具掙扎越過風高浪險的黑水溝，到達台灣。

這樣的移民，我們很容易可以觀察到他們個性上一些突出的共通點。

第一，　他們幾乎毫無例外都是窮苦人家，因為生計無著所以出走。

第二，　他們之所以選擇離鄉背井而不是苟活故土，表示他們對自己所擁有的能力具有強烈的信心，他們只能是樂觀主義者，相信在遠方那個島嶼上，可以找到更好的希望。只要有一點點悲觀的因素，都可能讓他們打消冒險遠走的念頭。

第三，　他們顯然都對權威與陳規抱持著反抗的態度，輕則不理，重則叛逆。國家設下許多嚴厲的禁制規定，卻都嚇阻不了他們，他們追求自主新生活的意志，遠高於國家集體秩序的號召。

第四，　他們具備面對陌生新環境的生理心理準備。早期的移民很自然地呈現懸殊的男女比例，非法偷渡者當然是以身強力壯的男人佔絕大多數，即使到後來開放合法渡航，依然是規定不准攜帶家眷。這些隻身赴台的男性，心裡還是抱著傳宗接代、綿延子嗣的強烈觀念，他們當中有許多人其實在上船之前就已經有了覺悟：此去想必只能接受在台灣當地「娶番為妻」的命運。連身邊的配偶都可以是非我族類，這樣的人，大概不容易對什麼陌生的事物感到驚異而無法接受罷。

第五，　在某些方面，他們和海盜有相通之處。他們大部分都出身於濱海地帶，雖然身受大陸性文明的養成，卻懂得如何接近海洋，如何利用

禁令	jìnlìng	prohibition; ban
公權力	gōngquánlì	government power
生計	shēngjì	livelihood
苟活故土	gǒuhuó gùtǔ	lead a wretched existence in one's native place
打消	dǎxiāo	give up; blot out
懸殊	xuánshū	entirely disparate
綿延	miányán	continuous and unbroken
子嗣	zǐsì	son; offspring
娶番為妻	qǔfānwéiqī	take a foreigner (i.e., native) as one's wife
非我族類	fēiwǒzúlèi	alien; not one of us
濱海	bīnhǎi	coastal

海洋。清朝征服鄭氏家族後，也摧毀了鄭家的海上艦隊勢力，把海洋讓給日本人及荷蘭人、葡萄牙人去縱橫來往，但移民社會的台灣，並沒有因此而徹底忘記海洋。

我們就是這種個性的人的兒孫。這些個性中許多成份至今還淌流在我們的血液裡。

尋找新餅的<u>拓邊</u>精神

一個移民的社會一定是個創造力飽滿的社會。移民最大的特點正在於無法把舊日生活裡所有既成的東西都隨身帶著飄洋過海。移民就是最大的捨棄。捨棄原來有的一切，到新的地方從頭開始。你沒有辦法帶太多舊東西來，你必須到新地方用新材料再製生活上的用具用品。

甚至連製造的技術都必須是新的。因為新的環境不見得能夠找到舊技術所需的材料與條件，你只能依照新環境提供的條件，去建造一個新家園。

所以，移民社會要成立，一定得學會在最短的時間內瞭解新環境，適應新環境。而且在新環境裡建造出來的新東西，會同時具備舊形式與新發明，變成一種混合的新樣式。

移民社會的價值裡，不會刻意去追求「純粹」，更不會逃避「混合」。移民社會如果還要<u>抱殘守缺</u>，執著於原來習慣的那一套，根本就無法生存下去。因此，在移民社會中，其他文明的概念與物品，都很容易被引進接受，不至於被唯我獨尊的價值壁壘<u>封殺</u>。

美國就是這樣的一個移民社會，所以他們能在「不純粹」中壯大成長，標榜做為世界各人種各文化的「大<u>融爐</u>」。台灣又何嘗不是一個這樣的移民社會，在過去一百年間成了多種文明的匯集點。

移民社會是由開拓新疆界開始的，因此它的世界觀當然和其他社會很不一樣。開拓新疆界事實上就是打破舊疆界。移民社會裡，疆界的概念

拓邊	tuòbiān	open up borderlands
抱殘守缺	bàocánshǒuquē	conservative; stick to old-fashioned ways
封殺	fēngshā	block and obliterate
融爐	rónglú	melting pot; crucible

不是死板固定的，而是隨時可以更動的，隨時都有人在想像疆界之外是不是另有一片沃饒的新天地。

　　拓邊精神和移民社會是二而一的。拓邊精神最有價值的地方就是它徹底打破「零和遊戲」的僵化概念。一個一般的社會裡，大家很容易傾向於把資源看成是固定的，桌上這塊就這麼大的餅，如果別人多分去一塊，就代表著我的份少了一塊。因此在這有限的空間裏，無所不用其極地進行掠奪競爭，甚至不惜做出事實上有害於整體社會運作的事。大家犄角相對，把所有的聰明才智和精力都耗竭在相互敵對爭鬥上。

　　移民社會的思考模式卻不是這樣。他們永遠不會相信餅就只有那麼一塊，這塊餅也許是這張桌上唯一的一塊，但總還有別的桌罷；就算這間房裡的確只有一張桌一塊餅，那總還有別間房罷。如果有人要霸佔這塊餅的大部分，剩下來的實在不足以吃飽，我們不見得只有跟他拼個你死我活這麼一個選擇，我們可以省下打架的力氣，去尋找新的餅，這個房間這道邊界以外的餅。

　　這是移民社會不斷活躍的精神泉源。也是台灣社會在歷史上接二連三遭遇強大挑戰，而終能成功回應的重要本錢。

(Cont.)

零和遊戲	línghéyóuxì	zero-sum game
無所不用其極	wúsuǒ búyòng qí jí	go to any length
犄角	jī jiǎo	horn

15. CONTEMPORARY SINO-JAPANESE RELATIONS

Excerpts from *Strategy and Management*

Throughout history, China and Japan have faced each other in a range of postures: teacher/pupil, victor/vanquished, partner/rival. From the earliest imperial embassies dispatched by Japan to learn about Chinese culture, to the Sino-Japanese War of 1895, when these roles were suddenly switched and Japan taught China the art of modern warfare; and from the nadir of the Nanjing Massacre to the busy trade channels of today, the two nations have always been "significant others" of a sort, bound together in a relationship which has rarely been casual. Equally constant down the years have been the sharp about-turns and flare-ups of impassioned feeling which have shaped their interaction. Nowadays, the exigencies of economics may make a degree of cooperation essential, but rivalry over who will rule the roost as East Asia's premier nation remains fierce. And any equilibrium which can be maintained between these drives is under constant threat from a core of redoubtable, and recurrent, problems which range from territorial rights over the Diaoyu (Senkaku) Islands to the manifold problems of shared history. Trickier still, each of these problems is a stand-alone flashpoint which has the power to turn the populace (and particularly the people of China) rowdy and indignant at short notice. This state of skittishness is especially apparent in the last few years, a period during which bilateral relations have spun like a weather vane from good to bad and back again.

That said, the bottom line of the relationship nowadays is, needless to say, economics; and here a certain pragmatism has continued to rule. Yong Deng observes that by 1993, Japan's Foreign Direct Investment (FDI) in China had already topped $3.39 billion,[1] and while economists may wrangle over the exact figures, investment has marched on. Moreover, the Japanese have poured funds into Chinese high-tech industries, thus enabling China's economy to step up a gear through value-added manufacturing. Meanwhile, Japan is China's most generous patron in the area of Official Development Assistance (ODA), a pattern of giving which continues at a volume that is "unprecedented,"[2] particularly given that China overtook Japan as the world's second biggest economy in 2010. Yet the real grist for such symbiosis is trade. Japan's imports from China have been exceeding those from the United States since 2002, while China is Japan's second biggest export market; and as Wu Xinbo puts it, these reciprocal economic interactions provide "the kind of grease that can

---

1. Yong Deng, "Chinese Relations with Japan: Implications for Asia-Pacific Regionalism," 378.

2. Christopher B. Johnstone, "Japan's China Policy: Implications for U.S.-Japan Relations," 1073.

smooth any frictions that may arise over political and security issues."[3]

But while bilateral trade may be booming like never before, the political and security issues to which Wu refers have grown thornier in the same approximate time frame. In blunt terms, both nations are fearful of the other, a wariness which is the flipside of the desire of each for regional dominance. For China, Japan's steady swing to the political right throughout the 1990s, and the hawkish demands to revise the postwar pacifist constitution which accompanied it, were unsettling because of what they said about Japan's renewed desire to be a potent global presence. In 1991, Japan's famously untried Self Defense Forces undertook their first mission overseas; and the reaffirmation of the US-Japan security alliance in 1995 further beefed up Japan's role and capabilities on the East Asian stage. In the eyes of many Chinese, this smacked of conspiracy and containment. Japan's willingness to defend Taiwan's corner against Chinese saber-rattling in recent years has fleshed out this hypothesis, and fed a sense that China is being corralled by jealous rivals. Yet for Japan, of course, it is China who is the real threat. A defense budget which swells year on year, regular nuclear testing, and threatening maneuvers in the Taiwan Strait all make Japan's attempts to achieve normal nation status look tame by comparison. Of course, Japan is long used to being the success story of East Asia—burst bubbles notwithstanding—and it does not relish surrendering this status to China. But just like the United States and its Janus-faced fear of China, Japan is exercised not just by the prospect of China's success, but also by the possibility of its failure. China's rise, if mismanaged, threatens all kinds of spillage for Japan— mass immigration, ruptured trade, and regional instability—and many doubt the plausibility of a new Pax Sinica.

If an uneasy balance between economic partnership and political rivalry forms the deep structure of Sino-Japanese relations in the contemporary period, then—as mentioned above—it is a nexus of linked disputes which constantly threatens to throw this balance off-kilter. Territorial squabbles make up the lesser part of this contention. In particular, ownership of the Diaoyu Islands is something of a running battle. The Diaoyu, a tiny archipelago of uninhabited rocks and islets, are claimed by China, Taiwan, and Japan, partly because they lie next to a continental shelf which is believed to contain up to 100 billion barrels of oil, and partly because they have become a rallying cry for patriotic sentiment.[4] Tension flared up over the islands in 1990, 1996, and again in 2010; but in each case, the Chinese government kept a close eye on demonstrations of patriotism, presumably with a view to keeping economic cooperation on track.

---

3. Wu Xinbo, "The Security Dimension of Sino-Japanese Relations: Warily Watching One Another," 309.
4. See Erica Strecker Downs and Phillip C. Saunders, "Legitimacy and the Limits of Nationalism: China and the Diaoyu Islands," 126.

Such pragmatism has, however, proved far more elusive whenever the so-called "history problem" (历史问题 *lishi wenti*) rears its head. The history problem is the many-sided scourge of Sino-Japanese relations, ranging over the Yasukuni shrine, the "truth" about the Nanjing Massacre and the comfort women, and the rumbling textbook saga. The Yasukuni shrine is the symbolic final resting place of nearly 2.5 million souls who lost their lives fighting for Japan's empire—including a small number of class A war criminals. In 1975, Miki Takeo became the first postwar prime minister to visit Yasukuni, and since then six have followed suit, usually in their capacity as private citizens.[5] Yet for many across the rest of East Asia, Yasukuni is a symbol of aggression, ethnocentrism, ultranationalism, and religious fanaticism, and these visits by incumbent prime ministers are an affront to already bruised sensibilities. Further fuelling indignation is the revisionist push in recent Japanese public life, and the appearance of a noisy breed of holocaust deniers who argue that the "comfort women" were "voluntary" prostitutes, and that the Nanjing Massacre is a hoax. Revisionist claims also stoke the slow-burning furor over the government-approved history textbooks used in Japan's secondary schools. Different versions of these textbooks have inflamed Japan's neighbors over the years, but all are alike in the neutral, whitewashed gloss they put on Japan's imperial-era depredations. Naturally enough, Japan has a rather different take on the intractable problem of history. Many Japanese are now suffering "history fatigue," tired of being excoriated for the sins of their fathers while their taxes are funneled off to pay for ODA to China. Just as prevalent is cynicism about China's motives for endlessly playing the history card. History equals leverage in the eyes of Japanese skeptics: it justifies demands for continued aid at a time when China can more than stand on its own two feet, and it keeps Japan hamstrung in its criticism of CCP conduct from Tiananmen downwards. Above all, there is a suspicion that the Chinese government plays fast and loose with history for reasons of its own. Fifty years and untold resources have been invested in nurturing Japanophobia, and a chief aim of this project has been to turn Japan-bashing into a tool for "patriotic education." The CCP—which rode to triumph on the back of its bloody resistance against the Japanese—routinely uses history to shore up its mandate in the present, and many in Japan wonder when the demonology will end.

Either way, perhaps the most telling point about the history problem is its own inner momentum: once the past is invoked, deliberately or otherwise, the managers of bilateral relations often find it slipping out of their control. Events over the last few years illustrate this vividly. The turn of the millennium saw a gentle upswing in bilateral relations: daily dealings

---

5. For an analysis of this stance, see John Nelson, "Social Memory as Ritual Practice: Commemorating Spirits of the Military Dead at Yasukuni Shinto Shrine," 456-58.

between the two governments had become a matter of course; Japanese citizens were being admitted to China without visas; and Chinese officials were even mooting the idea of renaming the Nanjing Massacre Memorial Museum the softer-sounding "Nanjing International Peace Centre." This warm glow was generated in part by the ascension to China's paramount leadership of Hu Jintao, whose advocacy of "China's peaceful rise" (see chap. 16) acknowledges the need for alliance with Japan. Rapprochement (接近 *jiejin*) became the motto of the moment, and its virtues were analyzed in a series of articles which appeared in the influential government-sponsored journal *Strategy and Management* (战略与管理 Zhanlüe yu guanli) in the first half of 2003.[6] The texts excerpted in this chapter are taken from the series, and they exemplify its stance. Yet by the latter part of 2003, "history" was already dampening this friendly ambience. The accidental unearthing of poison gas canisters abandoned by the Japanese army in Heilongjiang in August, the three-day "mass orgy" between Japanese tourists and local women in the southern city of Zhuhai a month later, and a racist skit performed by Japanese students in Xi'an in October all brought back memories of invasion and brutality. By 2004, Chinese fans were openly jeering at the Japanese football team at the Asian Cup finals in Beijing, and in 2005, a new textbook-related drama seized the stage, leading to full-blown anti-Japanese riots across numerous cities in which Japanese embassies, consulates, restaurants, and supermarkets were attacked. The years since have seen a slight subsiding of tension, particularly since the departure of the maverick Japanese prime minister Koizumi Jun'ichirō—whose visits to Yasukuni were annual throughout his tenure. But as East Asia attempts, for the first time in its history, to accommodate two closely matched economic and political powers, it would surely be rash to assume that this détente will blossom into permanent alliance. Bruising clashes over the Diaoyu Islands in late 2010 simply prove the point.

Shi Yanhong. "Zhong-Ri jiejin yu 'waijiao geming'." *Zhanlüe yu guanli* 2/57 (2003), 71-3.

Xue Li. "Zhong-Ri guanxi neng fou chaoguo lishi wenti." *Zhanlüe yu guanli* 4/59 (2003), 28-9.

Further Reading

Dirlik, Arif. "'Past Experience, If Not Forgotten, Is a Guide to the Future': Or, What Is in a Text? The Politics of History in Chinese-Japanese Relations." *boundary 2* 18/3 (1991), 29-58.

---

6. The journal was closed down in September 2004 after it published an article on China's relationship with North Korea which jeopardized relations with Pyongyang.

Downs, Erica Strecker, and Phillip C. Saunders. "Legitimacy and the Limits of Nationalism: China and the Diaoyu Islands." *International Security* 23/3 (1999), 114-146.

Garrett, Banning, and Bonnie Glaser. "Chinese Apprehensions about Revitalization of the U.S.-Japan Alliance." *Asian Survey* 37/4 (1997), 383-402.

Hilpert, Hanns-Günther, and René Haak, eds. *Japan and China: Cooperation, Competition, and Conflict.* Basingstoke: Palgrave, 2002.

Johnstone, Christopher B. "Japan's China Policy: Implications for U.S.-Japan Relations." *Asian Survey* 38/11 (1998), 1067-85.

Ming Wan. *Sino-Japanese Relations: Interaction, Logic, and Transformation.* Stanford: Stanford University Press, 2006.

———. "Tensions in Recent Sino-Japanese Relations: The May 2002 Shenyang Incident." *Asian Survey* 43/5 (2003), 826-44.

Nelson, John. "Social Memory as Ritual Practice: Commemorating Spirits of the Military Dead at Yasukuni Shinto Shrine." *Journal of Asian Studies* 62/2 (2003), 443-67.

Newby, Laura. *Sino-Japanese Relations: China's Perspective.* London: Routledge, 1988.

Rose, Caroline. *Sino-Japanese Relations: Facing the Past, Looking to the Future?* London: RoutledgeCurzon, 2005.

———. "The Textbook Issue: Domestic Sources of Japan's Foreign Policy." *Japan Forum* 11/2 (1999), 205-16.

Wakabayashi, Bob Tadashi. "The Nanking 100-Man Killing Contest Debate: War Guilt amid Fabricated Illusions, 1971-75." *Journal of Japanese Studies* 26/2 (2000), 307-40.

Whiting, Allen S. *China Eyes Japan.* Berkeley: University of California Press, 1989.

Wu Xinbo. "The Security Dimension of Sino-Japanese Relations: Warily Watching One Another." *Asian Survey,* 40/2 (2000), 296-310.

Yang, Daqing. "Convergence or Divergence? Recent Historical Writings on the Rape of Nanjing." *American Historical Review* 104/3 (1999), 842-65.

Yong Deng. "Chinese Relations with Japan: Implications for Asia-Pacific Regionalism." *Pacific Affairs* 70/3 (1997), 373-91.

时殷弘：中日接近与"外交革命"

一

近年来，中日关系中相当经久、广泛和深刻的紧张构成了中国对外关系中很少数特别令人担忧、也特别催人思索的方面或问题之一。不仅如此，尤其具有<u>忧患</u>意味的是，这紧张的最突出、也最具深远危险性的特征，在于中日两国各自很大部分国民之间（甚或略为夸张地说是中日两个民族之间）近年迅速增长着的互厌和敌意，亦即一位中国作者最近一篇重要文章的副标题所说，是"中日民间之忧"。该文以某种<u>报道文学</u>似的<u>生动</u>有力的方式，加上冷静的理性思考，<u>列举</u>、警示和谈论种种现象，那是我们大多数人总的来说其实都相当熟悉，但往往远不那么勇敢地予以正视和深思的。在此，只需要从并非<u>罕见</u>的有关<u>民意</u>测验资料中，举出其公正性无可怀疑的单单一项<u>调查</u>，来<u>印证</u>事态发展的严重性。中国社会科学院和日本《朝日新闻》合作，于2002年8月末到9月中旬分别在中日两国进行了被称为全国范围的民意调查，结果显示：(1) 50%的中国回应者和45%的日本回应者认为中日关系状况不好，而持相反看法的中日回应者则分别占22%和41%；与1997年进行的前一次同样的测验相比，认为中日关系状况不好的中日回应者分别增加了21%和5%；(2) 80%的中国回应者将"历史认识"列为影响中日关系的<u>头号</u>负面因素，而在40%的日本回应者那里，这样的因素是"缺乏互相理解"和"政治制度不同"。总之，情况如报道这次民意测验的《朝日新闻》所说，"大多数日本人和中国人觉得他们两国间的关系不好"，因而同先前一些年里的情况相比，"中日关系正在恶化"。

由于近年中国公众的对日情绪和<u>舆论</u>氛围，加上有关的媒体报道和研

忧患	yōuhuàn	concern; worry; solicitude
报道文学	bàodào wénxué	reportage literature
生动	shēngdòng	lively; vivid
列举	lièjǔ	list; cite item by item
罕见	hǎnjiàn	rare
民意	mínyì	popular will; public opinion
印证	yìnzhèng	verify; confirm
头号	tóuhào	number one; first-rate; the largest
舆论	yúlùn	public opinion

究工作中的重大缺陷，一般中国人对于日本公众一段时间以来的对华情绪和对华看法，连同其日本国内政治影响，几乎完全缺乏了解。就此，读一下英国《经济学家》杂志2001年初的一篇专题文章肯定是有益的。其中写道："这些日子里……尽管有（中日两国）官方的要人放心的表示，（中日）关系却不好，而且愈益更糟。为此，日本人怪罪中国在贸易和对外政策方面的咄咄逼人。然而，相当大一部分原因可以在日本国内找到。在那里，同中国'交往'(engaging) 的老政策正受到新一代张扬(assertive)的政客、学者和报人的持续抨击。甚至外务省官员也已开始予以注意。官方的对华政策已突然开始强硬起来。"在日本各界和公众中间，"对华鹰派有一群竖耳聆听他们讲话的听众……日本病态的经济和高失业率在煽着沙文主义的火焰。"此外，中国的对日谴责和要求、中国公众中相当流行的厌日反日舆论、两国间的贸易摩擦和领土争端、来自中国的非法移民、部分旅日中国人的刑事犯罪和黑社会活动等，在该文看来都有助于日本"形形色色的民族主义者"在一定的公众同情和呼应基础上，"要求实行一种更为张扬的对华政策"，而石原慎太郎之流右翼鹰派"正在得到愈益增长的赞同，尤其在比较年轻的日本人中间"。此类状况的原因如该文所述，相当复杂，日本自身国内的经济、政治、心理原因总的来说很可能是首要的。然而无可讳言，中国从民间到政府的某些对日基本态势和行为也跻身于原因之列，无论它们有多大部分有怎样的确实正义的理由，而中国可做的首先是优化自己的有关战略和态势，从而为中国自己至关紧要的利益促进大幅度改善中日关系。

《经济学家》	Jīngjìxuéjiā	*The Economist* magazine
咄咄逼人	duōduōbīrén	overbearing
抨击	pēngjī	attack verbally or in writing
外务省	Wàiwùshěng	Japanese Foreign Ministry
鹰派	yīngpài	hawkish parties
竖耳聆听	shù'ěrlíngtīng	listen attentively
沙文主义	shāwénzhǔyì	chauvinism
谴责	qiǎnzé	censure
石原慎太郎	Ishihara Shintarō	maverick politician and author, governor of Tokyo since 1999 (1932-)
无可讳言	wúkěhuìyán	there is no hiding the fact
跻身	jīshēn	ranked among
至关紧要	zhìguānjǐnyào	of the utmost importance

二

日本邻近中国，有1亿以上人口，经济实力和技术水平处于世界最前列，并且因此具有成为军事大强国的很大一部分客观条件。因此，完全可以认为中日两国多数人民之间近年迅速增长着的互厌和敌意不受制止地发展下去，对中国的中长期未来相当危险。讲穿了，这危险之一就在于恶性发展下去，石原慎太郎之类反华、排外、极端民族主义和政治／军事<u>扩张主义</u>的极右势力就有可能有朝一日控制日本政治和对外政策方向。中国领导人多次十分正确地强调要"<u>高瞻远瞩</u>"地对待中日关系，很大部分意义大概就在于此。<u>鉴于</u>这样的危险，也鉴于中国在东亚的外部总体安全环境比较严峻，大力尝试中日接近、尽可能避免或缓解中日之间的"安全两难"就其本身来说至关重要。中国大陆经不起在一个往往敌对的美国、敌对的台湾以及可能敌对的印度之外，还面对一个敌对的日本。从全局观念出发，具有根本意义的战略集中原则要求大力争取改善中日关系、实现中日接近，以便中国能够主要在中长期安全意义上尽可能集中应对美国实在和潜在的对华<u>防范</u>、压力与威胁，连同集中致力于台湾问题上的<u>阻独促统</u>重任。

近两三年来，尤其是"9.11"事件以来，美国的巨大力量优势和在世界政治中的霸权态势达到了可称<u>史无前例</u>的地步，它对中国真正崛起的戒备，它阻滞中国具备强国的军事力量和国际政治影响的倾向，也发展到了可称前所未有的程度，尽管美国行政当局的对华意图、态势和政策行为可以发生显著的<u>局部</u>良性变化，也尽管中美两国之间长远来看也有真正的希望争取形成总的和平协调与协作前景。与此同时，虽然近年来的一项基本方针——以对美关系为重中之重，尽可能（甚至不时在相当程度上<u>忍辱</u>

扩张主义	kuòzhāngzhǔyì	expansionism
高瞻远瞩	gāozhānyuǎnzhǔ	far-sighted
鉴于	jiànyú	in view of
防范	fángfàn	on guard; vigilance
阻独促统	zǔdúcùtǒng	prevent (Taiwanese) independence and promote reunification
史无前例	shǐwúqiánlì	unprecedented
局部	júbù	partial; part
忍辱负重	rěnrǔfùzhòng	endure humiliation to carry out an important task

负重）维持中美良性关系——出于中国国家利益的必需，并且总的来说产生了对中国至关紧要的有利效果，但是单凭这一基本方针，显然不足以真正<u>实质性</u>地大幅度改善（至少在当前<u>共和党</u>行政当局执政期间）美国的对华基本观念、基本政策和战略态势以及中国的中长期外部安全环境。不仅如此，中国已经可以相当强烈地感觉到，这一方针有两项代价：第一，对美外交的<u>回旋余地</u>必不可免地受到颇大限制，并且因而在多项重大的国际问题（一定意义上乃至某些国内问题）上的回旋余地也受到不利的制约；而且，由于国际政治军事形势的局部紧张化和美俄两国的显著接近，这种受限情势在某些方面进一步加剧；第二，在具体实施中被不少中国公众往往不正确地看作<u>未免</u>一味"示弱""示软"的对美态势有损于国家对外政策所需的、比较广泛的国内公众支持，而在中国"大众政治"随改革和社会发展愈趋形成的情况下，这种公众支持愈益重要。在所有这些情况下，至关重要的战略<u>灵活性</u>原则要求中国局部调整自己的大国外交构局，有力地缓解某些重要方面的对美被动境地，显著增强对美外交<u>杠杆</u>，营造一种大有助于促使美国政府乃至美国舆论朝良性方向多反思、多改善对华态势的国际氛围压力。就此目的而言，中日接近是一项（在能够比较明确预计的时期里甚至很可能是唯一的一项）可以有很大分量的外交举措。

然而与此同时，必须认识到日本是美国在东亚的首要盟国，并且缺乏外交独立传统；不可设想在可明确预见的时期内，日美间现有和可能出现的矛盾会发展到实质性地动摇日美军事／政治同盟的地步。不仅如此，有许多原因使日本会对中国的外部困难感到<u>庆幸</u>，也有许多原因决定它会对中国的力量增进和中日间的"权势转移"（power transition）怀抱疑惧：所有这些将使日本不愿接受、并且<u>警惕</u>任何在战略上明显地图谋中日协作<u>制衡</u>

实质性	shízhìxìng	substantive
共和党	Gònghédǎng	Republican Party
回旋余地	huíxuán yúdì	leeway; room to maneuver
未免	wèimiǎn	rather; inevitably
灵活性	línghuóxìng	flexibility
杠杆	gànggǎn	lever
庆幸	qìngxìng	rejoice
警惕	jǐngtì	on guard; vigilant
制衡	zhìhéng	checks and balances

美国的"外交革命"。这近似于1890年后的奥地利几乎全无可能成为法国或俄国制衡德国的伙伴。

可是与此同时，还有若干重大因素很可能使日本像中国一样，可以变得认真地、甚或比较强烈地<u>企盼</u>中日接近。它们包括：与中国相邻的地理位置和由此而来对于中日敌对的担忧；在经济长期衰退中特别突出的对华贸易和投资需求；在因为中国经济<u>勃然</u>兴起而改变了的东亚经济格局中维持日本影响的需要，而这分明只有通过与中国的协调和协作才能做到；在东亚国际政治、特别是东北亚区域安全方面与中国协调和协作的同样大的重要性，它们对于日本维持足够的安全感和实现区域政治大国抱负显然<u>必不可少</u>；二战后日本国内<u>准和平主义</u>的"贸易国"政治文化虽受一定<u>侵蚀</u>、却仍然占有的主流地位；日本对于美国的一种可有或必有的担忧，即东亚稳定与日本自身安全将由于美国（一个过分霸权主义、<u>单边主义</u>甚至<u>黩武主义</u>的美国）可能不时太具威胁性和太<u>莽撞</u>的对华态势而遭到损害；日本关于自身一种基本处境的必有愿望，那就是改变它虽然位于东亚、却与各主要邻国（首先是巨大和愈益重要的中国）长期保持心理和情感上严重疏离的那种很不自在的状况。只要中日关系有大幅度进展，只要实现了中日接近，中国对美外交和战略地位的显著改善几乎是其必然或"自动"的副产品。中日接近可以是一种虽然在程度上打了折扣、但仍不失其原来意义的"外交革命"。

如上所述，在通过中日接近显著改善安全处境以及外交地位方面，中国有非常重大的利益。而且，中国对于中日关系大为改善的实际需求应当认为超过日本在这方面的需求。然而另一方面，中日关系由于历史、民族

企盼	qǐpàn	eagerly hope for
勃然	bórán	vigorously; suddenly
必不可少	bìbùkěshǎo	essential; indispensable
准和平主义	zhǔnhépíngzhǔyì	quasi-pacifist
侵蚀	qīnshí	erode
单边主义	dānbiānzhǔyì	unilateralist
黩武主义	dúwǔzhǔyì	militaristic
莽撞	mǎngzhuàng	rash; impetuous

心理和东亚国际政治构造等方面原因，原本就多有困难，而近年来与两国政府政策和公众舆论（或许尤其是与中国公众舆论）相关，相当显著地趋于恶化。利益大，但困难也大，这就需要中国政府本着真正创新性的国策思维和很大的战略决心，主动地以看似重大的代价（或者说依靠对日态度、态势和政策行为的主动的大调整）来谋求中日接近，何况现行的某些对日态势和政策的基本无效更突出了这么做的必要。

薛力： 中日关系能否超越历史问题

2002年8月底中国社会科学院与《朝日新闻》社联合进行的一项调查显示，80%的中国人将历史问题看作是影响中日关系的第一因素。无疑，切实执行中日双方达成的＂以史为鉴，面向未来＂的共识是解决历史问题的根本途径，但日本的历史观与政治潮流则显示：日本难以如德国般反省二战历史。这就引出了本文的写作目的：在这种情况下，中日关系能否超越历史问题？本人的看法是：中方应当采取进一步的措施，超越历史问题，为了国家的总体和长远利益，这可能是中国不得不吞下的一枚苦果。

这个观点的得出，乃基于对以下几个问题的分析而得出的逻辑判断。

一 日本的历史观；来源是什么？与德国有可比性吗？有可能改变吗？

在开始讨论之前，先明确两个概念。

中日关系中的历史问题，是指部分日本人基于他们对二战及相关问题的认识而采取的行动，具体包括日本首相参拜供有二战甲级战犯的靖国神社、日本官方不肯就侵华战争作出正式的（书面的）抱歉、日本的一些政界人士不时就侵华战争发表自己的＂个人见解＂、右翼势力通过大众媒体（广播、电影、电视、互联网（网络）、漫画、书籍等）表达他们对那场战争的看法、右翼势力对揭露战争真相者的攻击与迫害、一些人要求修改中学历史教科书并编纂代表他们观点的历史教科书、右翼通过遍布全国的战争资料展览鼓吹日本是受害者等。修宪的努力、派兵海外、有事法案、

以史为鉴， 　面向未来	yǐ shǐ wéi jiàn, 　miànxiàng wèilái	take history as the mirror while 　looking to the future
吞下一枚苦果	tūnxià yìméi kǔguǒ	swallow a bitter pill
参拜	cānbài	make a formal visit
甲级战犯	jiǎjí zhànfàn	class A war criminal
靖国神社	Jìngguó shénshè	Yasukuni shrine
编纂	biānzuǎn	compile
鼓吹	gǔchuī	play up; advocate; preach
修宪	xiūxiàn	amend a constitution
有事法案	Yǒushì Fǎ'àn	the Contingency Bills: recent 　legislation which expands the 　autonomy of Japan's self- 　defense forces to participate in 　military actions outside the 　country

211

钓鱼岛争端等虽然严格说来不属于上述历史问题，但因为右翼人士在这些
事项中常常比较活跃，这些事件又与历史问题交替发生或纠缠在一起。所
以，它们常带有历史问题的影子。

　　本文中的日本历史观，特指部分日本人对二战及相关问题的认识，这
种认识往往与中、韩、朝、东盟成员国等亚洲受害国的一般观点相异乃至
相左。如认为大和民族优越、是 " 大东亚战争 " 不是侵略战争，天皇对战
争不负责任、新一代不应对过去的事情负责、中韩批评日本是 " 对其内部
事务揪住不放 " 等等。这种历史观之所以成为中日关系中的历史问题，目
前而言，主要源于中老年右翼人士、相当部分年轻一代政治家的推动。日
本共产党、社会党、公明党， " 中国归还者联络会 " 成员，东史郎、小川

钓鱼岛	Diàoyúdǎo	Diaoyu/Senkaku islands
大和民族	Dàhé mínzú	*Yamato minzoku*: nationalistic term for the Japanese people
天皇	tiānhuáng	emperor of Japan
公明党	Gōngmíngdǎng	Komeitō: Japanese political party
中国归还者 联络会	Zhōngguó Guīhuán-zhě Liánluòhuì	Association of Returnees from China, a group of former soldiers interned in China after WWII who admit their war guilt and promote peace between China and Japan
东史郎	Azuma Shirô	Japanese soldier (1912-2006) who openly admitted taking part in atrocities against the Chinese during WWII, and published a diary detailing his involvement in the Nanjing Massacre
小川武满	Ogawa Takemitsu	Japanese medical doctor (1913-) posted to China during WWII who wrote a memoir describing the brutality of the Japanese military command, and who also admitted his involvement in the Nanjing Massacre

武满等退役老兵，仓桥凌子等老兵亲属，＂孩子与21世纪全国网络＂成员，＂日本教职员组合＂成员，＂亚洲历史问题恳谈会＂成员等的观点与周围国家相同或相近，故不属于本文所指的＂日本历史观＂（他们的观点如果成了日本社会的共识，则中日关系中的历史问题可能不复存在）。调查显示：普通民众认识到那是一场侵略战争，日本伤害了周围国家，应当反省、道歉并做出某种补偿，但总体看来，普通民众的反省是不彻底的，这是＂日本历史观＂形成的社会心理基础。

1．为什么形成这种历史观？

(1) 文化、历史与宗教原因。神道教与武士道背景使得日本人对历史缺乏独立的思考判断能力、无法进行彻底的反思，国家缺乏包容性，民众有明显的跟风心理。所以，对广岛、长崎核攻击的反省仅止于认定自己是核弹的唯一受害者，而没意识到自己是＂加害者＂甚于＂受害者＂。又比如，在西方发达国家中，日本是吸收外来移民最少的。在难民问题上，政府奉行的＂原则上不接收难民＂政策使日本显得缺乏大国应有的包容度。

督教徒认为上帝是不会犯错误的，日本人则不但认为天皇不会犯错误，而且认为＂天皇是日本国民的象征、是国民宗教生活的核心、是超宗

仓桥凌子	Kurahashi Ayako	daughter of Ōsawa Yūkichi, a former military policeman who confessed to participation in a "war of aggression"; Kurahashi went public with his apology
孩子与21世纪 　全国网络…	Háizi yǔ 21 shìjì 　quánguó wǎngluò…	Japanese organizations which promote honest discussion of the war and its commemoration
亚洲历史问题 　恳谈会	Yàzhōu lìshǐ wèntí 　kěntánhuì	
日本教职员组合	Rìběn jiàozhíyuán 　zǔhé	Japanese teachers' union, well-known for its left-wing orientation and opposition to revisionist textbooks
补偿	bǔcháng	make recompense
神道教	Shéndàojiào	Shintoism
武士道	wǔshìdào	*bushidō*: the martial spirit
跟风心理	gēnfēng xīnlǐ	"me-tooist" mentality
奉行	fèngxíng	pursue a course or policy

教的信仰对象 " ，所以，日本人会建 " <u>八纮一宇</u> " 塔，但不会喊出像 " 上帝死了 " 这样的话；可以向天皇认错，向强者低头，不会向弱者认错、向<u>公理</u>低头。

八纮一宇塔	bāhóngyìyǔtǎ	"Hakkô ichiu" tower in Miyazaki prefecture: *hakkō ichiu*, or "all the eight corners of the world," was a slogan drawn from Japan's creation myth which was promoted during the militarist era as a justification for the nation's aggressive war in Asia
公理	gōnglǐ	rule of law; justice

16. CHINA'S PEACEFUL RISE

The New Path of China's Peaceful Rise and the Future of Asia *and*
The New Path of China's Peaceful Rise and Sino-US Relations
Zheng Bijian

Some time in the late 1990s, the world began to wake up to China's burgeoning economic power. The China that Western media had always portrayed as a communist state and an infringer of human rights began, article by article, news item by news item, to be viewed as a powerful economic entity that was rapidly climbing the world rankings. When China's GDP began to chase that of Japan, jitters in financial think tanks and academic publications became mainstream questions. As the Chinese stock exchange grew, soaring internal investment and double-digit annual inflation prompted questions in the foreign financial press. Could such growth be sustained? What effect would a Chinese slow-down have on the world economy? China's purchase of US debt might underpin US budget deficits, but at what cost? Could America's Mid-west industries survive Chinese competition? The tensions of containing China's growth were sharpened as whole cities of high-rise buildings seem to appear almost overnight on the eastern seaboard, and images of thick smog raised still more fears: could China cope with the effects of its consumer power—and could the planet itself cope with China's energy demands and costs?

As the new millennium began, both China and the rest of the world took stock of these shifting power relations. G8 membership and WTO entry took the political center stage. A China-India axis suddenly became the object of attention. Asian neighbors became proactive in their quest for regional alliances. Sino-Japanese relations cooled as vocal patriots expressed their Chinese nationalism in "spontaneous" demonstrations over such issues as war reparations and textbook history. The open wound of Taiwanese independence remained as sore as ever. China's support for dubious regimes from North Korea to Zimbabwe was scrutinized as its economic clout began to raise questions of how China would wield the new geopolitical power that it had acquired. All of these international relationships now took on new contours as China began to be perceived as a potential superpower. On the positive side, China promoted debate on "globalization," which provided a key shared term for discourse. And when China persuaded North Korea to return to the negotiating table with the United States over nuclear testing in April 2007, and then later that year helped to curb the violence in Burma, Western democratic nations had much to be thankful for in China's new process of engagement. China's international orientation has continued throughout the first decade of the new century with the roll-out from 2004 onward of the Confucius Institute program and its promotion of Chinese language across the world, and with the Beijing Olympics handing China a golden opportunity to assert itself globally at a more popular level.

If economic power ushered in a new era of foreign policy, it also created a raft of domestic questions. The liberalization which had allowed non–state sector growth and private entrepreneurship was paying huge economic dividends, but doubts lingered over how the transition to a market economy could be finessed internally. Although "Reform and Opening Up" had greatly changed the political landscape in the two decades since its inception in 1978, the perceived need for Party policy, rhetoric, and direction to integrate Marxist-Leninist-Maoist thought remained. The mark of a new policy had always been a newly minted slogan or guiding thought, from "Without the Communist Party there will be no new China" during the early days of CCP rule, to "Socialism with Chinese characteristics" in the Dengist era. The new leadership of Hu Jintao and Wen Jiabao still needed to convince Party and country alike that they were developing an inherited communist vision.

Into this matrix came Zheng Bijian 郑必坚 (1932-), who in late 2003 articulated a new framework for China's foreign policy and dubbed it "China's peaceful rise" (和平崛起 *heping jueqi*). Zheng's involvement and the subsequent (if short-lived) adoption of the slogan points to a greater openness in Chinese policy formulation. Zheng, who had been vice-president of the Central Party School and an erstwhile speechwriter for Deng Xiaoping, was no longer a government member, but was the head of a research unit, the China Reform Forum. Following a fact-finding trip to the United States in late 2002, Zheng became convinced that fear of China and divided views on its rise could have negative effects on China's future status as a major world power. In a report submitted to the Central Committee, he proposed setting up a multi-body task force to research the question of how Chinese-style socialism could integrate with regional and global neighbors. After a conglomerate of research units had pursued the question, Zheng developed their ideas in a series of speeches. These speeches pick up different angles, exploring China's relationship with the United States, Europe, and Asia respectively.

The formula of China's "peaceful rise" can be seen as both descriptive and prescriptive. It was intended to set the course of China's development, and to provide assurances to the outside world about that course. Part of its novelty was that the theory specifically located China within the wider world; it was not a policy which described her own development to herself, as had so many previous slogans. A dawning awareness of the import of foreign perception had grown alongside China's participation in world affairs. Given that China had the media legacy of Tiananmen to contend with throughout the nineties, incursions into territorial disputes and saber-rattling over Taiwan did nothing to improve the nation's image or its relations with near neighbors, and China had already begun to initiate overtures toward adjoining states, a process which led to "qualitative improvements in China's bilateral and multilateral diplomacy in Asia."[1] The West, meanwhile, was still engaged in debates on whether China posed a threat to US dominance or whether its economy might implode first. China responded to both strands of the debate, and "peaceful rise" can be seen as an attempt to address such fears at the same time as asserting China's new confidence.

Zheng Bijian chose the Boao Forum, held on Hainan in November 2003, to make the first presentation of his ideas. Key themes recur throughout his speeches, which were picked up and reiterated by politicians. Zheng sets out from the premise that China is a developing country, but one which wishes to attain the same standard of living as developed countries for its citizens by the middle of the twenty-first century. The difficulties of managing a state of 1.3 billion citizens cannot be overlooked, since great wealth would have to be distributed thinly. China will have to be self-reliant in its development. It will, however, seek to develop in step with the contemporary world, putting economic construction in the fore. The plan is that internal reform of the socialist market economy and external opening will develop in concert with drives to raise the level of civilization (文明 *wenming*) of China's people. A program of coordinated management of paired relations, such as between rural and urban growth, and between people and the environment, is also crucial to Zheng's policy. His speeches acknowledge to foreign listeners the threats that rising states can pose. Yet he contends that warfare is always a route to failure. China will spare no effort to rise (奋力崛起 *fenli jueqi*), but will also maintain peace, steadfastly following a path of "not striving for supremacy." In Asia, China's "peaceful rise" will be a force for stability and security.

A new rhetoric of coexistence with capitalist states marked a move away from standard PRC discourse. Another nicety of the formulation "development path with a peaceful rise" was its broad chronological span, which covers the entire period from the 11th Central Committee (1978) through to the middle of the current century. "Peaceful rise" theoretically allowed for China to continue along Deng Xiaoping's path of economic prosperity, building on the achievement of "basic comfort" (小康 *xiaokang*) for all which was heralded in the early 1990s. When both Premier Wen Jiabao and President Hu Jintao adopted the term "peaceful rise" in speeches during December 2003, it seemed that the new policy had been espoused at the highest levels. At a later speech to the National People's Congress in March 2004, Wen outlined four aspects of "peaceful rise:" China's role in safeguarding world peace while ensuring her own

---

1. Bonnie S. Glaser and Evan S. Medeiros, "The Changing Ecology of Foreign Policy-Making in China," 293.

development; China's blend of self-reliance and economic interdependence with the rest of the world; the long time span needed for her rise; and the lack of any threat posed to other nations. By April, however, Hu Jintao had adopted the term "peaceful development," thus signaling a distancing from the "peaceful rise" motif.

It later transpired that although "peaceful rise" remained an acceptable research concept, a Politburo standing committee had taken the decision to shelve the term in Party and government documents.[2] Criticisms had appeared from sundry quarters, and had evidently taken politicians by surprise. Both "peaceful" and "rise" were attacked. Some argued that no country had ever risen peacefully; it was a void concept. Indeed, militarists wanted China to retain a war option and limit its pacifist rhetoric, especially given the precarious Taiwan situation. People's Liberation Army experts feared the effects on military spending should the policy take hold. Others were more concerned about the potential misreading of the term, especially the *jue* of *jueqi*, with its connotations of an abrupt mountain face, which might suggest aggression—particularly to China's East Asian neighbors. There were also fears that the slogan could incite nationalism within China itself. Yet others argued that the concept was premature, and touted a false sense of China's importance.

Although "peaceful rise" dropped out of frontline political usage, others have continued to develop the concept. A newspaper article in 2007 by Shi Yinhong 时殷弘, professor of international relations at Renmin University, discusses "peaceful rise," linking it to Joseph Nye's well-known concept of "soft power." Shi's article reiterates China's peaceful development in both the economic and the diplomatic spheres, while chiding the United States for its "colossal mistake" in adopting a containment strategy and beefing up its military presence in the mid- and West Pacific during the late 1990s.[3] Chinese and Western academics have continued to debate the term, using it to examine wider questions of regime stability, the continued legitimacy and authority of the CCP, and bilateral foreign policy perspectives.[4]

Further Reading

Garrett, Banning. "US-China Relations in the Era of Globalization and

---

2. Glaser and Medeiros, "The Changing Ecology of Foreign Policy-Making in China," 300.

3. Shi Yinhong, "China's Peaceful Rise Is All About Soft Power,' *China Daily*, 14 June 2007.

4. On the latter, see Baogang Guo, "China's Peaceful Development, Regime Stability and Political Legitimacy," and Xuetang Guo, "Maintaining an Asymmetric but Stable China-US Military Relationship," in Sujian Guo, ed. *China's "Peaceful Rise" in the 21st Century*, 39-60 and 159-182 respectively.

Terror: A Framework for Analysis.' *Journal of Contemporary China* 15/48 (2006), 389-415.

Glaser, Bonnie S., and Evan S. Medeiros. "The Changing Ecology of Foreign Policy-Making in China: The Ascension and Demise of the Theory of 'Peaceful Rise.'" *China Quarterly* 190 (2007), 291-310.

Guo Sujian, ed. *China's "Peaceful Rise" in the 21st Century*. London: Ashgate, 2006.

Lampton, David M. *The Making of Chinese Foreign and Security Policy*. Stanford: Stanford University Press, 2002.

Lu Ning. *The Dynamics of Foreign Policy Decision-Making in China*. Boulder: Westview Press, 1997.

Shi Yinhong, "China's Peaceful Rise Is All About Soft Power,' *China Daily*, 14 June 2007.

Shirk, Susan. *China: Fragile Superpower: How China's Internal Politics Could Derail Its Peaceful Rise*. Oxford: Oxford University Press, 2007.

Spence, Jonathan, Zbigniew Brzezinski, et al. "China Rising: How the Asian Colossus Is Changing Our World." *Foreign Policy Magazine* (January/February 2005), 43-58.

Suettinger, Robert. "The Rise and Descent of 'Peaceful Rise.'" *China Leadership Monitor* 12/4 (2004), 1-10.

Sutter, Robert. "The Taiwan Problem in the Second George W. Bush Administration —US Officials' Views and Their Implications for US Policy.' *Journal of Contemporary China* 15/48 (2006), 417-44.

Wang Hongying. "National Image Building and Chinese Foreign Policy." *China: An International Journal* 1/1 (2003), 46-72.

Zheng Bijian. *China's Peaceful Rise, the Speeches of Zheng Bijian*. Washington, DC: Brookings Institute Press, 2006.

———. "China's 'Peaceful Rise' to Great Power Status." *Foreign Affairs* 84.5 (2005), 18-24.

Zhu Tianbao. "Nationalism and Chinese Foreign Policy." *China Review* 1/1 (2001), 1-27.

中国和平崛起新道路和亚洲的未来

尊敬的主席先生，女士们、先生们：

很高兴同各位朋友见面，我今天讲演的题目是：中国和 平崛起新道路和亚洲的未来。

我想用尽可能短的时间，以尽可能节约的方式，向各位陈述我关于下列问题的若干思考：

怎样看中国的发展问题，

怎样看中国的崛起道路，

怎样看中国崛起同亚洲的关系。

中国实行改革开放，到今天整整 25 年，刚好是四分之一个世纪。在这 25 年中，中国取得了一系列新的重大进步和发展。到本世纪初，中国进入小康社会，现在正在为全面建设小康社会而努力。

但是与此同时，我们又清醒地估计到，中国现在达到的小康，还是低水平的、不全面的、发展很不平衡的小康。中国仍然远未摆脱不发达状态，仍是一个发展中国家，而且是一个面临一系列大规模难题的发展中国家。

什么叫"大规模难题"呢？

这里有两道最简单的数学题，一道乘法，一道除法。

乘法题是：无论看似多么小的因而可以忽略的经济和社会发展难点，只要乘以 13 亿，那就成了一个大规模的，甚至可能是超大规模的问题。

而除法题是：无论绝对数量多么可观的财力、物力，只要除以 13 亿，那就成为相当低的，甚至很低很低的人均水平了。

我想各位都很清楚，这里说的 13 亿，是指的中国人口太多。而中国的人口高峰还在前头，大约要到 2040 年前后，达到 15 亿，尔后才会逐渐有所下降。

崛起	juéqǐ	rise abruptly; appear on horizon
小康	xiǎokāng	comfortable standard of living
摆脱	bǎituō	cast off
乘法	chéngfǎ	multiplication
除法	chúfǎ	division

当然，事情还有另一方面。中国改革开放 25 年以来的实践证明，中国活跃起来，把一切可以调动的<u>积极因素</u>愈益充分地调动起来，那么中国庞大的劳动力、创新力、购买力形成的<u>凝聚力</u>和增长动力，以及由此而给世界带来的增长动力，又是多么大一个数量级呢？看来这是又一个方面的，联系于 13 亿到 15 亿的数学题。

所以，中国的发展和崛起，包括问题的方面和动力的方面，归根到底，都离不开这个 13 亿到 15 亿。而中国为解决发展问题的一切努力，无论经济、政治、文化工作，也无论内政、外交、<u>国防</u>，归根到底，都是为了使我们的 13 亿以至 15 亿人民过上好日子，并且越来越好，越来越富裕，越来越文明，越来越符合人性，到本世纪中叶达到中等发达国家的水平，尔后当然还要继续提高。

我认为这就是我们当代中国人，从领导层到全体人民，一个共同的<u>雄心壮志</u>。单单这件事，就够我们从现在算起的两到三代中国人，很忙很忙的了！

把占全人类五分之一的人口的生活提到相当高的文明境界，这难道不是中国理应为人类发展承担起的<u>无与伦比</u>的重大责任吗？

那么中国有没有办法来解决这样的问题呢？

朋友们大约都知道，世界上对此议论纷纷。而我认为，从总体来说，中国的发展成就本身，已经和正在有力地回答这个问题，并且还将更加明白有力地回答这个问题。

这里最根本的一条就在于：中国实行改革开放的 25 年来，已经开创出一条适合中国国情又适合时代特征的战略道路。这就是：

在同<u>经济全球化</u>相联系而不是相脱离的进程中独立自主地建设中国特色社会主义，这样一条和平崛起新道路。

关于这条道路，我首先要强调一点：同经济全球化相联系而不是相脱

(调动)积极因素	jījí yīnsù	(mobilize) positive factors
凝聚力	níngjùlì	cohesive force
国防	guófáng	national defense
雄心壮志	xióngxīn zhuàngzhì	lofty aspirations and great ideals
无与伦比	wú yú lún bǐ	incomparable
经济全球化	jīngjì quánqiúhuà	economic globalization

离，这本身就是中国人的一个重大的历史性战略抉择。

这个抉择，是在上世纪 70 年代摆在中国人面前的。当时，世界范围新科技革命和新一轮经济全球化浪潮蓬勃兴起。中国领导人把握住这个动向，作出了"当今的世界是开放的世界，中国的发展离不开世界"的重大判断，决心抓住历史机遇，把全部工作转到以经济建设为中心的轨道上来，实行对内改革和对外开放，并以农村包产到户和在沿海设立 4 个经济特区及 14 个开放城市作为起步，发展国内市场，走向国际市场。这样，才开创了中国改革开放的新时期。

在此之后，到了上世纪 90 年代，中国面临又一次历史性战略抉择。这就是经济全球化同反全球化两股潮流的对抗，以及亚洲金融危机的发生。中国领导人注意分析经济全球化的正面和负面，果断地确定了进一步积极参与经济全球化而又"趋利避害"的战略方针。这样，又把中国的改革开放推进到新的水平。

关于这条道路，其次我要强调一点：在积极参与经济全球化的同时，走独立自主的发展道路。

像中国这样的十几亿人口的发展中国家，不应当也不可能设想依赖国际社会，而必须也只能把事情主要放在自己力量的基点上。

就是说，更加充分自觉地依靠自身的体制创新，依靠开发越来越大的国内市场，依靠把庞大的居民储蓄转化为投资，依靠国民素质的提高和科技进步来解决资源和环境问题。总之，依靠调动一切可以调动的积极因素来实现我们的雄心壮志。

关于这条道路，第三我还要强调一点：这是一条奋力崛起而又坚持和平、坚持不争霸的道路。

抉择	juézé	choice
蓬勃兴起	péngbó xīng qǐ	surge forward; spring up
包产到户	bāochǎn dàohù	fixing farm output quotas at household level
趋利避害	"qū lì bì hài"	"tend toward benefit and avoid harm"
战略方针	zhànlüè fāngzhēn	strategic principle
储蓄	chǔxù	savings
争霸	zhēngbà	contend for hegemony

近代以来的历史反复说明，一个<u>后兴大国</u>的崛起，往往导致国际格局和世界秩序的<u>急剧变动</u>，甚至引发大战。这里一个重要原因，就是后兴大国走了一条依靠发动侵略战争打破原有国际体系，实行对外扩张以争夺霸权的道路。而这样的道路，总是以失败告终。

那么在今天新的时代条件下，我们亚洲国家包括中国，难道还会重复这种完全错误的、害人终害己的道路吗！？

我们的抉择只能是：奋力崛起，而且是和平的崛起。也就是下定决心，争取和平的国际环境发展自己，又以自身的发展来维护世界和平。围绕这条道路，最重要的战略方针有三条：一是<u>毫不动摇</u>地<u>锐意</u>推进以<u>社会主义市场经济</u>和社会主义民主政治为基本内涵的经济和政治体制改革，以形成实现和平崛起的制度保证；二是大胆<u>借鉴</u>吸收人类文明成果而又坚持弘扬中华文明，以形成实现和平崛起的精神<u>支柱</u>；三是周到细致地<u>统筹兼顾</u>各种利益关系，包括统筹城乡发展、统筹区域发展、统筹经济社会发展、统筹人与自然和谐发展、统筹国内发展和对外开放，以形成实现和平崛起的社会环境。

朋友们还会注意到，过去 25 年，中国的改革开放并非<u>风平浪静</u>，经历过多次考验。但是，中国人对这条和平崛起新道路从来没有动摇过。这个基本事实有力地表明：改革开放、和平发展，已经深深<u>扎根</u>在当代中国人的生活和文化之中。这已经形成为和平崛起战略道路不可逆转的大气候。

各位朋友，

从上个世纪六、七十年代以来，亚洲一些国家和地区成为世界上经济和社会发展最活跃的地区之一。紧接着从 70 年代末叶起，中国实行改革开

后兴大国	hòuxīngdàguó	late developing superpower
急剧变动	jíjù biàndòng	sharp fluctuation, change
毫不动摇	háo bú dòngyáo	without the slightest waver
锐意	ruìyì	with keen determination
社会主义市场经济	shèhuì zhǔyì shìchǎng jīngjì	socialist market economy
借鉴	jièjiàn	draw on the experience of
支柱	zhīzhù	mainstay; prop
统筹兼顾	tǒngchóu jiāngù	give overall consideration to; plan as a whole
风平浪静	fēngpíng làngjìng	smooth sailing; calm
扎根	zhāgēn	take root

放，经济迅猛增长，社会全面进步。中国同亚洲其他国家的经贸联系越来越紧密，亚洲在世界经济中的比重也越来越大。

仅就中国同东盟的经贸关系而言，过去 10 年，双边贸易额增长了 6 倍多，去年更达到 547.7 亿美元，预计到 2005 年，将突破 1000 亿美元。中国——东盟自由贸易区建立之后，双方的经贸合作将更加紧密。中国有句老话："远亲不如近邻。"我们高兴地看到，在中国与亚洲国家之间，已经形成一种互促、互利、互助、互补的新型合作关系。

作为一个研究者、观察者，我愿根据历史和现状的发展大局，提出这样一个判断：总体而言，未来十几年、二十几年，或者说 21 世纪前期，亚洲正面临着世界历史上一个极为难得的和平崛起的重大机遇。而和平崛起中的中国，则是亚洲和平崛起的一部分。这不仅意味着中国的改革开放与和平崛起得益于亚洲其他国家的经验与发展，而且意味着中国作为亚洲一员，将会对亚洲其他国家首先是周边国家的发展、繁荣和稳定，发挥愈益积极有益的作用。

谢谢大家。

2. 中国和平崛起新道路与中美关系

这两年，美国政界和各大思想库的专家以及媒体，就中国的和平崛起会不会威胁美国的全球利益问题，展开了热烈讨论。为加深了解，扩大共识，增信释疑，推动中美关系向着更加积极、更加稳定的方向发展，就中国和平崛起新道路与中美关系，谈十点看法：

第一点，过去二十多年的事实告诉我们，中国的和平崛起对美国不是威胁，而是机遇。

中国自上世纪 70 年代末实行改革开放以来，就选择了一条争取和平的国际环境来发展自己、又以自身的发展来维护世界和平的发展道路。中国和平崛起意味着这既是一条国家发展道路又是一个国家发展目标。所谓发展道路，就是要在同经济全球化相联系而不是相脱离的进程中，在同国际

东盟	dōngméng	ASEAN (Association of Southeast Asian Nations)
思想库	sīxiǎngkù	think tank
释疑	shìyí	dispel doubts

社会实现互利共赢的进程中，独立自主地建设中国特色社会主义。所谓发展目标，就是要在 21 世纪中叶基本实现现代化，使中国摆脱不发达状态，达到中等发达国家水平。

我们说中国的现代化进程同经济全球化相联系，就是积极参与经济全球化，而不主张用暴烈的手段去改变国际秩序、国际格局；我们说独立自主地建设中国特色社会主义，就是主要依靠自己的力量解决发展的难题，不给别人制造麻烦。20 多年来的实践表明，中国的这条和平崛起发展道路是能够走得通的。在中国和平崛起进程中，中国的实力不断壮大，美国也仍然保持强劲的发展势头，二者实现了同步发展，互利双赢；中美关系也已从过去主要是政治上的合作变为政治、经济、文化乃至军事安全等全方位的交流与合作。

第二点，随着中美关系的深入发展，美国对中国和平崛起的认识也在逐步加深。

最近，美国一些很有影响的媒体，发表了不少对中国和平崛起客观、正面的评价或报道。美国国会关于积极推动中美关系的呼声开始多了起来，布什总统最近有关中国问题的答问，基调相当积极。他强调，中国的崛起是"神奇的故事"；强调中国是"巨大市场"、"经济机遇"和"安全伙伴"；强调美中关系的"复杂性"，力避简单化。所有这些都表明，美国朝野和社会

互利共赢	hùlì gòng yíng	mutual benefit to the gain of all; win-win
暴烈	bàoliè	violent
秩序	zhìxù	order
格局	géjú	setup; structure
势头	shìtou	impetus; momentum
美国国会	Měiguó Guóhuì	US Congress
布什总统	Bùshí Zǒngtǒng	President Bush
基调	jīdiào	key tone; keynote
神奇(的)故事	shénqí de gùshi	magical story; legend
机遇	jīyù	opportunity; favorable circumstance
安全伙伴	ānquán huǒbàn	security companion
力避	lìbì	do all one can to avoid
朝野	cháo yě	the government and the people

各界，已有越来越多的有识之士开始正视并积极思考如何同和平崛起的中国打交道。

第三点，中国领导层对于和平崛起进程中已经遇到的和可能会遇到的问题十分<u>清醒</u>。

一个13亿至15亿人口的大国要实现和平崛起，绝非易事。特别是21世纪上半叶，中国既面临"<u>黄金发展期</u>"，又面对"<u>矛盾凸显期</u>"，其中，带根本性的是"三大<u>挑战</u>"：一是资源特别是能源的挑战；二是生态环境的挑战；三是经济与社会协调发展过程中一系列两难问题的挑战，比如沿海与内地的发展不平衡问题、公平与效益的矛盾问题、城乡差别和贫富差距问题、改革与稳定的关系问题，等等。这"三大挑战"如果不能有效解决，不仅你们的担忧不能解除，中国的和平崛起也将非常困难。

第四点，至关重要的是，中国已经开始应对这"三大挑战"的"三大战略"。

一是超越旧式工业化道路，推进新型工业化。二是超越近代以来后兴大国传统的崛起之路和以意识形态划线的冷战思维，积极参与经济全球化。三是超越不合时宜的社会治理模式，继续致力于构建社会主义<u>和谐社会</u>。这三大战略，归结起来，就是在坚持对外和平与对内和谐及其相互结合、相互促进的基础上，引导13亿至15亿中国人，在同世界的互利共赢中使自己的日子过得好一些，对人类的贡献大一些。

第五点，这"三大战略"以及中国和平崛起的发展道路，具有一个鲜明的特点，就是主要依靠自己的力量来解决问题。

这叫做"中国特色"，这就叫做中国对内对外方针的相统一。就是说，我们把对外强调的和平崛起同对内的社会变革、社会改造联系在一起，<u>着眼</u>

清醒	qīngxǐng	clear-minded; sober
黄金发展期	huángjīn fāzhǎnqī	golden period of development
矛盾凸显期	máodùn tūxiǎnqī	period of emerging contradictions
挑战	tiǎozhàn	challenge
和谐社会	héxié shèhuì	"harmonious society"
着眼于	zhuóyǎn yú	with an eye to; with aim of

于构建中国特色社会主义现代化的和谐社会。一是中国特色的节约型社会；二是中国特色的城市化社会；三是中国特色的学习型社会；四是中国特色的地区协调发展社会。

第六点，概括起来，中国和平崛起所做的只是"中国梦"，而绝不是别的什么梦。

比如在能源消耗上，我们就做不起"美国梦"；在人口流动上，我们也不会做"欧洲梦"；在增强综合国力上，我们也不想做"苏联梦"。

第七点，中国走和平崛起发展道路，所追求的绝不是成为一个争霸世界的军事大国，而是要建成一个市场大国、文明大国、在国际社会起建设性作用的负责任的大国。

以市场大国来说，20年前，中国被称为"最大的潜在市场"，而今天，中国庞大的市场能量已开始显现，特别是1997年亚洲金融危机以来，中国对世界贸易增长和GDP增长作出了积极贡献。以文明大国来说，中国的崛起就是要使中华民族的素质得到历史性的提高，使中华民族的文明得到伟大复兴。正如新加坡内阁资政李光耀所说，"中国的和平崛起不会给任何国家造成威胁，而是要用其富有活力的高尚的民族文化，去点燃人类文明之光！"

我们毫不动摇地坚持走和平崛起的发展道路，就是要成为"富强、民主、文明"的社会主义现代化国家，成为"不称霸、不争霸、不当头、也不当附庸"，在国际事务中充分发挥建设性作用的负责任大国。

第八点，面对这样的中国共产党，面对中国这样的和平崛起发展道路，美国有什么可以担心的呢？

节约	jiéyuē	economizing; thrifty
消耗	xiāohào	consumption; depletion
潜在	qiánzài	potential
亚洲金融危机	Yàzhōu jīnróng wēijī	Asian financial crisis
李光耀	Lǐ Guāngyào	Lee Kuan Yew, Singaporean "Minister Mentor" (1923-)
点燃	diǎnrán	kindle; light
称霸	chēngbà	dominate; bully
附庸	fùyōng	vassal; dependent

欧盟委员会前主席普罗迪先生最近在中国的博鳌亚洲论坛上说过，在目前这个阶段，我们不需要计量经济学的预测家们来预测哪一年中国将成为世界第一或第二工业产品制造国，或者哪一年会成为世界第一或第二出口国。我们真正想要了解的是，中国将采用哪些价值观。美国人要搞清楚中国的和平崛起会不会威胁美国的全球利益，首先应当了解中共十一届三中全会以来中国领导层的新理念。

关于这个问题，我要郑重提请各位高度重视以下五个关键点：一是邓小平先生在他生命的晚年，把"中国现在不称霸，即使将来强大起来了也不能称霸，要以此来教育我们的子孙后代"作为政治交代；他还一再强调，中国要坚定不移地长期实行全面改革开放，坚持这条基本路线 100 年不动摇。

二是江泽民提出的"三个代表"重要思想同邓小平理论一脉相承，并更加强调了经济全球化是不可逆转的时代潮流，中国要积极参与经济全球化；强调世界是丰富多彩的，中国要积极借鉴人类文明的有益成果，同时又要使中华文明同人类文明交相辉映。

三是以胡锦涛为总书记的中国新一届领导集体，进一步解放思想、实

普罗迪	Pǔluódí	Romano Prodi, president of European Commission 1999-2004
中共十一 届三中全会	Zhōng-Gòng Shíyī Jiè Sān Zhōng Quánhuì	Third Plenum of the 11th Central Committee of the CCP, held Dec. 1978
三个代表	Sān ge Dàibiǎo	"Three Represents": the Party must represent the development of China's advanced productive forces, the orientation of China's advanced culture, and the fundamental interests of the broad masses of the Chinese people
一脉相承	yīmài xiāngchéng	run in a single line; derive from the same origin
逆转	nìzhuǎn	be reversed; deteriorate
交相辉映	jiāoxiānghuīyìng	enhance each other
胡锦涛	Hú Jǐntāo	general secretary of CCP (1942-)

事求是、与时俱进，奉行"对外和平、对内和谐"、同时谋求对台和解的<u>核心理念</u>，这对中国的内政外交已经、正在并将继续产生至关重要的影响。

四是中国要在 21 世纪中叶实现和平崛起，我们只能集中力量干好这件事，根本没有精力也从来没有想过要去威胁任何人。

五是中国是新一轮经济全球化的<u>受益者</u>，中国主张用改革的方式而不是暴烈的手段来建设国际政治、经济新秩序。如果看不到中国领导层的这些顺应世界潮流的重要理念、核心理念，就会对中国在 21 世纪的根本走向发生严重的战略<u>误判</u>，其结果将会犯历史性错误。

第九点，只要换一种思维、换一种<u>胸襟</u>、换一个角度，就会发现中美之间发展各方面交流与合作的内在机遇很多，中美关系的前景很光明。不要把中美关系看成"外力推动型"，似乎冷战时期争霸世界的"<u>北极熊</u>"和策动"9·11"的<u>本·拉丹</u>，才是中美关系的"<u>粘合剂</u>"，似乎一旦那个"北极熊"消失了，恐怖主义威胁基本摆平了，中美关系就又要出问题了。有人说，崛起的大国必然要搞<u>鹰派</u>外交、持久冷战和损人利己。这是在用老眼光和旧理论看问题。<u>布热津斯基</u>先生不久前在<u>卡内基国际和平基金会</u>谈论中国和平崛起时说，"当理论被证明不符合现实的时候，理论就应该修正。"曾在<u>布鲁金斯学会</u>工作过的<u>理查德·哈斯</u>说："中国只向世界输出电脑，而没有输出革

核心理念	héxīn lǐniàn	core idea
受益者	shòuyìzhě	beneficiary
误判	wùpàn	misjudge; give an erroneous judgment
胸襟	xiōngjīn	state of mind; mood
北极熊	beǐjíxióng	polar bear, i.e., Soviet Union
本·拉丹	Běn Lādān	Osama Bin Laden
粘合剂	niánhéjì	adhesive; bonding agent
鹰派	yīngpài	hawks; hawkish
布热津斯基	Bùrèjīnsījī	Zbigniew Brzezinski, national security advisor to Jimmy Carter, 1977-81
卡内基国际和平基金会	Kǎnèijī Guójì Hépíng Jījīnhuì	Carnegie Endowment for International Peace
布鲁金斯学会	Bùlǔjīnsī Xuéhuì	Brookings Institution (non-profit thinktank)
理查德·哈斯	Lǐchádé Hāsī	Richard Haass, president of the Council on Foreign Relations, 2003-

命，也没有输出意识形态。"这些清醒的声音值得肯定。无论从当前还是从长远的观点来看，中美关系都具有相当广阔的"同步发展空间"和发展机遇。中美关系的第一个机遇，来自全球化时代两国利益的深度捆绑和互有所求。中美双方形成了轻易拆解不开的利益共同体和利害共同体。如果美方能够本着"非政治化"的原则来处理两国经贸问题，中美经贸关系必然会赢来又一次大发展，而绝不会是又一次大倒退。

中美关系的第二个机遇来自随着非传统安全威胁上升所带来的"大国合作"的新安全观。恐怖主义、大规模杀伤性武器扩散等非传统安全威胁成为我们共同的主要威胁和凶恶敌人。我们完全有条件在战略安全领域进一步展开深度合作。关键是建立战略互信。

中美关系的第三个机遇来自两国重视处理地区热点问题和维护国际秩序的共同努力。亚太地区是中美共同发展的舞台。中美既面临清除冷战遗产的历史任务，又面对避免热战发生的现实挑战。中美两个大国如果能从这样的大视野看问题，就有可能排除"中国在搞亚洲版门罗主义排挤美国利益"这样的思想干扰，务实地携手解决现实冲突、思考未来布局，在兼顾各自利益的基础上谋求共生、共处、共同发展与共同和平。至于在维护国际秩序的稳定和共同推动国际秩序的改革方面，中美两国更加义不容辞和责无旁贷。我们应当以开放的胸襟共同探索新的国际经济、金融、政治、安全机制。中美关系的第四大机遇来自中美两大文明的共存与交汇。全球化时代不是"文明冲突"的时代，而是文化交流的时代、文明和谐的时代。现在，中美在文化资源和文化产业方面的交流与合作，已成为中国文化市场

同步	tóngbù	synchronized; simultaneous
捆绑	kǔnbǎng	truss up; bind together
非政治	fēizhèngzhì	apolitical; non-political
大规模杀伤性武器	dàguīmó shāshāngxìng wǔqì	weapons of mass destruction
(亚洲版)门罗主义	Yàzhōubǎn Ménluózhǔyì	"Asian Monroe Doctrine" i.e., China should not interfere in affairs of neighbors
义不容辞	yìbùróngcí	sense of duty
责无旁贷	zéwúpángdài	duty which cannot be shirked
交汇	jiāohuì	converge; meet

兴起和发展的重要组成部分。对美国来 说，深入了解中国文化也日益成为两国和谐相处的重要基础。

第十点，我还想强调，机遇不是<u>等来的</u>，而是共同创造出来的。前不久，一位美国前政要说，中美两国如果加强合作，21 世纪将是非常美好的世纪，反之，中美关系如果发生倒退，21 世纪对两国和世界来说将是非常糟糕的世纪。美国在如何看待中国崛起和如何发展中美关系上，要实现"<u>三个超越</u>"：一是超越以意识形态和社会制度<u>划线</u>的冷战思维，因为用这种思维看问题，很容易对中国特色社会主义和中国共产党发生战略误判；二是要超越以价值观划线的"文化优越论"，因为当代世界已是多种文明长期共存、不同文化相互<u>激荡</u>的新时代；三是要超越后起大国必然挑战现存霸权的传统理论，因为它解释不了中国和平崛起的新道路和中国的崛起是维护世界和平坚定力量的新现实。

等来的	děng lái de	something which comes from waiting
三个超越	sān ge chāoyuè	"three transcendents"; three (errors to) transcend
划线	huàxiàn	gauge; demarcate
激荡	jīdàng	excite; stimulate